MY THIRTY YEARS
BACKSTAIRS
AT THE WHITE HOUSE

MY THIRTY YEARS
BACKSTAIRS
AT THE WHITE HOUSE

LILLIAN ROGERS PARKS
In Collaboration With
FRANCES SPATZ LEIGHTON

FLEET PUBLISHING CORPORATION

230 PARK AVENUE, NEW YORK 17, NEW YORK

To Maggie, My Mother,
Who Urged Me to Complete
The Backstairs Story of the White House,
Which She Began So Long Ago
When She Bore the Proud Title
Of Number One White House Maid.

CONTENTS

PART THREE

THE WHITE HOUSE THROUGH THE EYE OF MY NEEDLE

TO HELP YOU GET
THE PICTURE . . .

In a little house, on a quiet street in Washington, D.C., lives "Little Lillian"—as she was known at the White House—among her souvenirs.

As you pass under the trees and into the hall, you do feel as though you were entering a little corner of the White House. Look up the broad, carpeted stairs on both sides, and you will see, neatly framed, all the old familiar faces of First Ladies and Presidents, whose lives touched hers or her mother's during the past half century. For Lillian Parks is that rare person, a White House maid whose mother had been a White House maid.

Lillian first saw the inside of the White House when, as a tiny child, crippled by polio, her mother brought her along, because she had no place to leave her, while she worked for President and Mrs. Howard Taft. Her mother, "Maggie" Rogers, worked through the tragic Wilson administration, the strange Harding era, and the impish Coolidge years. She was one person who *did* hear "Silent Cal" talk.

Lillian would sometimes come to the White House during those years, to deliver the sewing she had done at home for the First Family. Then when the Hoovers arrived, Maggie was told to bring "Little Lillian"—still only four feet ten—to be both seamstress and maid at the Executive Mansion. Those were the most difficult years.

Then came the "Wild and Wooly" Roosevelts, the "Pepper Pot" Trumans and the "Puzzling" Eisenhowers. Their lives, as she saw them, and the lives of Mrs. Taft, the two Mrs. Wilsons, Mrs. Harding and Mrs. Coolidge, as her mother had seen them, make up this wonderful book, which Lillian began shortly after her recent retirement from the White House.

Her size does not prevent Lillian from waxing a bit peppery too, and in these memoirs, she really exercises "free speech," along with a host of White House tales and anecdotes—some sad and some amusing, others tragic or marvelously funny. Over a half century of White House history is chronicled in these pages, and only "Little Lillian" could have done it so well.

—FRANCES SPATZ LEIGHTON

PART ONE

I'LL REMEMBER MAMIE

AND

"BESS T"

"ELEANOR R"

"LOU H"

"IF A CAT MAY LOOK
AT A QUEEN . . ."

I recently read in the newspapers that a man who had been released from a mental hospital in California came to the White House with a ladder, a bucket of red paint, and a brush. He placed the ladder against the fence, and climbed over and was caught just as he was walking over the South lawn putting green. He was headed for the President's office. He planned to paint on the wall "I quit."

I laughed uproariously. It was so typical of the wacky, sometimes funny, sometimes sad things that are forever happening at 1600 Pennsylvania Avenue.

For a moment, I felt that I could turn to the other maids, and compare this character with some we remembered from administrations past. And then it struck me! I was no longer at the White House, and suddenly I was so terrifyingly lonely, that I felt I could die.

It is strange to know that never again will I be at the White House to compare notes with my backstairs friends or to greet a new First Lady.

No more embarrassing moments like the time when

I was crawling around on the floor, making blackout curtains, and FDR rolled in. No more listening to inside jokes that circulate in the White House: "Have you heard the latest? You'll never believe it! George (houseman) was sitting cross-legged on the floor in the sitting room, reading President Truman's Bible to Sarver (another houseman), and the President himself walks in. Oh my, Sarver couldn't even signal him to pipe down."

No more First Ladies to call "Madam."

No more "Mr. President."

No more little David Eisenhower, who wanted to sell me his own story— "It's the true story of my life, Lillian, and how I had to take care of all these visiting little kids, and I was the King and had to administer the punishments." And no more little Peter Hoover, then three or four, who startled everyone by appearing at the window of the hallowed White House wearing a hat— and nothing but a hat. No more little Roosevelt grandchildren, learning to walk by lifting themselves up on my crutch.

No more of living at the White House as if it were my second home. No more of sharing the lives, the laughter, the sicknesses, the sorrows and the secrets of the Presidential families. I have retired after thirty years of viewing the First Families through the eye of my needle— sewing needle, that is. Yet as I write these memoirs, I am still a part of the most exciting household in the world.

Some day soon, I would like to organize a small museum in Washington, where private citizens can browse among the objects which the Presidents and their First Ladies once held dear, or which had some significance at the White House.

I have enough items to start this museum, or room of a museum— fans from Mrs. Taft; walking canes that held FDR aloft, so that people thought he could walk; two pictures and a tray made entirely of butterfly wings from Mrs.

Hoover; a lock of hair from Amelia Earhart, which she snipped off herself during her last visit to the White House; book ends; vases; perfumes in cases; autographed pictures, White House scenes . . . things of which you'd never dream . . . a bar of soap that was used by the Prince of Wales when he lunched with Coolidge, and a framed prayer written by— you'd never guess— pepper-tongued Harry Truman. And a million more items. I look at them, and I dread to think what would become of them if something happened to me, and no one were there to explain their significance.

My mother, who was a White House maid before me, used to lie in her sickbed after she had retired during the Roosevelt administration, and prod me to write "our" memoirs— hers and mine— as soon as I had retired from the White House. I would say, "Why, Mama, why? People will think it is presumptuous for a maid to write about a First Lady."

Mama, who had worked at the White House from the fourth day of the Taft Administration in 1909, would get very angry with me. "Lillian," she would say, "Just remember this. If a cat may look at a Queen in England, a maid may write about a First Lady in America. This is a free Republic."

I hope that Mrs. Kennedy will read this, because a few things may be of value to her in the life she is about to enter. A few things may surprise her, and a few things may amuse her. I hope that other ladies will be reading this too, so that they may compare their own lives with that of a First Lady, and see that they themselves are not too badly off. Most of all, I hope that, looking through the eye of my needle with me, they can see that First Ladies are not Pollyannas but real flesh-and-blood women like themselves, with tempers and problems, and superstitions and fears, and the desire to succeed.

I know it will take the new First Lady months to get used to the mausoleum feeling of the rooms, which belong to her, and yet don't belong to her.

She will be terrified at those first State dinners. Mrs. Truman never did learn to really enjoy formal functions, and her hands would perspire from nervousness. I hope that the new First Lady won't overdo it, and try to make every dinner or small tea the greatest of its kind. Backstairs, we used to feel sorry for Mrs. Eisenhower, because she tried so hard, that it sometimes seemed she was trying to make history by outdoing Dolley Madison in the perfection of her entertainment.

Most of all, I sympathize with the new First Lady, because I know that never for a moment will she be completely free of the fear of danger to her children and her husband. It goes with the job, as a special hazard, and no matter how many Secret Service men are around, she will never feel completely secure.

Somewhere along the line, the new First Lady will wonder aloud whom the public elected— the President or her. She will be shocked to find out how much is expected of her. She will wonder if she can endure it for four years— and then maybe another four.

I can predict so many of the things that will happen to the new First Lady, and so many of her reactions. She will be amazed, and a little bit annoyed, when she finds that things wear out at the White House, even as elsewhere. Somehow, this always seems to come as a surprise. In the Eisenhower administration, it got to the point where I had to use adhesive tape to hold the drapery together in the Rose Room, where Queen Elizabeth had stayed, and to wonder aloud if I would have to supply my own thread, before money for supplies was forthcoming.

I can predict that the new First Lady will be shocked when she finds out how much is pilfered from the White

House as souvenirs— not by the servants, but by the guests. Tea napkins seem to be the favorite item, but silverware and even a silver tray have had to be retrieved— once from a lady's suitcase.

I can predict that she will feel hurt when she discovers that whatever she does, and no matter how hard she tries, the new First Lady is going to be under attack. She will know, as she stands receiving guests, that some people who are saying nice things as they shake her hand are going to be saying nasty things a little later when they go to the powder room. I know, because my duties included helping the guests in the powder room, both for evening and for daytime entertainment.

If it will be of any comfort to her, FDR once comforted *his* wife, after she had been attacked in the press on one of many occasions, by reminding her of what her uncle, Teddy Roosevelt, had said to them— that he only expected to be supported 75 per cent of the time, and if he were attacked only 25 per cent of the time, he felt successful.

The best advice I can give the new First Lady, before it is too late, is to find the thickest set of invisible armor and put it on. She will need it to let the arrows of false accusations and needless criticism bounce off her.

I've heard the accusations that Mrs. Eisenhower acted drunk; that Mrs. Truman was a nag, and wouldn't let her husband wear the pants in the family; that Mrs. Roosevelt gave money to men, and that Mrs. Coolidge purposely "got lost" in the woods with a Secret Service man. Well, ignorance thrives on gossip.

Some unkind souls couldn't even wait to see whether Mrs. Kennedy or Mrs. Nixon would move into the White House. They started criticizing as soon as the nominations were made.

Of Mrs. Kennedy, they demanded to know whether she would go bare-legged in the White House; why she wore her hair in a "floor-mop" hairdo; why she wore "tight pants" on vacation, and wild pink ones at that, which "clashed" with her orange sweater.

Of Mrs. Nixon, they demanded to know why she didn't insist that her husband make clear his "religious affiliation." Was he really a good Quaker, or was he a Methodist, and if he had turned Methodist, why didn't he formally join the church, and if not, why didn't he attend Quaker Meetings?

The wives of both nominees tried to avoid controversial matters, and kept silent. But the pride of Jacqueline Kennedy was unbearably stung when she was accused of spending more money on clothes than did Pat Nixon. She rose to her own defense by pointing out that Mrs. Nixon bought her clothes at Elizabeth Arden, which made them more expensive than her own. She promptly went out and bought herself a set of maternity dresses, none of which cost more than $34.50. Mrs. Nixon admitted to buying one dress at Elizabeth Arden, and the battle was finished.

Then President Truman made us feel he was somehow back in the White House when, characteristically defending the ladies, he charged into the field. He said emphatically that he didn't think it "proper, decent, or polite to bring the candidates' families" into the campaign. He said he thought both ladies were "wonderful." The candidates themselves said nothing.

We remembered what Truman had said when asked how he thought his wife looked in her new hairdo. He said, "I think she looks just like she ought to look."

Yes, it seems like yesterday when people were complaining about Mrs. Truman's new poodle cut. "What does she think she is, a little girl or a poodle dog?" they were asking caustically. And eventually, the poodle cut became the rage— with no credit given to Bess "T"— when it was suddenly "invented" by Italian and French stylists.

And what about Mrs. Eisenhower's bangs? People said to me, "You work at the White House. Why does Mamie wear those awful bangs? Why doesn't somebody like you send her an anonymous note to get rid of them?"

First of all, I would like to assure those people that there are no anonymous notes at the White House. One poor messenger who "anonymously" placed an amateurish painting he had made of Queen Elizabeth in her room, when she was visiting in 1939, almost lost his job. It's hard to keep a secret at the White House.

And secondly, much of the criticism of the First Ladies is just a lot of talk. I have to laugh when I remember a particular woman at the White House who complained the loudest in the powder room about Mrs. Roosevelt's travels, and ended with the usual, "Why doesn't Eleanor stay home and take care of her husband?" It came to pass that Mrs. Roosevelt invited that same woman to go along on a trip, and she didn't hesitate for a moment to accept, leaving her husband behind!

Along the same line, I have seen many ladies who criticized Mamie Eisenhower's bangs in my powder room later wearing them.

In spite of the criticism she is bound to encounter, I would hate to see the First Lady try to escape criticism by hiding away, and staying out of the limelight. No, I think a First Lady can do more than any other woman in the country to increase respect for women generally, and to be a pacemaker.

As just a tiny example of what a First Lady can do, let's take the matter of smoking. Mrs. Roosevelt felt that women had as much right to smoke as men, and ordered cigarettes for the ladies at the table. After the meal, she would light a cigarette, and thus gave the stamp of approval to women smoking in public. After she had won her point, and had helped women across the nation bring smoking into the open, she quit smoking after meals, because she actually didn't care for the habit.

We maids at the White House watched Mrs. Roosevelt take an interest in national and international problems and make recommendations to the President that he considered valuable. Characteristically, she always left them at his bedside table.

Socially, she showed what could be done for the national good when her sponsorship of the March of Dimes paid for the work done by Dr. Jonas Salk, and resulted in the conquest of polio. If she had not encouraged and attended the President's Birthday Balls, would polio be conquered today? It's a good question. In the servants' area of the White House, we talked about the amazing power a First Lady has.

From my thirty years of observation within the White House, I believe that a good First Lady must typify the good things of America. If there is anything that symbolizes a nation, it is its most important citizens.

The First Family must set an example. And as a social leader, the First Lady must demonstrate, in her own life and actions, such American virtues as religious tolerance and concern for the poor and the sick. Furthermore, she must, by her own interest, foster the arts and encourage education. Her lead will be followed. As proof of the interest the public takes in the wife of a candidate, there actually was an organized "Put Pat Nixon in the White House" campaign.

And yet a First Lady is still a woman who must set a good example in her home life as well as her public one. I am frequently asked what kind of mothers and grandmothers the First Ladies made. What kind of family atmosphere prevailed in the White House? Who were the best hostesses? Did any "wear the pants" in the family?

First, let me touch upon the subject of motherhood. The

staff at the White House have a theory that the Roosevelt boys may have felt they lacked maternal love, which caused them to be mixed up in their own lives and loves. Of course, Mrs. Roosevelt loved them and showed it, but they seemed to feel that there was nothing exclusive about it, and that they had to share her with the world. She loved them, but she also loved a lot of other children not related to her.

One Roosevelt boy was overheard saying, "To Mother, all the world's a classroom, and she's teacher." And another son said, rather plaintively, "She has time for everyone except us."

It is true that to some extent, there was an impersonal quality in Mrs. Roosevelt's family relationships. She wanted to be a buddy to her boys, and she was the one they came to with problems, but they couldn't get as close to her as they wanted to.

When she did arrive, there would be a "duty" feeling about it; she would greet them in a great hurry, and rush out to take care of others outside the family. Even her warmth was impersonal. She kissed all her family and in-laws when they arrived, but she did the same in greeting close friends. The consensus backstairs was and is that she spread herself too thin, and that her sons are still going through life trying to feel important and exclusive to someone, as they never could to her.

Therefore, we could understand his feelings when Congressman James Roosevelt married his secretary. She had saved every clipping about him from schooldays on, before she had ever met him.

Later, when the Trumans came, we used to say that if the Roosevelt boys could have known the warm love Margaret knew, they might have been happier men. Never have I seen greater three-way devotion than existed between Margaret, her mother, and her father. There was nothing impersonal about it, and each had a great interest in everything the others did.

They put up a little barrier against the world to protect their privacy. Whether this was good or bad, I do not know. I do believe that Mrs. "T" made a mistake in not having press conferences like Mrs. Roosevelt, because the nation did not get a chance to see the real Mrs. Truman, and formed an impression of a rather cold woman.

There was nothing cold about Bess Truman in the heart of her family, as the White House servants saw them. When Mrs. "T" played table tennis with Margaret, both of them laughed and kidded like classmates.

I remember how any two of the threesome would gang up on the third member of the family to play some prank. The President once hid Margaret's Bible and substituted the Koran, and Margaret pretended to go into a rage over it, to the amusement of her parents. She, in turn, would throw bits of bread at her father at the table till Mrs. "T" would put a stop to it.

And yet there was a strange protectiveness toward Margaret that was hard to understand until we were told that when she was a small child, and the President was a young judge, a kidnapping attempt had been made on her. It had happened at school, and had been foiled when the teacher did not permit her to leave with the strange man who supposedly had been sent for her. Ever since that time, she was never out of their sight, or the sight of some trusted adult.

As "backstairs psychologists," we felt that this special protectiveness, which started way back with the kidnapping attempt in Independence, Missouri, was the cause of the fiercely angry letter the President sent the music critic who panned Margaret's voice. Now that I am no longer at the White House, I feel that I have the right to give my personal opinion, which is that the President erred. As long as he is in office, a President should never step down to the level of private citizen in order to do something that takes away from the dignity of the Presidential office. Let's face it. A President cannot be a private citizen.

Though I disapproved, others backstairs applauded, and Margaret herself, though seemingly embarrassed by the incident, said she was grateful.

Margaret had a feeling that all kinds of hard luck followed her around. She used to say that the only time her dad lost an election was the year she was born. She laughed about it, but I had an idea she took it rather seriously anyway. Every once in a while, I almost had to agree about her luck, as when someone she knew died in the audience one night when she was singing; and also when she developed pneumonia just when she was supposed to go on the air for the first time.

But when it was *her* piano leg that went through the ceiling, proving that the White House was about to cave in, I had to disagree with her about bad luck coming her way, and join many of the White House staff who pointed out that her piano might have saved the President's life, and ours too. For after the piano incident, the men came running immediately with a pole to hold up my linen room, the ceiling of which, they said, was about to collapse.

Mrs. Eisenhower was a devoted mother and grandmother, but somehow she showed a strange coolness as an aunt. Whereas Mrs. Roosevelt had given a coming-out party at the White House for her brother Hall's daughter, and even for the daughters of friends, Mamie Eisenhower did not choose to do this for her niece, Ruth Eisenhower, the daughter of Milton, when she had come of age in nearby Baltimore.

Nor did she give parties for her own sister's children, one of whom, Mamie Moore, had been named for her, until just before she left the White House. Having seen how much White House sponsorship has meant to others in bygone years, we domestics sometimes wished that we could again hear the White House ring with young laughter— this time the laughter of the Eisenhower clan. But when I retired from the White House, I reflected sadly that only son John Eisenhower, and his wife, Barbara, had been permitted to have a party for their friends.

The White House is big and roomy, and built for dancing and fun as well as serious matters, and I hope that the new First Lady will keep this in mind. I can assure her that the White House staff, and the nation, will enjoy the parties almost as much as she will. So let there be laughter in the White House!

Of course, before I seem too hard on Mrs. Eisenhower, it is only fair to explain that her health is not at all good. Few people realized what an effort she had to put forth before any White House affair. The day of a party, she had to go to bed and stay there till the last minute.

Many times she attended an affair elsewhere, putting in an appearance, and leaving as soon as possible, because her head was splitting, or her asthma troubling her. I remember that once when she went to a rally with her husband at Madison Square Garden, she was so sick she could hardly stand. Her throat was sore, and she was feverish. Yet she put a fur scarf around her neck, and a smile on her lips to hide her condition from the press. A newspaper photograph showed her alert and smiling, and no one knew that the little white fur scarf protected a raw throat.

Not only did the First Lady have a heart condition, dating from childhood, but a disturbance of the inner ear that at times upset her equilibrium and made her footing uncertain. That is why the false rumor occasionally arose that Mrs. Eisenhower drank to excess. I can truthfully say I have never seen her drink or seen any after-effects of alcohol, nor have I ever noticed the odor of alcohol. I would get very disgusted when people kept asking me if Mamie drank, and I would explain patiently that any trouble with her balance came from the impairment in her inner ear.

It was for this reason that she did not fly with the President if she could help it. High altitudes affected the ear condition. The President always gave her his arm to help her walk, and because standing tired her, a chair was usually placed within her reach so that she could steady herself, or rest during a reception.

Even worse insinuations were made about Mrs. Roosevelt, because she tried to help people get on their feet. Surely she helped some men go into business, or simply lent or gave them money, but she also did the same for women. I remember, in particular, one female dancer whom she helped, and who named her daughter Eleanor, after her. I would get so angry when people implied that Mrs. Roosevelt was romantically interested just because she was helping a man! I would tell people who asked me that they didn't know Mrs. Roosevelt, because if they knew her, they'd realize how silly that sounded.

Only Mrs. Truman escaped scandalmongers, and even so, some people claimed that she must be the one who dominated the family. Again, this was untrue. The President called his wife "Boss" as a joke, just as he called his grown daughter "My Baby." I assure you that both the First Lady and Margaret tried to make him stop. The "Boss" wasn't even *boss* enough to get him to quit using this nickname she hated. And if she had really been boss, he would never have sent the vitriolic letter that made him look so undignified.

As far as I can see, no recent First Lady has acted as a domestic tyrant. Even FDR, who was in a wheel chair, and whose wife was known for her independence, was the complete boss of the family. It was he who decided whether or not the family would dress for dinner. It was he who

cracked down occasionally on household expenses, criticized repetitious menus, and made the First Lady toe the
mark.

As for President Eisenhower, he hadn't been a military
commander for nothing. He made the decisions of the
family, and Mrs. Eisenhower could move him to change
his mind only with sweet words and coaxing.

We used to talk backstairs about the fact that the White
House was the first real married home for the three First
Ladies prior to Mrs. Kennedy. To Mrs. Truman, home
had always meant the home of her mother, and that is
where she and the former President live today. Only after
her mother's death, during Truman's administration, was
Mrs. Truman able to change the house to suit herself.

Mrs. Eisenhower, as everyone knows, led a transient life,
following her soldier husband to various posts, or waiting
somewhere for him as he climbed the ladder to military
success. The White House was the first real home she could
count on occupying for at least four years with him— and
Gettysburg was her second.

As for Mrs. Roosevelt, her mother-in-law's home, Hyde
Park, had been "home," though Mrs. James Roosevelt
supervised to the extent that she even hired the servants.
Though she had once escaped her mother-in-law at Hyde
Park when her husband was Governor of New York, it was
not until she got as far away as the District of Columbia,
that she dared to take her stand and become the mistress of
her own home.

A maid was present when the President's mother arrived
to help her son get settled in the White House, and give her
usual advice as to its running. The maid overheard the
senior Mrs. Roosevelt criticizing her daughter-in-law for
using colored help instead of white help, as was the custom
at Hyde Park, and then she started in on other complaints.

The First Lady said in a tense but controlled voice,

"Mother, I have never told you this before, but I must tell you now. You run your house, and I'll run mine."

And run it to suit herself she did, opening its doors to everyone.

Living in the White House is like being on the stage, where tragedies and comedies play alternately. And we, the servants of the White House, are the supporting cast. Like actors after a première, we too always watched for the critics' reviews in the newspapers. Would "Eleanor" and "Bess" and "Mamie" win the hearts of the audience? We supported one another, hoping for rave notices. We bit players protected our stars, the President and the First Lady, and in no way did we embarrass any member of the cast.

Even now, after the show is over, and I am home, a retired actress, so to speak, I would say nothing that would violate any personal confidence that has been given me. Any little inside story that may seem at first glance to be a little harsh is related here with no malice intended, but only to help you understand the First Ladies as I did, and the problems they lived with or overcame.

IF THERE'S ANYTHING
I'VE LEARNED . . .

If there's anything I've learned, in my thirty years at the White House as a maid and seamstress, and from the stories my mother told me of *her* thirty years, starting with Mrs. Taft, it is to expect that things will never be placid, and that they are never as they appear to those on the outside.

Take Mrs. Truman. "Isn't she a sour puss?" I was frequently asked. "I'll bet she could bite your head off if you made a single mistake!" That was absolutely wrong. The maids at the White House saw a Bess Truman who acted as if she had invented laughter. She was one of the wittiest women imaginable, and would get on the telephone and talk and laugh for a half hour with her bridge friends.

Nor was she ready to bite your head off if you made a mistake. Once, when a butler came in with the cake plate and stumbled on the rug, scattering little cakes in all directions, Mrs. Truman laughed and laughed. Then she said jovially, "Well, as food for thought, what *was* the dessert?"

The butler regained his dignity and replied that only the little cakes were missing—the sherbet was right behind!

A lot of things happened at the White House— a lot to laugh about and a lot to cry about . . . and a lot that could have ended up tragically, but fortunately didn't.

Mrs. Truman will probably learn here, for the first time, about a near tragedy that happened in her last few months in the White House. The family had moved from Blair House not too many months before, and workmen were still checking the air conditioning system, which wasn't working right and had, in fact, broken down the first day they entertained. To get to the core of the trouble, an engineer had to go into the wall of a third-floor guest room closet through a panel that opened with a key.

Mrs. Truman had some distant relatives as house guests the particular day that the engineer went into the wall to work. The relatives had two little girls, who watched in fascination as the man opened the magic door. Then the little girls closed the magic door and refused to let the man out. He pounded and he pounded. But the little girls had wandered away to play elsewhere on the third floor.

Eventually, some maids heard a strange noise in the wall and came to investigate. When they let the man out, he refused to go back in until the house guests had left the White House for home— they stayed about a week. The maids decided not to tell Mrs. Truman, because there was no sense in distressing her when she would soon be leaving— and no one wants to be a tattletale, especially in the White House.

I wish I could take a walk through her new home with the new First Lady, and tell her all that I know of the things that have happened there, and what she might do to make the staff happy and the guests happy and comfortable. I wish I could tell her the pitfalls to avoid and the things that we folks backstairs at the White House consider important in the making of a good First Lady.

My opinions have been formed slowly over the years since I came to work at the White House at the beginning of the Hoover Administration. I had grown up steeped in the traditions of the White House, because my mother had been a White House maid for so many years.

I was mistaken once for a little White House ghost, because I came in my little white dress with my mother when she was turning down President Taft's bed at twilight. Sometimes she didn't know what else to do with me, so she would bring me along to the Executive Mansion, keeping me out of sight as best she could. I had had polio as a child and wore a brace, so I was used to staying put.

President Taft himself caught me sitting in his room, waiting for Mama to come back from another bedroom to get me. I made him promise "not to tell Mama." To my knowledge, he never did, but eventually she repeated to me a new rumor of a child's ghost at the White House. She used to bring home a White House story almost every night to delight me. When she told me this one, I had a pretty good idea as to who the ghost might be, but did not venture an opinion for fear I'd never get back in the White House again.

I did get back in, however, through my skill as a seamstress— a skill which I had developed to compensate for the polio handicap. One of the places where I had sewed was the dress shop opened by a friend of Alice Longworth, daughter of Teddy Roosevelt— the President who is still remembered around the White House as the loudest talker ever there. After the First World War, it became fashionable to "do something," and four ladies, who had been debs at the same time, had banded together to help one of their number who had been widowed by the influenza epidemic, which had taken so many lives, and had been left with four children to support.

For a while, Mama would bring home sewing work from the White House for me to do, and my greatest thrills came when I could go to the big mansion to deliver some rush job of mended linen or a hemmed dress. An operation had gotten rid of the brace, but I still used crutches. I would arrive at the most beautiful house I have ever seen, inwardly bemoaning my crutches, which kept me from running up and down steps and being a maid like Mama.

You can imagine how thrilled I was when Mrs. Hoover sent word that "Maggie's little girl" could come to the White House to sew and do light maid's work. That was the only name she ever knew me by— "Maggie's little girl." I never did grow taller than the four feet, ten inches I was then, or heavier than 106 pounds. Somehow, Mrs. Hoover made a project of fattening me up, sending her desserts to me by the butler, who stood over me until I had eaten the last morsel. Poor me! I had to sit there and eat it, afraid to say that I had already eaten one dessert.

Had Mr. Hoover won a second term, she might have succeeded. I remember how sad I suddenly was on FDR's Inaugural Day to see this kindly woman go, and I went up on the roof to cry a few private tears and take a look at the new First Family, the Roosevelts, who were arriving at the reviewing stand on Pennsylvania Avenue.

But I didn't get to cry. As I came up into the cold fresh air, I encountered the hilarious sight of another person, who had also come up for a look— a butler. Upon his head, to protect himself from the cold, he had plopped one of Mrs. Hoover's old hats— a perfectly huge brown one— that she had left behind. We stood there and laughed until we could hardly stand, and then we went down to start work for our new family.

In a way, that first laughter was prophetic, because we

descended into the happiest, most relaxed and laughter-filled administration that Mama or I had ever seen. Herbert Hoover had never spoken to me, even at the Christmas party, and had only spoken to my mother once— to ask where Mrs. Hoover was. Suddenly I was confronted by a President who spoke jovially to the servants and wanted to know exactly what I did.

Undoubtedly, we servants worked harder under the Roosevelts than during any other administration, but, because of that relaxed atmosphere and the happy acceptance of everyone, including the staff, into the Roosevelt family, nobody minded the extra work. But don't get the idea that Eleanor Roosevelt was the perfect person to work for. One of the maids summed it up nicely when she said, "If you get Mrs. R mad, she's dangerous. She's good to work for till you get her angry."

It was true. If you angered her, you were a dead duck. And the things that did *not* get her angry were the things that *really* made you wonder. For example, once we got all ready for a tea party, and no guests arrived. Mrs. Roosevelt checked and found that the invitations had not been mailed. We held our breaths, waiting for someone to be squelched for the oversight. But, instead, she laughed and said, "Well, just pack up that food and send it to the boys at Walter Reed."

But let one servant prove himself "unable to get along with the rest of the help," let him be caught quarrelsome or irritable, and out he would go. Mrs. "R" had no patience with people who "couldn't get along."

By comparison, Mrs. Eisenhower lost her temper frequently, but got over it just as quickly, and did not fire anyone. In fact, she would be exceptionally nice to make up for it. The thing that would get her angry quickest was not getting something done *fast* enough. She was an utter perfectionist, and impatient if things were not done instantly.

Once, on a Thursday, I was given two foam rubber cushions to cover with heavy material for the President's study in Gettysburg, and by cutting them out immediately and working hard, I managed to get one finished that night. But the next morning Mrs. "E" decided to go to the farm, and wanted to take the cushions with her. She was much put out when she saw I had only one done. "It seems that I can never get anything done when I want it," she said. I was hurt because I had been proud of my speed. After all, I had just cut them out late the day before.

But when the First Lady got back to the White House from Gettysburg, she seemed to have forgotten all about it, and went out of her way to say something nice to me about my sewing.

I think the behavior of Mrs. Truman toward the White House servants set the best example for any future First Lady. She was neither too sentimental, nor too harsh. She didn't keep looking over our shoulders, as Mrs. Eisenhower did; and she didn't ignore the work that was done, as Mrs. Roosevelt did.

Mrs. Truman gave you a job, assumed you knew what you were doing, and left you alone until you had done it. If she ran into you, she would not investigate your progress, but would show only a friendly interest. She would praise a job when it was done. She had such dignity that some of it rubbed off on you when you were working near her.

She was also the most considerate First Lady in recent decades. Dozens of times at the White House, before it was air conditioned, and at the un-air conditioned Blair House, I heard her say, "Bluette . . ." or "Vietta . . ." or my own name, "Lillian . . . finish what you're doing and rest a while. It's too hot to work today." If it wasn't hot, she'd say, "You've been working too long. Stop now." Never have I heard Mrs. Roosevelt or Mrs. Eisenhower tell anyone to rest. And if Mrs. Truman saw that someone didn't feel well, she was also much concerned.

It used to trouble us in the servants' area that Mrs. Roosevelt didn't care enough about the most important building in the country, which had been entrusted to her care. We felt that it should be kept in as good condition as possible at all times. It would get so bad, that sometimes the curtains wouldn't match, or we would have to tell her about something that had been needed for a long time. She would say, "Oh, it will do. It doesn't matter." Though Mrs. "R" stayed the longest in the White House, she seemed to have the most temporary feeling about it.

Actually, we didn't fully appreciate her constant reminder to us not to forget that "This house belongs to all the people," until Mrs. Eisenhower came along with what we, the staff, considered a wrong impression that the house belonged only to her and the President. She would constantly refer to "my rug," "my drapery," and "my elevator." That wouldn't have bothered us so much if she hadn't also acted as if they were hers.

Rugs were her special obsession. She made the houseman carry the luggage by hand when guests came, because she didn't want the wheels of the little handcarts to roll on "my rug," even though they had been specially made not to hurt rugs. She didn't want reporters to walk on "my rug" when they came to survey the sparkling, flower-laden table in the State Dining Room. They had to stand in the doorway and only look in.

She did not like to see footprints on a rug. So before she went out, the rug had to be brushed so that she would not see anyone's footprints. And before she came back to the White House, her *own* footprints would be brushed off for her return. But Mrs. Eisenhower was democratic enough to give everyone the same royal treatment she demanded for herself, and every time there were guests, the last thing that would be done, at 7:30 before they arrived, was the brushing of the hall rug on the first floor, so that the guests coming in would be treated to a perfect rug— if they noticed.

Finally, before I left the White House, Mrs. Eisenhower didn't want anyone to use "my powder room." This was the library powder room on the ground floor, which had always been used by guests at formal affairs. She had had it all redecorated in "Mamie Pink," down to the towels and the carpeting. She wanted the guests to use another powder room way at the other end of the house, and Mr. West, the head usher, finally rebelled and ordered that the library "Pink Powder Room" be used, so that guests would not have to walk miles.

Mrs. Truman's own little idiosyncrasy in her house-keeping was new soap. We had to keep putting a new bar of soap in a room every time it was used. We never did figure out why. We just obeyed orders. When she had company who stayed a week, a fresh bar of soap had to be put in each bathroom every morning, even though only one person would be using it. It was the same as the rug fixation in a way— untouched soap and untouched rugs.

Mrs. Hoover kept the White House in the most turmoil. Things were always in such a state of flux that it would be quite true to say that she never did get *completely* settled in the White House. We used to remark that she was probably waiting for her second four years to enjoy the White House, but the second four years never came.

I can still remember that almost every room was in a torn-up state, and as soon as it was fixed one way, she would decide it would look better another way. Soon after her arrival, the Lincoln bed was taken up to storage— but later brought back again. We never knew what to expect next in the game of "musical chairs" she played with the furniture. But, in her defense, it must be said that some of the

things still at the White House are things that she purchased with her own money and left there.

I would say that of the four women of my era, Mrs.
Truman was the best at making the family quarters look
homelike and comfortable. She believed in moderation,
and she actually made the living quarters look quite wonderful, even before the White House was remodeled. In
fact, I am tempted to say it looked better before she moved
out than after we moved back, when it had taken on a bit
of an institutional look.

And not only was it institutional-looking, but it was shot
full of errors— some funny, some downright unforgivable.
In the pantry, the decorators had forgotten to check the
size of the dinner plates, and it was discovered that you
couldn't wash plates in the sinks. There were sinks all over
the place— they had been very generous with sinks, placing
them in every conceivable place where you could use one—
but not any sinks you could use for the most important
things of all. Fields, the chief butler, had them taken out,
and we settled for one good big sink.

The valets were fit to be tied when they discovered that
the pressing room for valets was in the basement. They refused to use it, because it would take them too far away
from the President, or the important guests when they
rang. Finally, one of the small rooms for the sleep-in
servants had to be converted for pressing.

The laundry was the most disappointing of all the so-
called improvements. I had pictured a long room with
shelves on the walls, where the girls could lay the sheets
and large tablecloths with ease after ironing, but instead,
there was a small room with two small metal cabinets and a
mangle that would take only a single sheet. The room next
to it had to be set up with a larger mangle, but the wall between could not be knocked out, and the arrangements
remained awkward.

The maids were up in arms when they discovered that their third-floor bath had been done away with in order to enlarge a cedar room. We were expected to go to the maids' room in the basement. Mrs. Truman took pity on us, and said we could use the bathroom of the visiting maid's room. This was fine, except that we had to go through her bedroom— impossible when a maid was in residence there during royal and official State visits.

No, the planners who supervised the plans for the remodeling of the White House certainly didn't have the servants in mind when they changed things around. They even took away two small tubs on the third floor that we had used constantly for small washing. But then, they didn't always have the comfort of the First Family in mind either.

For some inexplicable reason, they omitted air conditioning from the Solarium— the one place that Presidential families seem to enjoy the most. The President and Mrs. Truman had eaten breakfast and lunch on this porch every day, unless the weather was too hot. From the Coolidges on, it had been used. President Roosevelt, but not his wife, rested there. Mrs. Eisenhower loved the room so much, that she asked me to make a special felt pad for the table out there, so her bridge club could hold its sessions in the Solarium. When the bamboo chairs were tearing the ladies' stockings, I had to make special covers for them too.

I'd hate to estimate how much it cost to have the error in the Solarium corrected, but corrected it was, and somehow the press never found out so they could make a fuss about it.

There were other errors too, like the catches on the cabinets in the linen room that were high enough for giants, but Mrs. Truman made sure that one thing was installed properly. It was a full-length mirror in the linen room, so that she and Margaret could come for fittings, and I would not have to go to them all the time. But then we found out that in the sewing room, there was not a single outlet for an electric iron. Mrs. "T" was furious. She spoke bitterly of all the errors, and, in conclusion, she said to me, "No matter what you tell them, they are going to fix this White House to suit themselves."

I give Mrs. Truman much of the credit for the good taste in the decoration of the family quarters of the White House. Toward the end of the renovation, she was consulted on this section of the house, and always chose things in simple good taste.

From the public interest standpoint, I think Mrs. Truman's greatest historical contribution was to reassemble the Lincoln Room. The poor Lincoln bed had wandered all through the White House in the previous administrations. Some Presidents had brought it to their bedroom and slept in it. The second Mrs. Wilson had brought it to her room. In the Roosevelt administration, everyone had fought to sleep in it, but Col. Louis Howe, the top advisor to FDR, received the honor and had it installed in his Green Bedroom, the northwest room that Margaret Truman later slept in. She was succeeded by Mamie Eisenhower's mother, Mrs. John Doud, and then, of course, the Green Room was changed to a pastel pink for the ladies.

Mrs. Truman worked diligently to restore the Lincoln Room, in which the great man had signed the Emancipation Proclamation, with all the Lincoln furniture, which had been spread all over the house. She brought back the Lincoln bed to its rightful place, as well as Lincoln's old dresser and tables. She also found a couple of Lincoln chairs around the White House to complete the restoration.

Margaret Truman tried out the restored Lincoln Room with two girl friends. They found the bed so uncomfortable that they ended up the night sleeping on the floor instead. While they appreciated the honor of using the bed, they said that it would have been hard to explain this to their aching backs the next day.

The new First Lady might like to see the labor of love that another First Lady contributed to the Lincoln bed. It is a crocheted bedspread, which Mrs. Coolidge worked on for several years. It is packed away now, and has been since the Truman family moved to Blair House, and a quilted spread now covers the bed. But she has only to ask for it, and the crocheted spread will be brought out of storage for her inspection.

At the windows in the Lincoln Room, I am proud to say she will find some of the many curtains I have made for the White House. There they are embroidered net under green drapery. They are four yards and sixteen inches long from the top of the window to the floor. That is the kind of material lengths we worked with at the White House.

But getting back to the contributions of the First Ladies, rather than mine, Mrs. Eisenhower will be praised by history for her important job of assembling a sample of china, from each and every administration, into a great display in the China Room on the ground floor. It was a real task, and took more patience than she would have given to other projects.

Mrs. Hoover's real contribution to the White House was the restoration of the Monroe Room. A friend of hers, a Miss McMullun, and she searched the mansion and painstakingly studied old records to collect the furniture that had been used by James Monroe and his wife in their sitting room. This room is on the south side of the second floor, on the other side of the President's Oval Room study. Some of the Monroe pieces were found outside of the White House and brought back in triumph.

As for Mrs. Roosevelt's greatest contribution, I think it

was important but of an intangible nature. She threw the White House open to everyone, and, in every way, made the public feel that the White House belonged as much to them as to her. Sometimes, we servants worried that she might be carrying her "Open Door Policy" too far when she brought in ill-clad and ill-fed strays right off the Washington streets, and scared the Secret Service men half to death.

However, FDR made the tangible contribution to earn the decorating laurels of that administration. It was a strange twist that FDR, rather than the First Lady, would sometimes get interested in the decoration of the White House and order some individual touch, which was always an improvement. As examples, he designed a frieze to ornament the grand piano, which all the guests would see in the East Room, and he ordered an inscription carved over the State Dining Room fireplace. The words were from a prayer that John Adams, the first President to occupy the White House, had composed and sent to his wife before she joined him in Washington. It reads,

> "I pray heaven to bestow the best of blessings on this house and on all that shall hereafter inhabit it. May none but honest and wise men ever rule under this roof."

Right here I want to clear up a point on which Mrs. "R" was much maligned. Though she may have been a little careless about matching things in a room, or overlooking something that needed redecorating, she was a stickler for cleanliness. The public had a mistaken impression about this, and Mrs. "R" was once quite hurt when a woman sent a letter saying that the White House curtains looked dirty from the outside. That couldn't have been true. Mrs. "R" would have surprise inspections late at night, and we always made sure that even the linen and sewing rooms were spick-and-span before going home.

FDR was very sensitive to the feelings of others, a quality that made him most kind to the help.

President Truman used to kid us by saying that his wife was coming, and to hurry and "be sure to sweep the dirt under the rug."

President Eisenhower left the complete running of the house to his wife, except for his personal bouts in the kitchen with his cooking. He used to let the beef for his soup simmer in the kitchen next to my workroom for hours and hours until we would all be drooling. It had a most delicious odor. Every once in a while he would pop into the kitchen to check on it, and he would supervise the preparation of the vegetables until they were just so. He loved to don an apron and do his own mixing at the pot. Once, when he went to Palm Springs, California, for a rest, he took his whole container of soup with him because he hadn't had time to eat it at the White House. We loved this human touch in the dignified General-President.

President Eisenhower did not make an effort to know us all by name as Truman and FDR had. After President Eisenhower had incurred the mild stroke in November of 1957, he snapped out of it in a few days, and was up and walking around arm-in-arm with Mamie, talking and laughing. Enrique, one of the three housemen who are assigned to the First Lady, told me about it. "They were talking about you too, Lillian," he said.

"What did they say about me?" I demanded.

"They were in the Lincoln Room, and Miss Mamie was telling about the curtains you made," Enrique said. "The President wanted to know who 'Lillian' was, and he looked at the curtains and said, 'You mean to say that you have someone in this house who can do work like this?'

"Miss Mamie told him, 'You know the little girl who sews in the room next to your kitchen?' The President looked surprised and said, 'Oh, *she* is Lillian? I know *her.*' "

I thanked Enrique for telling me. And I noticed the President taking a good look at me one day soon after.

FDR used to ask me everytime he saw me, and after every election, when we would line up in the Oval Room to shake his hand and welcome him back to the White House, "Well, Little Girl (that was his nickname for me), how is everything in the linen room?" Then he'd throw back his head and laugh.

Eventually, we had a special joke between us, because I had made the blackout curtains for the whole third floor, and he had caught me sprawled out on hands and knees working on the bolts of black material. Everything was so covered with black, that he had kidded me about whether I would lose my eyesight or my mind first. I had joshed him right back about being the first person to have "blackout knee" instead of "housemaid's knee."

Before the President wheeled away from me and my bolts of black, he became very serious for a moment. "Little Girl, you know and I know that one can overcome anything."

I said, "Yes, Mr. President, we do."

Hardly anyone knew he really couldn't walk on his legs. He made it look like walking by using handrails so he could pull himself along one foot at a time, to help him look more robust. Handrails were always installed wherever he was going to speak.

Whenever I saw him, I felt so grateful to the dear Lord for letting me have one normal leg, even though the other was withered by polio.

Once, my common bond with the President—polio—almost got me into trouble. The war had begun, and because of the ever-present danger of attack on the White House, it was ordered that no one was to use the elevator except

the President. No one. We people backstairs were to stick
to the stairs and leave the elevator for him. Someone went
to the President and told him that "Little Lillian" could
not use the steps. The President said that an exception
should be made for me.

Somehow, my superiors got the impression that I had
asked for this special privilege, and I was in the dog house.
I didn't even know for what. Finally, I found out what was
going on, and explained that I could certainly walk up and
down the back steps like anyone else, and was not expecting favors.

People are always asking me what we do when the servants meet the President or First Lady in the halls. Do we
ignore them? Or call out a cheery "Hello, sir" or "Ma'am."
Or what? Strange as it may seem, we make ourselves as
scarce as possible. We try not to run into the President and
First Lady if we can possibly help it, in order to give them
a feeling of privacy.

Every President has faced the servant problem in a different way and with different reactions. The Hoovers were
fierce about servants being neither seen, nor heard, and
heaven help you if you were caught in the hall when the
President was coming. It was a sort of scandal around the
White House, the way we would dodge into a particular
closet so the President wouldn't see us. It was a closet
near the elevator on the second floor that was used mostly
for brooms and mops. But it was definitely for the help in
an emergency, and butlers with trays would pop in and fall
into a closetful of maids and housemen waiting for the
coast to be clear.

President Hoover was so emphatic about having "invisible" servants, that we tried very hard to disappear when
we heard the bells— three for the President, and two for the
First Lady— announcing that they were leaving their
second-floor quarters. Like jack-in-the-boxes, we would

jump in and out of hiding places, because maids and house-men would be severely scolded— on sight.

Yet, he could be thoughtful on occasion. The painters were painting the servants' dining room; a table for us had been set out in the hall, and the President had to pass it on the way to his own lunch. Out of respect, we stood when he appeared, but he stopped to say that he understood quite well that we were respectful of his office, and that we did not have to interrupt our meal by standing.

When the Roosevelts arrived and saw us popping into the closets, FDR gave the order to stop this and "just act natural."

Of course, we still tried to stay out of the way as much as possible. This is a White House tradition. But if we ran into them in the halls, we no longer had to be afraid of consequences.

Mr. Truman was the most insistent that we be at ease. But the yardmen hadn't heard of his attitude, and were still crouching behind the rose bushes when they saw the President approach on the way to his office. He asked, "Why are these people peeping at me?" After that, even the yardmen continued working when he passed.

When President Eisenhower came in, we again tried to stay out of his way until we knew just how easy-going he would be. Finally, Eisenhower asked, "Why don't I ever see anyone working?" When the White House tradi-tion was explained to him, he ordered, "Let these people do their work, and stop this foolishness about keeping out of sight."

And so we said farewell, without tears, to an old White House tradition.

THE ETERNAL CLOTHES
PROBLEM

I don't know how you feel, but I think you *can* tell something about people by their clothes— not only the clothes they wear, but the ones they don't— and what they do with their clothes.

You'd be surprised by the clothes problems some ladies have had in the White House. The First Lady I felt sorriest for, in the clothing department, was Mrs. Truman. The most conservative dresser herself, she was shocked at the wild clothes the President loved to deck himself out in.

She had to be a kind of watchdog. The funniest moment was when she was getting ready for a trip to Florida with the President, and caught Prettyman, Mr. Truman's valet, packing a pair of red trousers into the President's suitcase. They had been a gift, just as the million-and-one wild sport shirts had been, and she lived in mortal fear that he would some day wear them.

If he wanted to bring the bow tie back into style— which he succeeded in doing— she could stand that; and if he wanted to wear hibiscus-flowered sport shirts among his buddies in and out of the press, she could grit her teeth and bear that too; but the bright red slacks— no, never!

Every few weeks, the President would go over his wardrobe and throw out a lot of his clothing, including the dozens of neckties and shirts he would receive, and Mrs. "T" always hoped he'd include the wild red pants. He would put out the clothes he was discarding for the ushers, Secret Service men, butlers, and housemen to take.

When Mrs. "T" saw Prettyman packing those pants, she said that the red trousers were not going on any trip *she* was going on. So the pants stayed at the White House that time. But the very next time that the President made a trip to Florida without his wife, he wore those pants.

Mrs. Truman was also Margaret's watchdog on clothes; I suppose she hoped that her daugher would be as conservative as she. But Margaret was theatrical like her father, and wanted something with dash. There was one dress that Mrs. "T" could not stand on her daughter. It was black with bright red flowers, and was cut on Oriental lines with a Chinese neckline. Margaret tried to plan a way to please her mother and still save the dress.

She came to me with her problem. "Will you take off the Chinese collar?" she asked. "I think Mother will like it then." Mrs. Truman happened to come into the room when I had the collar off and was fitting the dress. She looked very displeased.

"What are you going to do with that dress?" she asked Margaret.

Margaret said, "Oh, Mother, when Lillian gets through, you won't know this dress."

Mrs. "T" gave the dress a look of disdain and said, "Well, when she gets through fixing it, tell her to dye it." And out she went.

Mrs. Truman would go up to New York when Margaret

was singing on the concert stage, and go through her wardrobe every once in a while, looking for anything that was not in good taste. Most of Margaret's dresses were beyond reproach, but there was one green one that prodded even me into using my own judgment. This particular green made Margaret look slightly green herself, and she had only worn it once, when she was bridesmaid at a wedding. She brought it to me to have the sleeves changed. "I can get some more wear from it that way," she said.

I took the dress and hid it as best I could at the back of the closet, still with its pins in, and hoped she would forget about it. I think she did, because I never heard another word about, and I'm happy to say I never saw her in it again.

As for her own clothes, Mrs. Truman was always simple and dignified. She went in for suits— even silk suits for teas. Her favorite color was black, and she used to tell me, "You can't go wrong with black."

Once I tried to argue with her, because she looked so well in blue, which matched her eyes, that I wanted her to wear it more often. I ventured to say, "Well, fashion claims that when you get older, you shouldn't wear too much black, because black makes one look tired." Mrs. "T" pondered that a moment.

"Well, Lillian," she repeated, "you can't go wrong with black."

Mrs. Roosevelt hated to be bothered with clothes. She would order up a supply at the beginning of a season, and that would be that. She always had a few lace dresses, because they could be tossed into a suitcase, and would not need ironing when unpacked.

Mrs. Roosevelt showed her true character when, after ordering identical blouses for herself and three of her secretaries, she told me, "Lillian, make theirs first." If she had a dress or blouse she particularly liked, she would hand it to me and say, "Please copy this," and I would make another in a different color. I could not take the garment apart to make a pattern, and my early training in copying any dress certainly came in handy.

The two women who were poles apart when it came to buying new dresses, or altering used ones, were Mrs. Roosevelt and Mrs. Eisenhower. Of all the women I have ever known, Mrs. Roosevelt cared the least about clothes, and Mrs. Eisenhower cared the most.

With only one exception, all the First Ladies whom Mama or I knew always gave their older dresses and accessories to the maids or other people in and out of the White House. But not Mrs. Eisenhower. Mrs. Roosevelt practically dressed a few members of her staff. Mrs. Truman was so kind, that when the family of one of her cooks sent word, all the way from the Philippines, that they had been burned out of their house, she gave the cook a bundle of her own dresses and other clothing to send to them.

Mrs. Eisenhower has been generous with other things, such as food, but not with her clothes. Only her daughter-in-law, Barbara, received anything. We were hurt until we saw the light. Then we ceased to hold it against the First Lady, because we finally understood what her clothes mean to her. Mrs. Eisenhower collects clothes as others collect demitasse cups or paintings. She knows and loves each dress, and, ten years later, brings out a dress which she wants to wear for some sentimental reason.

When I retired from the White House shortly before she left there, her evening gowns alone had grown so numerous, that she had appropriated two whole bedrooms in which to store them on clothes racks, covered with sheets. I believe history will record that she had more clothes than any lady who ever occupied the White House.

She did not go in for sheaths, and practically every dress had a very full skirt. I can remember only once when she wore black, and after that, the black velvet gown was put away, never to be brought out again. Her favorites were in solid colors and combinations, both bright and pastel. She was a genius at color selection, and knew exactly what would bring out the wonderful coloring of her complexion. She looked lovely in a lavender changeable silk and in the soft, flowered patterns she frequently wore.

It is true that Mamie Eisenhower loved pink. She wore a lot of pink, and she dressed in a pink dressing room (I made the pink draperies for it). Sometimes, when everything that arrived at the White House was pink or rose, or had a contrasting background with pink flowers, we kidded one another backstairs that we'd be living in a Pink Palace if it didn't stop.

One day, I sent Talmadge Baty, one of our helpers in the storeroom, to get five yards of flannel. I needed it to make bags to fit over the large mop that is used to clean the East Room floor, after the sight-seers had scuffed it. He brought me the flannel, and I looked at it aghast.

"Baty, why did you get pink flannel?" I asked him.

"It's for Mrs. E, isn't it?" he inquired bluntly.

"No," I snapped, "it's for the mop."

"Well," he said matter-of-factly, "everything else is pink around here, so we may as well have pink mops."

And we did.

I revolted once by making a green pincushion when a pink one had been ordered. It happened when, in a great rush, I was fixing up the "Pink Powder Room" for a Halloween party. The salmon-pink carpeting clashed with every other pink object in the room— wall, towels, and accessories. Mrs. Eisenhower was personally concerned that every bathroom detail be arranged in time, and a rush job on the carpeting was done at the last minute. When I saw all that pink, I saw red, and I disobeyed orders and made a green pincushion to give it a *little* contrast.

Future generations will be able to see how this particular First Lady felt about pink if they visit the Smithsonian Institution in Washington, and view the gown on display that she wore at the first Inaugural Ball. It is a pink *peau de soie,* sprinkled with pink stones. All the accessories were pink too— purse, shoes, and gloves. Someone made a count and found that over 3,000 pink beads had been used to decorate her accessories. That's a lot of pink for anyone.

She also wore more red than any First Lady I have seen, and went so far as to get a whole red outfit, including a coat. But with it she wore navy blue shoes. Mrs. Eisenhower did much to popularize the wearing of fabric shoes dyed to match her dresses. She had shoes for almost every dress.

Only once did Mrs. Eisenhower come to me with a dress that needed fitting, and make use of the mirror that Mrs. Truman had had installed in the linen room. The rest of the time, I would go to her dressing room, or her maid, Rosie, would put the pins in and bring the dress to me.

Mrs. "E" had a professional marking stand in her dressing room that was too heavy to take elsewhere. It was a metal pedestal on which you could stand, and attached to it was a hem-marker. I was happy that the First Lady ignored short-short styles and kept her hems at mid-calf. Had she worn them a bit shorter, I think the public would have objected. As it was, I overheard many adverse comments from the guests when I tended the powder room during parties.

Since I was always the girl who tended the powder room the guests used, and stood by with my needle and thread at receptions, dinners, and teas, I would cringe when I heard guests at the White House criticizing the youthful look of the dress their hostess was wearing.

Sometimes they would turn to me— as if I had some control over what the First Lady wore— and ask embarrassing questions. One woman said, "Why don't you stop Mamie from wearing those teen-age dresses?" I would say something to the effect that it was too bad they didn't like the First Lady's dress, as it had been designed by a very fine dress designer. But I longed to add that in openly discussing their hostess, their own taste was questionable.

Around the White House, we maids were convinced that many of the uncomplimentary statements we heard about the First Lady were simply the result of jealousy. Mrs. Eisenhower was determined to stay as young as she could as long as she could; other women wanted her to act like a grandmother just because she was one.

It is true that youthfulness meant a great deal to Mrs. Eisenhower, and we were all aware that it was a motivating factor in her life— she didn't want her grandchildren to call her "Grandma," but only "Mimi." Even her daughter-in-law, Barbara, had to call her "Mimi." She didn't want a dress that "makes me look old." She ate like a bird to keep her figure girlish, and went to Main Chance to be rejuvenated with health foods and beauty routines.

Mrs. Eisenhower is the only First Lady I have known who fought to remain youthful, and who had not resigned herself to being "matronly." Mrs. Roosevelt and Mrs. Truman automatically chose the matronly type of dress, and Mrs. Hoover emphasized it, and seemed to glory in her "grandmotherliness."

As far as the maids of the White House were concerned, we were on the side of Mrs. Eisenhower. We didn't tell our ages, and we were proud that a woman— and a First Lady at that— was proving that one could be young and lovely into the late fifties. To us, she symbolized the New Woman who does not have to grow old.

I'll never forget the time I gave Mrs. Eisenhower a little gift tied in a pink ribbon. The next morning, she was wearing the ribbon from the wrapping— she loved to wear ribbons around her hair, and did so almost every morning. "Oh, Lillian," she exclaimed, "that was the nicest French ribbon!" Then she thanked me for the gift too, a pink powder puff.

One of my proudest moments in the White House was when I was called in to make some change in the work of the experts. I remember when I did a quick job on a Sally Victor hat— Mrs. Eisenhower loved hats— changing the trimming from rose to pale pink. I had to send to the store to get my materials, and I had only two hours to do the job before a garden party. When Mrs. Walker, the housekeeper, brought me the hat, and I saw I would have to take off the crown, I asked Mrs. Walker, "Who told Mrs. E I could work on hats?"

Mrs. Walker said, "She didn't ask— she thinks that you can do anything."

I felt mighty good, mighty good. And for an extra reward, I noticed that "my hat" looked beautiful, prominently displayed in the newspapers the next day.

At the opposite end of the color chart was Lou Henry Hoover, who had beautiful white hair, which any woman would envy. And then Mrs. Hoover would ruin it by wearing the most drab, neutral colors— grey and muddy brown. We used to shudder at the money that was spent to make her look drab, when she could have looked radiant for half the amount.

My regular Government job at the White House covered a multitude of tasks, such as mending the linen, sewing the draperies, filling in for absent maids, taking care of resident or visiting children, and standing by with the

Secret Service men to check tourists' cameras and other gear.

The sewing and alteration that I did for the First Ladies was my extracurricular job, done after regular hours— and my favorite one. The only mending I did for a President was done as a favor to Moaney, Mr. Eisenhower's valet— I mended the President's woolen golf stockings.

But I'm proud to say I made one of Eisenhower's favorite garments— a cooking apron. It was made of most unusual fabric— a piece of tan material with the pictures of many Presidents of the United States, including himself and Harry Truman. He loved to wear the apron, and would sit down among his guests when he was cooking, still wearing it. I have kept a piece of the material, which shows Fillmore, Wilson, Taft, Lincoln, and Washington.

Mrs. Hoover used to want me to dream up collar-and-cuff combinations to change the appearance of her gowns, and I made dozens of large chiffon handkerchiefs to match all her evening gowns. Mrs. Roosevelt demanded the least alterations— if the hem were anywhere near where it should be, let it alone, there are more important things— that was her attitude.

Mrs. Truman hated shoulder pads, and it was my job to figure out how to get rid of them, whenever they appeared in a dress or suit, without spoiling the lines.

Mrs. Eisenhower would have a dress shortened if she felt it was off by one-quarter inch. She is by far the greatest perfectionist. No hook could be bad or zipper showing, or she'd change dresses.

I wasn't supposed to help the fitters who came to the White House in their work, because that was what they were paid for, and I had my own work to do. But I would always get involved anyway, because I love couturier work.

Once I almost got caught. We were all working at top speed around the White House, getting ready for the

Russian Premier, Khrushchev. The housekeeper came along with a rush order— "We are putting up clean curtains," she said. "You will have to make a new sunburst right away to go over the front door." These are the kind of orders that used to really vex me— last-minute stuff.

I had no sooner gotten started, than Mrs. McCaffree, Mrs. Eisenhower's social secretary, brought in Reda, the *little* French fitter— she was even smaller than I— and the dress that was being rushed for Mrs. Eisenhower to wear at the White House dinner for Khrushchev.

"Lillian," said Mrs. McCaffree, who did not know how Mrs. "E" felt about my helping the fitters, "will you give Reda a hand as she has to catch a 3:45 plane back to New York?" Reda worked with Arnold Scaasi, the young designer who introduced Mrs. "E" to the richest fabrics. I told her I would be happy to just as soon as I got the carpenter off my back who was waiting for the sunburst. That was the fastest sunburst I ever made. Then I settled happily to the task of helping Reda finish the gorgeous, long, gold, heavily-embossed brocade ball gown for the First Lady.

Just as I had finished, I went out in the hall to use the desk to hem some towels, so Reda could use my table to spread out the dress for the final inspection, and who should pop off the elevator at that moment but Mrs. Eisenhower. Her first question was, "Lillian, you are not helping her sew on my clothes, are you?"

What could I say? I said, "No, Madam."

Had she been five minutes earlier, she wouldn't have had to ask!

On another historic occasion, I had no choice but to get into the act when the fitters were there— from Arnold Constable of New York, I believe. When President Roosevelt died, and his closed casket was on display in the East Room, fitters were rushed down to fit a black costume for the First Lady to wear at the funeral service. I had just finished preparing a mourning hat for the President's daughter, Anna Boettiger— a hard job because all I had to work with were "beanie" hats. Anyway, just as I'd finished veiling a black beanie, Mrs. Roosevelt's fitters asked me how to thread my sewing machine. I ended up doing their sewing for them while they stood by helplessly and nervously. The funeral was to take place in a few hours, and I felt worse than they, but at the White House, one learns to carry on, no matter what.

On one of the occasions when President Eisenhower was stricken, and was being taken out of the White House in an ambulance, I had to keep one of Mrs. Eisenhower's fitters in my sewing room, to make sure she knew nothing of what was going on. She had been fitting Mrs. Eisenhower when it happened, and had been taken up to my room to "wait."

I talked guardedly on the phone, and I never let on what the delay was all about. The fitter went back to New York unaware that word of the President's illness would soon be flashed around the world. One year later, she came back to the White House for another fitting. I hoped she wouldn't remember, but the first thing she asked me was, "Did you know the President was sick?"

"Oh, no," I said.

When you work at the White House, your first and greatest duty is to the White House, and there silence is the code of ethics.

Naturally, among ourselves, we shared many a cozy private story about Presidents and their clothes habits. For example, Coolidge wanted his wife to dress elegantly while he wore oversized underwear, badly-fitted shirts, and suspenders much too wide for him. And thus he would wander about the White House in shirt sleeves. He didn't own a tailored suit till a mill finally sent him free material.

Hoover dressed expensively, but stiffly, and his dainty feet— size 7½— didn't help his appearance.

I don't know whether Truman or Eisenhower will go down in history as the best-dressed President. Possibly Eisenhower, because he is a little more conservative in his clothes.

As far as we were concerned, it was a big joke when FDR was named one of the best-dressed men. He was so clothes-"unconscious" that the day after the attempt on his life, when he was President-elect, he was about to put on the same "unlucky" tie, not even recognizing it as the one he had worn the day before. McDuffie, his valet, always used that as the supreme example of how little attention FDR paid to his clothes.

And when FDR died, several dozen sweaters were sitting in his room that had never been worn, and I myself counted thirty-five hats, as well as other hats I didn't bother to count, which were still in boxes. The sweaters he had worn were mended and remended, and his hats were battered.

Sartorially speaking, Eisenhower will go down in history for changing the inaugural garb from top hat to Homburg, and Truman for the return of the bow tie.

But in my heart, Truman will also go down in history for his attitude toward his undergarments— he *washed his own.*

GUNS, GIFTS, AND GHOSTS

I remember exactly where I was, of course, when the bullets that killed my favorite White House guard, Leslie Coffelt, started flying. I was one of the maids you read about who were looking out the third-floor window.

The President, I knew, was down below taking a nap. I was sitting all alone, making curtains in the front room of the third floor of Blair House, with my portable sewing machine resting partially on the wide window sill. It was a beautiful All Saints Day— November 1, 1950— and I was thinking about that as I looked across the street at the sunlight on the old State Department Building.

Rose Booker, the new maid, came to the door and said, "Is there anything you would like for me to do to help you?"

I said, "Oh no, come in and sit down a few minutes."

I guess I was feeling a bit lonesome. Rose sat down, and before we could even talk, we heard this "BANG, BANG, BANG, BANG!"

Both of us jumped up, and Rose said, "What's that?"

I said, "Shots," and did the wrong thing by hoisting the window, because the bullets were whizzing in all directions.

Rose and I looked out, and I realized the danger and jumped back and yelled, "Rose, take your head in!"

I was shaking like a leaf as I stood back and watched it all, and later, when Mrs. Truman went down and saw the blood and heard the story, she came back upstairs and cried. Then she pulled herself together and calmly phoned Margaret, who had a concert that night, to tell her everything was "all right," and to go ahead with her singing.

I had seen bravery before in First Ladies, and I was proud of her. I had seen Mrs. Roosevelt live twelve years in the White House with the knowledge that an attempt had been made against her husband, while he was still President-elect, and might be made again at any time. It had been made the month before his inauguration, and it could have happened again. Mayor Anton Cermak of Chicago was killed by that bullet.

Few people knew that the President slept with a gun under his pillow. Nor did they know that the Secret Service men had ordered Mrs. Roosevelt to carry a gun with her wherever she went. I used to see a storeroom helper, Mac, cleaning the First Lady's gun in the supply room run by the husband of the housekeeper, Henrietta Nesbitt.

Backstairs, we called the guns "His" and "Hers." In spite of the joke, however, we were much concerned about the welfare of our invalid boss and his on-the-go wife. Mrs. "R" was supposed to keep her gun handy because she traveled alone so much, and no Secret Service man could keep proper track of her. I was told by others that most of the time, the gun was simply kept in the glove compartment of her car.

I thought it foolhardy for Mrs. Roosevelt to let the White House be so open to the public, both to tourists and casual friends. One of my jobs, until the White House was closed to tourists at the time of the declaration of war, was to check the cameras and other gear of the visitors who entered. I stood with the guards and policemen, and I had to learn to remember faces, and to know a suspicious object when I saw one. If someone came back a second or third time, we watched him or her carefully.

We had many frightening, many funny, and many touching moments. From all over the country, it seemed that every crackpot came to see the Roosevelts— some of them bringing their own supply of food. Once it was a ticking clock that gave us a nightmarish time. It turned out that the man had simply gone shopping before coming to see the White House. Many a person who arrived in Washington to see the President found himself delayed by a trip to St. Elizabeths (the mental hospital) instead, where he was checked by psychiatrists. Harmless people got transportation home.

I was at this post four hours a day, and then I would go back to my other chores of sewing, mending, checking the White House linens, and doing a million-and-one other things.

Once, when I was checking tourists' cameras at the ground floor East Entrance, with a White House guard and Secret Service man, a call came from St. Elizabeths to watch out for a man in purple trunks who had escaped and was on his way to "clean out the White House." Fortunately, they got to him before he got to us, or what was more important, to the Roosevelts.

It is impossible to be too careful. There is always that unexplainable moment when the impossible happens— like the time, during the Franklin Roosevelts' residence, when a couple of tourists simply appeared wandering around the second-floor family quarters. We signaled the guard instantly, and it turned out that they were perfectly harmless, and had somehow just walked up the back stairs without even trying to be secretive.

But it reminded the old-timers of a more dangerous invasion that happened, before my time, to Teddy Roosevelt, and is still recalled around the servants' dining room. A man arrived one evening in full dress and top hat and ushered himself into the White House through a comedy of errors— which were not so comic when someone got fired for them. The President was called from his bedroom to see the man, waiting downstairs and looking very important. He frequently made late appointments, so it seemed natural enough.

When the President had talked to the man for only a few minutes, it was apparent that he was dangerous. Pretending to call for drinks, Teddy Roosevelt marched out of the room, muttering to the butler to "get that crackpot out of here." When the guards searched him, they found that the man was carrying a loaded gun, and could have been a very harmful "crackpot."

President Coolidge, who was just a little fellow, was least afraid, and gave his protectors the most headaches, because he thought it was a good game to sneak out without them. It was almost his way of getting exercise— running down the back steps, seeing if he could avoid being accompanied.

Because all knew the trouble the White House detail would be in with the Secret Service chief and, in fact, the nation, if the President got away and anything happened to him, everyone cooperated with the Secret Service in signaling which door Mr. Coolidge seemed to be headed for. The staff tracked his progress, and he could never figure out why his "shadow" was always waiting for him wherever he emerged.

Truman and Eisenhower were rough and tough and quite unafraid of any danger. Eisenhower went ahead and braved travel abroad when he was warned of possible danger to his life, and Truman hardly changed his schedule, even on the day when the shooting took place in the attempt on his life at Blair House.

Every President had his favorite Secret Service man. With President Eisenhower, it was Richard Flohr, who even accompanied the President on the golf course. Flohr ran the golf cart.

Col. Ed Starling— he was a Kentucky Colonel— was the Secret Service man Coolidge could most tolerate, and he would fall in with the President on his walks. He was also a favorite of President Harding, and used to keep track of all the bets at Harding's golf and poker sessions.

Starling was a big man— big in spirit and big in size. One morning, when I was coming in to work, the guards had in tow a man who claimed he had come to read poetry to the President. While the officers were talking to him, Colonel Starling came in, looked at the man, and spoke a few words to him. Then I heard Starling say, "Let him go. There is no anger there whatsoever."

It was said around the White House that Starling could tell whether a man was dangerous or not just by his expression. I believed it.

Secret Service Agent Mike Reilly was the favorite of FDR. He travelled with the President, and that took in a lot of territory. He was with Roosevelt at Casablanca and aboard the *Augusta,* in August of 1941, when the President met Churchill.

The next time Reilly saw Churchill was just after Pearl Harbor when the Prime Minister came to the White House. Churchill did not know that when he was leaving Washington, an attempt was made on his life. One of the American guards at the airplane that was waiting to fly him home had gone berserk and was about to shoot Churchill, who was getting out of the White House car. A Secret Service man named Howard Chandler grabbed the fellow's gun and had him hustled off before Churchill arrived at the plane. So quickly had the action taken place, that Churchill had not even noticed it, and he marched happily into the plane.

You can imagine how careful we became at the White House with two incidents hanging over us— the attempt on Roosevelt before he had even taken office, and the attempt on Churchill by someone obsessed with anglophobia — hatred of the British.

Joseph Zangara, the man who aimed at President-elect Roosevelt and killed Mayor Cermak, was electrocuted, and the man who tried to do the same to Churchill ended up in a mental institution.

The funniest story along this line— if such grim tales can be funny— is the case of the man who hung around in front of the White House for two weeks with murder in his mind before he was apprehended. The humor comes out in the way he was arrested.

It was war time— World War II— and the District of Columbia had just passed an ordinance calling for the arrest of those who crossed the street against the red light. The police were being very vigilant, and this man was caught crossing the street from Lafayette Square toward the White House.

As we heard the story afterward, the policeman said, "I'm going to take you to the station house." Whereupon, the man said, "You can't do that; I'm here to shoot the President."

He's still at St. Elizabeths, by the way.

During the Eisenhower administration, a nineteen-year-old Texas blonde tried to get in to see the President to protest a decision of a court that involved a Texas land claim. She would speak to no one but the President, or reporters— so she didn't get in. Then for ten days she laid siege to the White House by hanging around the sidewalk near the White House gates, while wearing a ten-pound

log chain, padlocked around her neck. It was a real atten-
tion-getter. The First Family did not appreciate the attention, but what could they do?

The girl sent the key to the padlock to President Eisenhower, so that he could come and unchain her, but the
President promptly sent it to the guards at the main gate,
without fanfare. She refused to take the key; then one day,
it started to rain. In a final fit of frustration, she retrieved
her key, unlocked her log chain, wrapped it around the
main gate, and locked it there. Then she left with the key,
never to return— we hope! Workmen had to cut the chain,
and we kidded about how the blonde had succeeded in
keeping the President away from his golf for three and a
half minutes— the length of time it took to break the chain.

Though the incident was amusing, the pretty girl was
lucky to get away in her own good time. This method of
attracting the President's attention is not recommended.
Others have gotten into real trouble using crackpot tactics.

Once, when a postal clerk found a bomb in a package
addressed to the President, he was at first highly praised.
He didn't deserve any laurels. It turned out he had sent
the bomb himself, and he ended up in a mental institution.

There are so many variations on the theme of attacking
the President, that the men of the Secret Service just develop a cynical attitude toward everything. The White
House is one place where visitors are not permitted to put
their hands in their pockets; the Secret Service is too afraid
of what they might pull out. Nor are visitors permitted to
walk too fast, or make sudden gestures.

More than one guest who waved an arm too wildly has
had the arm bumped by a man who was, unknown to him
or her, a member of the Secret Service. Once— I can't remember if it happened in the Truman or Roosevelt era—
a woman pulled out a tiny gun from her pocketbook and
was indignant when she was instantly surrounded by Secret

Service men. It turned out that the little gun was just a cigarette lighter.

Usually, anybody who has it in for the President or his family gives plenty of evidence that he is warped to the point of needing psychiatric treatment. This kind of person generally talks about his complaints time and again. People just pass it off as harmless sorehead talk, but at the White House, we never take a chance. Crackpots and soreheads are presumed dangerous until proven harmless.

When someone wants to see the President to read him poetry, or to give him a message from God, he is looked over very carefully, and he finds a good audience for his wild talk in the Secret Service men. When a man says "they" are out to get him, and only the President can handle the situation, they *really* pay attention. Almost every assassination of a President has been the result of a persecution complex in the would-be murderer's twisted brain.

The general public does not realize how many times attempts have been made upon the lives of the Presidents. Those you hear about are the ones that were successful— Lincoln, Garfield, and McKinley. But there are the ones that failed— the ones the Secret Service still talks about.

Did you know, for example, that Andrew Jackson was attacked by an assassin in the Capitol of the United States when he was President-elect? Fortunately, the gun jammed, and he lived to make history in the White House by inviting his rough, tough friends, who thought furniture was to stand on and rugs to spit upon.

And did you know that when Teddy Roosevelt was giving a speech (the time he was trying for a comeback for the Presidential office as a Bull Moose), he was shot in the chest and finished his speech in spite of the wound? The man who tried to kill Teddy Roosevelt died in an insane asylum during World War II.

All these would-be assassins had an unnatural and unreasonable hatred for the President, and had been heard talking in a threatening way about how they were "going to get the President." Few people knew it, but during World War II, the tall iron fence around the White House was wired for sound. After the war, it was unwired.

From time to time, all kinds of gadgets are tried for their value in ensuring security and in detecting whether anyone entering the White House grounds is carrying a gun. Once we heard of an X-ray type of machine that was being tried out for handling crowds. The gadget was discarded, because it was considered too indecent to be used on women, even though the women who passed through its beam wouldn't have known that they were being, you might say, "disrobed" by it.

Let me warn you— if you want to get a gift through to the White House, don't send a watch. Anything that ticks is assumed to have an explosive quality, and I'd like to have a penny for every watch and clock that has been smashed or dumped in oil.

And don't send food; most of it is destroyed. All food is sent to the Department of Agriculture to be checked for poison, but sometimes it is deemed best just to destroy the lot. Once, some poisoned fish arrived from Cuba, and it turned out that the sender was not the culprit. Someone else had gotten at the package.

Don't send anything that looks too mysterious. Once, such a package was destroyed, and it proved to be phonograph records that Churchill had sent. That was a hard one to explain.

Don't send nasty or threatening letters to the White House either. Every one is investigated, and occasionally, in times of stress, several thousand are received in a month. Before a President goes to any city, the Secret Service men have to determine where each poison-pen writer is, and some of them are watched all the time the President is in their town. Once, it took years to find a certain female letter-writer. But the Secret Service never gives up, and she was eventually nabbed right in the act at a corner mailbox.

The White House is probably the only home that actually needs whole rooms for gifts. No gift comes to the White House directly. It is inspected and X-rayed in the basement of the building next door, which used to be the State Department, but now is used for executive offices. Some suspicious items are taken out to the country in a bomb carrier and there examined and destroyed.

Probably the Eisenhowers have accepted more gifts than any other First Families. Gettysburg is an example of the rewards of popularity— a lawn of shrubbery, a barnful of prize livestock specimens.

When gifts come from strangers, however— little gifts like pot-holders, hand-wrought jewelry and Chinese scrolls— they are stored for one year in the gift rooms— either "His" or "Hers," as the case may be. Mrs. Roosevelt started this practice in self-defense, because gifts were rolling into the White House in unprecedented numbers during the Roosevelt administration, and were followed soon after by bills for the goods. The legal counsel advised her that if a giver did not call for his gift within a year, it really belonged to her.

I remember that once I wasted half a day hunting for a handkerchief that a woman had sent to Mrs. Roosevelt and then wanted back, because she disapproved of something the First Lady had said in her column. I almost lost my eyesight rummaging among the thousands of items until I finally came up with the hand-embroidered handkerchief.

We've received some weird presents at the White House, but the one that turned my stomach the most was a gruesome scroll that had been written in human blood and was sent from India. No matter how disgusting and how batty the gift, the White House secretaries must send a very sweet and gracious note acknowledging it. The last time I stopped by the gift department, two secretaries were employed full time simply sending "thank you" notes.

I may as well talk about ghosts, because everyone wants to know about ghosts in the White House. "Are there really ghosts?" I've been asked. "Do you see them, feel them, or hear them? Does Lincoln really 'inhabit' the White House?"

I can't help what the reader will think; I only know that two times I had frightening experiences along that line, and that people who live at the White House, and some who visit the White House, have also known strange goings on. I suppose that some of them are as unreal as mistaking me for a little ghost way back in the Taft administration, when as a child, I sat in my little dress, waiting for my mother to take me home. But there are other incidents that can't be explained so easily.

I remember that when I was working at the bed in the Rose Room, getting the spread fixed for Queen Elizabeth, I had an experience that sent me flying out of there so fast, I almost forgot my crutches. The spread was a little too long, and I was hemming it as it lay on the bed. I had finished one side, and was ready to start the other, when suddenly I felt that someone was looking at me, and my scalp tightened.

I could feel something coldish behind me, and I didn't have the courage to look. It's hard to explain. I went out of that room, and I didn't finish that spread until three years later.

I wasn't the only one who had an experience in that room. Katurah Brooks, who used to work with Mama on the second floor, was doing her chores there when she heard laughter coming from the bed. It was loud laughter and had a hollow sound, and it couldn't have come from any other place, because she was the only person in the room.

The Rose Room is the one that is always reserved for queens and famous female guests, and the bed there is the one that was used by Andrew Jackson.

I am not an expert on ESP, and I do not know if there are such things as ghosts. And so far, nobody else does either. But all I can do is tell you what stories I have heard around the White House, and what happened to Mama and me at various times.

Once, during the Roosevelt administration, I was in the small room in the northwest corner of the house (later Margaret Truman's bedroom), getting the room put together after the painters had finished with it. It was summer, and the house was almost empty, because some of the maids had gone to Hyde Park with the Roosevelts.

I had to go through the big room to get to the small room. The Lincoln bed and most of the furniture was in the big room at the time. This had been Col. Louis Howe's suite when he was living. All the time I was working, I could hear footsteps coming right to the door. When I looked that way, I never saw anyone.

After an hour, I went to the third floor and found a houseman. I asked him, "Why do you keep walking across the floor in the Lincoln Room without coming in?"

He informed me, "I just came on duty and haven't been on that floor. That was Abe you heard."

He was perfectly serious, and he wasn't trying to be funny.

I don't want to frighten the new tenants, but any number of persons in the White House believe in the ghost of Lincoln. It was rumored backstairs that Queen Wilhelmina had seen the ghost of Lincoln when she opened the door to a strange knock. The next morning, she is supposed to have told it to FDR, who was not too surprised, because his wife had felt something strange also.

Mrs. Roosevelt mentioned several times that when she was working at her desk in the room that had been Lincoln's bedroom, she would feel a presence behind her. She was braver than I, and did turn around, but she couldn't get rid of the feeling.

There is a certain window in the Oval Room where Lincoln was supposed to have stood looking out toward Virginia, while he worried about the Civil War. That is where Lincoln's ghost has been seen most often by White House servants. Mama said that even Mrs. Coolidge saw him there.

Another person who saw Lincoln's ghost was Mary Eben, who was a secretary to Roosevelt, and who didn't make up stories. I used to sew for her, and I would go to her home at the Wardman Park— now the Sheraton Park Hotel— for the fittings. Miss Eben told me she saw Lincoln putting his boots on at his bedside.

Truman may have been awakened by Lincoln's ghost, because he too heard a strange knocking at his door. He opened it, so we were told, and found no one there, but he had been awakened by a rapping and was sure it was not a dream.

Lincoln is supposed to have marched up and down the second-floor hall, where the President sleeps, and where his old room is now used as a guest room.

Once, when Mama brought a breakfast tray to a house guest during the Roosevelt administration, she was shocked to find the woman all packed to go. The woman said, "I am leaving. I will never spend another night in this room." Another guest insisted that a ghost had tried to set her bed on fire and had kept her up all night. She too was ready to leave.

The one who told me about the latter incident, and some of his own adventures with ghosts, was Cesar Carrera, who took Mama's place as chief houseman on the second and third floors when she retired as head maid of the family quarters. Later Cesar became valet to FDR when George Fields went into the Navy. As a matter of fact, Cesar and his wife shared a house with me— they took one floor and I the other— and I know his character. He was convinced that the White House was haunted, and he was a man who would not lie about such a thing.

He had heard someone calling him in a strange, far-off voice in the Yellow Room, and telling him that his name was "Mr. Burns." He had thought that possibly it was someone trying to play a joke on him, but in his research, he discovered that a Burns had actually given the land on which the White House was built to the Government. Cesar told me that he also had seen the ghost of Lincoln.

Every administration has had its ghost stories. Back in Harding's time, when Mrs. Harding lay deathly ill, Mama was carrying laundry from the second to the third floor when she heard a terrible, ghostly groaning, like a woman suffering. She refused to go a step further. I asked her why she wouldn't go see who it was, which made her very angry. But, when I went to the White House, I too heard an odd noise, and suddenly I was no longer interested in checking up on Mama's report.

The ghosts of several First Ladies are supposed to return now and then. Dolley Madison is said to have been an angry ghost when the second Mrs. Wilson ordered her old flower garden dug up, and Abigail Adams is a busy ghost, fooling around with her laundry in the East Room.

Mrs. Hoover had a little fun with the latter story when she gave a shower for one of her three secretaries, who was leaving to be married. She suggested that all the guests bring linen, and all this ghostly array was strung up on a clothesline in the East Room. Shades of Abigail Adams.

Then there has been the ghost of Mrs. Cleveland, who gave birth to the first child of a President to be born in the White House. Some of the moaning such as Mama heard is supposed to be the echo of her childbirth pangs.

I don't know what the White House does to its occupants, but even little Fala, Roosevelt's beloved dog, saw a ghost when his master died. The maids, who were with the President in Georgia when he died, swear that Fala saw the spirit of the President leaving the "Little White House" at the instant of death. Fala rushed, howling, straight into the screen door, as if following the ghost of his master. The screen door opened, or someone opened it, and Fala pursued the unseen for quite a while till he gave up.

Then at the President's funeral service at the White House, the only funeral at which I've ever seen a dog in attendance, Fala made such a strange crying noise, as if he wanted to get nearer to something that only he could see, that he had to be taken from the room. He didn't want to leave. I know, because I was there.

Does that mean FDR is also at the White House? If so, no one human has seen him yet.

Backstairs, we were aware of all kinds of family superstitions. For example, Lizzie McDuffie, one of the maids who was at the Little White House when FDR died, and whose husband, Irvin McDuffie, was valet to FDR, told me that a bird found in the house was a bad luck omen in the Roosevelt family. She said that a bird was found in the "Little White House" just before Roosevelt's mother died, and another was found there just before the President died. Strangely enough, the dinnerware used by the Roosevelts had a design of three feathers. And the man who had designed this pattern was Franklin Delano Roosevelt.

DON'T ENVY A FIRST LADY

To the reader I say, "Don't envy a First Lady."

Many a guest and tourist at the White House has told me she wishes she could know what it's like to be married to a President.

How would you like to be married to a man who eats twice as fast as his guests and leaves the table before they have finished? That was Hoover. And how would you like to be married to a man who tells you whom you may see and whom you may not; who embarrasses you by pulling the guests along in the reception line so fast that they almost feel unwelcome; and who simply refuses to talk to people, leaving you holding the conversational bag? That was Coolidge.

Would you like to be First Lady to a man who speaks so bluntly and writes such nasty letters, without your knowing it, that you can hardly face your friends? That was Truman. Or to a man who is idolized by millions, but has such a bad temper that you live in fear that he will burst out at the wrong time? That was Eisenhower. Or to a man who has great personal wealth and gives the impression of great generosity, but is a little penny-pinching with you? That was FDR.

So, you see, maybe you're a lot better off married to an average American. As far as I can see, no average man ever became President. Our Presidents have been tremendous individualists, with tremendous drive, whether they showed it or not. And to balance their less endearing traits, each one had some special good trait that the nation was looking for at the time. We used to wonder if each President could have been elected at any other time in his history.

We at the White House learned to have great respect for the man and, yes, his wife who finally made it to the big mansion. I add the wife, because I've seen how hard she works during elections and re-elections, even when it seems that she does nothing but smile and stand by. She does her part when her head is aching and her feet too, and the weather is bad, and she is inadequately dressed, and she fears the crowd, which is pushing her, and she cringes at the close inspection she gets and the catcalls her husband receives, which are more painful to her than to him.

So she deserves a four-year rest at the White House. But it's no rest. It's a great strain to entertain constantly, and make meaningful small talk with people with whom you have absolutely nothing in common, and who find it as painful as you do. And then there are those guests who hardly speak your language at all and require the presence of an interpreter. Oh, that's quite a conversation you can hold!

Mrs. Truman tried to bridge the gulf by learning Spanish. But there are a lot of languages in the world, and it's a little too late to wait till you get into the White House to start learning them.

And it isn't only languages! How would you like to entertain visiting dignitaries from cultures so unlike your own that it puts you in a tizzy trying to figure out how to handle the situation? True, you have loads of servants, but you are the one who looks bad if anything goes wrong. You are still the hostess.

Backstairs, we had a million-and-one laughs at the little stories that would circulate about each new guest, and the problems of taking care of him or her. And, believe me, some things you can't even take for granted. When Mme. Chiang Kai-shek was staying at the White House, a valet asked one member of her party, "May I draw your bath, sir?"

It turned out that the "sir" was a niece of Madame Chiang who had arrived dressed in boy's clothes.

Russia's Khrushchev brought his own food-taster, and King Ibn Saud of Arabia had two bodyguards sleeping on the floor in the hall outside his room. That was no lesson in democracy, we folks backstairs agreed.

Newspapers carried stories of how hard it had been to get goats' milk for the first visit Ibn Saud made some years ago. It fell to Victoria Geaney, the housekeeper for the President's guests in Blair House, to get the milk. And she got it too, after personally scouting the countryside clear to Baltimore. But what the papers didn't tell is that far from being grateful for his darned goats' milk, Saud called for Cokes and more Cokes. Backstairs, we laughed and laughed, but we admired the amazing, unshockable Mrs. Geaney, who has saved the day more times than I have space to tell.

And if you think a First Lady's problems are confined to dealing with foreign dignitaries, you are sadly mistaken. The classic example of domestic diplomacy, I think, is the case of the Congressman and the decapitated fish— one of the few times, incidentally, that I was glad to have a bit of sewing at the White House done by someone else.

During the Hoover administration, a Congressman sent a tremendous fish to the White House by a trusted aide, and then hurried over to be photographed with it and the President. The Congressman arrived, but where was the fish, which had been a present from the people of Maine? Poor Mrs. Hoover! Naturally, she assumed that a fish is for eating, and had had someone take it to the kitchen. Already its head was missing.

One of the men sewed the head back on, and I was grateful to be able to sit out that sewing assignment. The picture was taken, and the people of Maine never knew the difference, but backstairs we added it to our list of stories that prove it is better just to work in the White House than to be its hostess.

Everyone thinks of the White House formal dinners as being the ultimate in timing and perfection— and they are. But, once in a blue moon, we would have a dinner that was absolutely jinxed. The *supreme* example was the Supreme Court dinner that was the kick-off for the 1958-59 social season. I was there with my needle and thread at my station in the powder room. When I heard that the ranking guest of honor, Chief Justice Earl Warren, had been stricken with a virus and couldn't make it to his own dinner, I said, "Oh, oh."

Then Mrs. Warren, who left her husband home sick in bed, to fulfill her duty, arrived at the last minute, tripped at the entrance, and ripped her coral chiffon gown. But she could not come to me to have it fixed— there was no time.

The guests sat down to dinner, but before the dinner was half over, the wife of the president of a railroad (Mrs. Howard E. Simpson, Baltimore and Ohio) suffered a minor heart attack, and was escorted from the table by her husband and an usher to Dr. Howard Snyder's office on the ground floor.

General Snyder was called at home, and was at the White House in a few minutes. I went to the door to see if I could be of any assistance, but there was little I could do, and I went back to my needles and pins in the powder room.

When I got back there, I had a surprise visitor. A Newport socialite, Mrs. Harold Tinney, had collapsed at the table and was receiving emergency help in my powder room from Mrs. Wiley Buchanan, wife of the Chief of Protocol. Mrs. Buchanan applied wet towels to Mrs. Tinney's throat to keep her from fainting.

As I was leaving to check again at the doctor's office, a third lady was brought from the table and helped to a second sofa in my powder room, where another friend was giving her a pill.

Things were moving so fast, I didn't even find out her name.

It was midnight before Mrs. Simpson was well enough to leave, and her husband asked me for a shoehorn so she could put on her slippers. There was no time to go to the third floor to get one, so I got a large spoon from the kitchen and gave it to Mr. Simpson instead. It did the trick, and he was most grateful.

As the guests started to leave, after the entertainment by the National Capital Harp Ensemble, I realized that this distinguished assembly, which included Mrs. Frederick J. Manning (whom my mother had served in the White House when she was Helen Taft), Elizabeth Arden, Mrs. Harvey Firestone, Mrs. Richard Mellon, and Mrs. Pierre S. duPont, didn't know what had happened. They were happily chatting about what a "lovely party" it had been, and one woman used the word "heavenly."

Naturally, I didn't tell any of the guests how close to the real heaven it had been. With seventy-eight people seated at a table, it is hard to see what is going on except in your immediate vicinity.

I had to take a lot of kidding after that night, especially

from General Snyder's assistant, Col. Walter Tkach, who announced to one and all, "Lillian is my new assistant— she takes care of the patients for me." Thereafter, he would call to me as he passed by to ask, "Any business tonight?"

Definitely that dinner was the most jinxed since the one at which Lincoln got locked out of the State Dining Room during a Civil War celebration, and ladies swooned with hunger as they waited for the key to be "found." Someone among the help who had Confederate sympathies had hidden the key, and made backstairs history that is still chuckled over. But, at the time, it was a very serious social matter, which further harassed the already-harassed Mary Todd Lincoln. Instead of receiving sympathy for what had happened, she was accused of having fun in the White House while the soldiers were cold and miserable in their camps.

It isn't only security problems and timing at a party that cause shivers backstairs; it's also the embarrassing moment when a lady's intimate garment can somehow escape its moorings and slide to the floor. It wasn't so bad when one of Washington's favorite radio personalities, WRC-NBC's Patty Cavin, was so startled by Mrs. Eisenhower, that she dropped her gloves right at the First Lady's feet, but it was a lot worse when a society lady, who shall remain nameless, dropped her slip.

I once knew a horrible moment when I realized I was to blame, because I had not noticed when a woman left my powder room with her voluminous skirts caught in her girdle, and had walked into the Reception Room with her undergarments plainly visible in the back. I still wake up in a sweat over that incident, which, I was sure, would lose me my job before I had a chance to retire.

Of course, no one will remember that an embarrassing incident happened when *I* was responsible for helping ladies in the powder room. No, they will remember that someone came out with their backside exposed during one of *Mrs. Eisenhower's* parties.

As to the aftermath of the slip incident, the problem was what to do with it. Would the owner be happier never seeing it again, or should it be returned to her? It was decided to return it to her, carefully boxed and wrapped, and I heard that she wished the White House hadn't bothered, because it just made her feel embarrassed all over again.

So, you see, whatever she did, Mrs. Eisenhower couldn't win. Nor can any First Lady.

Mrs. Eisenhower isn't the only First Lady who has had to cope with embarrassment and snide laughter over such an incident at a serious formal affair. The most embarrassing moment happened at a Roosevelt party, when a wife of a foreign diplomat actually lost her panties right in the middle of a diplomatic reception. It was made more conspicuous, because it happened while she was walking forward in the line to be received by the President and Mrs. Roosevelt.

What could she do! She stepped out of the panties and moved aside, trying to pretend that they weren't hers. Everybody else did likewise, stepping around the fancy satin panties as they marched by trying not to look.

The man who saved the day was John Mays, a doorman who had worked at the White House four days longer than Mama. He made a little bow to the people who were walking around the shiny silk object, and leaning down at their feet, he put the panties over his arm, so that they looked more like a fancy towel than a lady's unmentionables, and carried them away with his usual dignity.

When FDR heard about the incident, he was gleeful about it and called for all the details. And we congratulated John Mays for "diplomatic action" beyond the call of duty.

We did have the heart to feel sorry for Mrs. Roosevelt, who always seemed to be at the butt end of jokes. I don't know if Mrs. "R" ever got used to the jokes made at her expense, but we cringed for her when we saw a cartoon that showed a man emerging excitedly from a sewer manhole and saying, "Hey, I just met Eleanor!" After all, she was always traveling on serious business for the President, and trying to do a serious job.

One of the things Mrs. Eisenhower was criticized about was the "quality" of the entertainment she brought into the White House. The critics felt that music such as that of Lawrence Welk was too lowbrow for the Chief Executive.

I had to laugh because I remembered that when King George VI of England was visiting the Roosevelts, he wanted to hear Kate Smith sing, "When the Moon Comes Over the Mountain." No one can call *that* highbrow music.

In my thirty years at the White House, I have certainly found that the importance of the guests, or their position, has nothing to do with the quality of their taste in entertainment. Sometimes, the higher their position was, the more they would indulge their taste for what is known as "corny" music, without having to make a pretense of being highbrow.

I felt sorry for Mrs. Eisenhower because of this unjust criticism.

We felt sorry for Mrs. Truman too at every reception she gave, knowing her agony. She was so timid about people and crowds, that her hands perspired when she had to stand in the receiving line. She tried wearing gloves for this reason, and then was criticized for what seemed like "an unfriendly way of shaking hands." One critic said to me, "When I see Mrs. Truman, all I see is big white gloves."

Mrs. Roosevelt had a great fear that anyone would think she was "shirking her duty." She would go to any lengths to do her "duty," flying hundreds of miles to be present when her sons arrived, remembering every birthday and anniversary, going anywhere, and any time, at the drop of a hat if the President were to suggest that she check on some situation for him.

So, it was no surprise that Mrs. "R" was greatly hurt when Chief Usher Ike Hoover, in writing about her just before he died, put the phrase "no housekeeper" beside her name. He never got to finish the thought, and it was printed in his memoirs that way. I remember that she fretted over the insinuation that she had been "shirking her duty" until someone kindly pointed out that Mr. Hoover had probably not meant that at all, but only that she had lacked a housekeeper when she came to the White House to live, and had filled the vacancy with Henrietta Nesbitt.

Mrs. Hoover had a terrible fear that everything would not go smoothly, and she drove us all crazy with the hand signals she would practice to keep lines moving, and solve other problems in "smoothness." She did not trust anyone else's judgment, and had to give all directions herself by dropping handkerchiefs, raising three fingers, touching the nose, and using other signals.

Once, for "smoothness," she wanted to find a particular tune that the musicians could play to signal the adjournment of the company to the other room. All the Cabinet officers would have to know and recognize the tune, and, in checking with the Cabinet wives, she found that only the "Blue Danube" waltz and the "National Anthem" would be recognized by one of the Cabinet members. She had to settle for the "Blue Danube," because if the band were to have played the "National Anthem," it would have meant the end of the entertainment and the time to go home.

She went to extreme lengths to achieve perfection. And for her pains in trying to have everything "smooth," she was accused of trying to turn the White House into another Buckingham Palace.

No First Lady has escaped gossip, not even the gentle Grace Coolidge. While vacationing in the Black Hills of South Dakota, Mrs. Coolidge went for a walk with a Secret Service man, and didn't return for hours. The President was frantic. A searching party was finally sent out into the Black Hills, and it met the returning couple. Though they had simply gotten lost, a big rumor was started that this had been some kind of romantic tryst.

The Secret Service man, Jim Haley, was transferred, and someone else was given the job of protecting the First Lady. It took years for the gossip to die down. At the White House, the sympathy of Mama and the other maids was evenly divided between the First Lady and the Secret Service man. What made it even more ridiculous was that the Secret Service man was engaged to be married, and they knew that he thought of no one but his fiancée.

The funniest happening calculated to ruin a reputation at the White House did not involve a First Lady, but a poor President, who probably didn't even hear about it. A woman came to the White House and insisted she had been made pregnant by— of all people— President Hoover.

Of course, the woman was slightly balmy. But accusations; visits from cranks and the mentally disturbed; visits from friends and foes, and everyone under the sun between —this is the lot of the First Ladies. And so it always shall be.

IT'S A FAMILY AFFAIR

While Mrs. Roosevelt thought the White House belonged to "the people," and Mrs. Eisenhower thought it belonged to her— temporarily— we, the backstairs crew who ran it, *knew* it belonged to us.

The First Families swept in and out like the tide; administrations arrived and departed. Only we remained, and because we knew our jobs, we continued to run the White House.

It's really strange when the First Lady, whom we think of as the complete boss, suddenly goes out the door for the last time. Immediately we must forget how she and her husband wanted things done, and we start thinking, "What will it be now?"

The cardinal rule at the White House is never to tell a new First Lady how her predecessor did things, unless she asks. Each First Lady has her own ideas as to how the White House should be run, and her own set of idiosyncrasies.

Mrs. Truman couldn't stand the sight of an electric sweeper sitting in a hall. While the housemen were waiting to get into a room to sweep, she would kick the machine they had left in the hall as she went by.

Under the Hoovers, we had to whisper and not make a sound in the pantry while they were eating. But the Roosevelts, who loved noise and talked excitedly and loudly, never wanted us to stop working just because they were eating— the Roosevelts wouldn't have heard us anyway.

Mrs. Coolidge couldn't stand to hear female voices on the radio, and Mama had to switch stations instantly until she had located a masculine voice or some music. The Eisenhowers loved TV and all its voices.

It takes almost a year to get used to the new whims and desires of a First Family. Under the Eisenhowers, the electrician, John Muffler, would wind all the clocks. But President Truman was a clockwinder, and when we lived at Blair House, he made a daily ritual of winding his favorite clock on the mantlepiece.

Mrs. Eisenhower couldn't stand to hear us call one another by nicknames backstairs, and so we had to be careful to use our proper names. She didn't like slang either. Although "Ike" was a cross she had to bear, she didn't think it was proper and said so.

President Roosevelt would patiently explain over and over how he wanted something done until he was sure you understood, and he seemed to enjoy explaining it. President Truman said something once, and that was it. He hated to repeat himself. He talked so fast, everyone really had to listen carefully to get his directions straight the first time. President Eisenhower was more military in issuing directives, and you got your orders through a chain of command.

We actually grew to have a great family feeling for each First Family, and we loved them for their good qualities and bad. Though we complained about their frailties

among ourselves, what we knew remained backstairs at
the White House.

We never talked to outsiders about the little disagree-
ments between Presidents and First Ladies; they were no
different from those engaged in by other husbands and
wives in less spectacular homes. But we knew that Mrs.
Truman was displeased about the Truman letter to the
music critic. We knew that FDR would get a little out of
patience if his wife would go over his head and take her
request to a Government agency after the President had
refused to help her on some project. We saw more bits of
temperament in both President and Mrs. Eisenhower than
any other Presidential couple, but each knew exactly how
to soothe and handle the other.

When "Ike" was displeased by something— rarely by
her, but usually by reports in the papers that misconstrued
his meaning or made him look bad— the First Lady would
put her arm around him and talk softly to him, and soon
he'd grin and be all over it. At such times, she called him
"Dearie" and "Sweetie." The President always called her
"Mamie." He was tender with her, and always concerned
about her health. He would always tell people to "look
after Mamie." Those who showed acts of kindness to her
were "in" with him.

The public thought that FDR and Eleanor were quite
formal with each other, but the servants would hear them
call each other "Darling" all the time in private.

FDR was a little put out with his wife when in her
"My Day" column, she told the story of how the butler
fell with a tray at Hyde Park when the King and Queen
of England were visiting. He disapproved, because it held
the butler up to ridicule before the whole nation, and he
pointed out to her how hard the butlers had worked on
that occasion. Mrs. "R" defended herself by explaining

that she had seen only the humor of the situation, and had not thought feelings would be hurt.

We certainly did love FDR for his sensitivity and tremendous concern for us. I remember the last election at which I would ever see him alive. After he had returned from voting, we were invited to step outside and greet him there, because it would have been too taxing to his health to shake all our hands, as was usual in the White House. But when we greeted him outside, *en masse,* the President insisted we go back into the White House and have the usual handshaking ceremony.

I happened to be the first in line, and I waited for him to adjust his cigarette in his famous cigarette holder and take a puff, throwing back his head in the well-known mannerism. "Well, Little Girl, how is everything in the linen room?" he asked.

It was the same old question, but my heart ached, because I saw for the first time how he had shrunk in size and how tired he looked. I longed to tell him to get some new shirts that would be tighter at the collar, so that his neck wouldn't look so bad in the newspaper pictures, but, of course, I didn't. I shook hands and said, "Just fine, Mr. President," and moved aside for the next person.

Nobody among the help knew how badly off the President was or how near death. And I'm sure his wife didn't either, or she would never have gone to a luncheon in Washington on the day he collapsed at Warm Springs, Georgia. They had called to tell her that the President had fainted, and she had told them the place where they could reach her if the President didn't feel well soon and needed her.

What she was really worried about that day was little Johnny Boettiger, who was at the hospital with his mother. It was Johnny's second time at Bethesda Naval Hospital. Once before, they had had a real scare; they thought that

Johnny might have polio like his famous grandfather, and he had been rushed away. Johnny, who had just started school, had sensed this concern for his health, and had learned to fake sickness so he wouldn't have to go to school. On this particular occasion, they had again thought Johnny was faking, but it turned out he *was* sick; he had been in the hospital for about a week, and Mrs. "R" was worried about him.

When the word first came to the White House that a tragedy had just occurred, many servants instantly thought it was Johnny. Then came the second shock, when we learned that it was the President. I remember how pleased I was to read in the papers that Johnny Boettiger had married, and, in the accompanying picture, his grandmother, Eleanor, was kissing the bride.

It is both sad and thrilling to see these children of the White House, whom I once held dear, grown up, and living their adult lives, and facing their adult problems. I remember when baby Nina Roosevelt, the thirteenth Roosevelt grandchild— John's daughter— learned to walk by pulling herself up on my crutch. She couldn't even talk, but I'd stand still, and she'd crawl to me every time she saw me, and stand up. "Mrs. John," as we called Anne Clark Roosevelt, used to say that Nina got more use out of my crutches than I did.

Close in time to the wedding in the Boettiger family was the tragic death of Nina's little sister, Sally, who fell from a horse at summer camp in New York at the age of thirteen. I never saw Sally, who was born after the Roosevelts had left the Executive Mansion, but Mrs. Roosevelt's former maid, Mabel Webster, who still lives in Washington, called me on the phone to talk about it, and burst into tears. The tragedies of the First Families became our own, no matter how far away or long ago they happened.

When the Eisenhower grandchildren came to stay the

first time, Mrs. Eisenhower entered my sewing room door and said, "Lillian, you are going to have some babies around the White House, but they are *good* babies," and off she had gone with a tinkling laugh.

Barbara Ann— who insisted we call her "Ann" and leave off the "Barbara"— used to ask to borrow my crutches. All through the Eisenhower years, she loved to hobble around on them, and would measure herself on them to see how much she had grown.

The last time I saw her at the White House, when she was almost twelve, she took my crutches and suddenly said quite sadly, "Oh, Lillian, something will have to be added." She was now taller than I, and had outgrown my crutches. I felt a certain sadness as another era closed. Had she been only *three* when I first laid eyes on her?

David won us over immediately and completely, though at five, he was already showing signs of being boss of the little girls. I'll cherish his confidence to me, one day, that he really didn't care about golf the way his grandfather did, but didn't want to hurt his feelings by not playing with him.

His passion, he explained, was baseball. He didn't have to tell me— his baseball cards, which he had gotten with bubble gum wrappers, were lined all the way up and down the halls, and no one was supposed to touch them.

When David and Ann were in school, and Susie was still too young, her mother confessed to me that she was being driven out of her mind with the chatter. "If she would just stop talking!" Miss Barbara exclaimed with feeling. "She nearly drives me crazy. She talks all the time, and won't give me a moment's peace."

I made it a point to become friendly with poor lonely Susie, and soon she was coming to the linen room to "help." She wanted to sew. I helped her make a hat. Then nothing would do but that a fancy box had to be fixed to keep the hat in. She would bring all her dolls and put them to bed in my linen room. When she started school, the linen room became a classroom, and Susie was always a tough teacher, imitating— I'm afraid— her brother more than her own teacher.

Oh yes, I'll remember the children, and all the funny little things, going way back to little Peter Hoover, the President's grandchild, who made history at the White House one day by wearing nothing but a hat. And Diana Hopkins, who came to the White House as a child, and packed her clothes for visiting, not in a suitcase, but in a laundry basket. Diana used to hide in my sewing room to get away from her French governess.

People ask me if it is true that Barbara, the daughter-in-law of a President, did her own housework. She certainly did, and it was also true that the grandchildren of the President learned to do housework. Mrs. Eisenhower came back from Thanksgiving dinner at the John Eisenhowers' and laughingly reported to me on Susie's efforts to serve dinner. All the children had helped serve the meal, and Susie had to pass the butter. She asked her grandmother if she wanted some, and Mrs. Eisenhower said no, she didn't care for butter. Susie promptly took the butter out to the kitchen, and threw it in the garbage pail.

You can see why I'll remember the children. But I'll also remember the dogs— oh those dogs! A book could be written about the Roosevelt dogs alone, from Blaze, who blazed across the nation's headlines for stealing a soldier's seat on a plane, to Fala, who of all dogs I have known, endeared himself the most. His heart was true, and he made it clear he had only one master, FDR.

There were some very funny dogs. Meg, who bit a newspaperwoman on the nose, had to be exiled to Hyde Park— though it wasn't funny to Mrs. "R" at the time.

And the mate, Duchess, who came to keep Blaze company and was not housebroken (to the detriment of a certain red rug for which she had a fondness) also had to be exiled to Hyde Park. That wasn't so funny either while it was happening.

Nor was it amusing, except in retrospect, when all the maids had to carry feather dusters to ward off a horsey-looking Great Dane and Major, a German Shepherd who had come from Hyde Park, and belonged to Franklin, Jr. It was worth your life to make a bed if Major or the Great Dane were around, and Elliott's Blaze was no angel either.

Fala paid no attention to these loutish dogs— not even the barking champion, Susie, a French poodle, who came from New York to live at the White House with Harry Hopkins' bride, Louise Macy. Fala, a gentleman in every sense of the word, would cock his head to one side like his master, listen a moment, and go about his business. He knew they were passing shadows, and that he would outlast them all.

Dogs didn't play a big part in the Eisenhower or Truman households, though they came and went. David's dog, Spunkie, is a stiff old fellow now. There was one that mugged for the camera when it should have been guarding President Truman, and all the delighted news photographers swarmed around as the dog posed alone and un-aided. "This dog could win an election," one photographer said.

The main pets for Margaret were a pair of "loudmouth" canaries, who never quit singing. Margaret loved to listen to them, but their main purpose was to provide company for her grandmother, Mrs. David Wallace, who was in poor health. When Mrs. Wallace died, the canaries were given to the maids Julia and Bluette.

One of my most touching memories is of Mrs. Wallace,

who never knew about the attempt on her son-in-law's life. She was living at Blair House with the Trumans, and when the shooting took place, she asked Bluette, who helped take care of her, what had happened. After she had gone to find out, Bluette choked back the tears, and reported that it was "Nothing. They're working on the street."

Mrs. Wallace's sight was so bad that Bluette and Vietta, another maid, took turns reading to her, and both carefully omitted anything about the assassination attempt.

I must confess that backstairs, there is a little matter of a caste system among the help, based on position and seniority. For a time, we even took our positions at our long dining table according to this system. I sat "high."

I was lucky because my mother had been at the White House longer than anyone but John Mays, the butler, who had preceded her by a mere four days, at the very beginning of the Taft administration. And she had risen to Number One maid, a post that my crutches kept me from achieving.

However, I had the prestige of sewing for the White House, with its aura of history, and enjoying the atmosphere of administrations past and present. Working for the First Ladies and their families also lent a little glamor to my life and position backstairs. And, incidentally, I was paid by the First Ladies themselves for the personal sewing I did after Government hours.

I don't know of any similar situation in which a mother and daughter spanned a half century of history working at the White House. Ten of our years there overlapped.

Because of the length of time we had been there, Mama and I would be called upon to do some of the more unusual jobs. In fact, after she had left, Mama was still called back from time to time.

You might say that working for First Ladies has been

a tradition in our family. Even my brother, before he went into the military service, worked on the grounds of the White House, and a cousin, Lucy Keys, worked for Mrs. Roosevelt at Hyde Park for three years.

It's a pity that John Mays didn't live to write his White House memoirs. He died in 1958, in his eighties, after a three-year illness.

The story of Mays is touching. He was a gentle soul, a wonderful, formal man. He even called mother Margaret instead of "Maggie," as everyone else did. Mays was one of the four original doormen hired by Mrs. Taft. Before that, the door had been manned by policemen. Mrs. Taft thought colored doormen would look less frightening to guests. Mays worked at that job for forty-seven years. The Presidents would have to sign special extensions to permit a man his age to stay on.

As a side job, Mays worked as a barber to Coolidge, and continued to cut hair for other Presidents. All through the Truman administration, I used to have to save old linen towels for Mays so he could have the softest cloths for the Truman shaves. When the Eisenhowers came in, he did not cut hair any more, but was still a doorman.

One day he cut his leg with a razor blade. It became infected, and the leg had to be amputated. Eventually, he died. He had no will to live after that happened to him. The saddest part of the story is that like the Coolidge tragedy, it needn't have happened.

Mays had once before done the same thing that caused his death— he cut his foot while removing a callus with a razor blade. At that time, the White House doctors had pulled him through and had warned him that his system could not survive another such poisoning. But he did it again, and this time, he had to leave his job and retire. He could never get used to the artificial leg.

After he was gone, and we were reminiscing about him

backstairs, someone told us how Mays had been the victim of a Coolidge practical joke, before he found out that the President was a great kidder. Coolidge had taken him on a camping trip and had ordered Mays, who knew nothing about culinary matters, to scrub off the brown spots on string beans, to get them ready for cooking. Poor Mays was scrubbing away when someone tipped him off that the President was pulling his leg. Mays was so dignified he wouldn't even look at "The Little Fellow" reproachfully. He just ignored it.

Another wonderful and sad story was that of the chief usher, Howell G. Crim, who had retired from the White House full of high hopes of spending many years raising roses on his farm, only to die in two years at the age of sixty-two. He was the man who had prepared the White House budget, managed State receptions and worried over the floral arrangements. He was the man who introduced strangers to the President. And most important to us, he was the one to whom we could take our personal problems.

When he retired in '57, after working at the White House twenty-seven years, friends backstairs asked him if he were going to write a book. He said, "No, I'm not a kiss-and-tell boy. I never kept notes." He undoubtedly took to the grave many secrets of great men that will never be revealed, or will be revealed by others who feel that the public has the right to know anything which is a part of history, or will not injure the nation in any way.

Everyone backstairs was invited to Crim's funeral on May 12, 1959. It took ten White House cars to carry us all. I was in the Number One car with Charles Fricklin, the White House maître d'hôtel; Ray Hare, an usher, the most nonchalant man in the White House; Viola Wise, who tends the China Room and keeps the priceless historic china collection sparkling, and O'Neal Phillips of the carpentry shop, who always gave me a ride home from the White House on rainy days.

We were struck by the fact that Crim had died the same day the King of Belgium was arriving at the White House. Someone said, "A king is coming, and a friend is going." It brought tears to our eyes.

We remembered how he had been ill now and then with the recurrence of a blood ailment, and how President Truman, who had been so fond of him, had gone to the hospital many times to see him and cheer him up.

With the passing of Crim and John Mays, a whole White House era had vanished.

I am always asked about the honesty of the White House domestics. They are always so honest that it hurts— especially if their work goes unnoticed and unpraised.

Mrs. Hoover used to have a large diamond ring that she would take off and put down anywhere she happened to be. It was just a habit she had, and nine times out of ten, she would walk off without it. Housemen would come running back and ask us maids, "Have you seen the ring?" Sometimes we'd find it behind the sofa pillows. She drove us almost crazy with that ring and her "find the ring" game.

Mrs. Lou Hoover also kept a $1,000 bill lying on her dresser at all times. We would dust around the bill. Everybody backstairs tried to figure out the significance of the $1,000 bill, but we never did.

Once, a workman came in to fix something in her bedroom, and Mama, who was standing guard (a maid or other authorized person must always be in the room with a workman) saw him looking bug-eyed at that bill casually lying there. "Is that a $1,000 bill, a real one?" he asked. Mama said, "Yes, but don't put your hand on it; you can inspect one next door at the Treasury Department."

President Truman left a $1,000 bill in his pocket when

he was having his suit pressed, and it stayed unnoticed overnight in the valets' pressing room. Another time, he left a $100 bill in the pocket of the sport shirt that was laundered aboard the *Williamsburg*. Truman was generous and gave rewards of autographed dollar bills— ten of them in the second instance. I'm sure he realized that the reward would be more valuable for the signature some day than the amount found and returned.

People are always asking whether any economy is practiced in the White House, or if it is all extravagance. If people knew how much economy is practiced there, they would be amazed.

I have cut down dozens and dozens of curtains and draperies to make new ones of the remaining good material. All old draperies are stored in boxes in the attic, and the material comes in handy for making other things. For example, the butlers needed silent cloths to deaden sound on the small round tables that are used when we have to set up for about one hundred ladies at luncheon. I took a bunch of old drapery apart, and used the flannel of the interlining to make round, silent cloths. That was about eighteen years ago, and they are still in use today.

Old pillowcases are not thrown out at the White House; I would take them apart and restitch them to cover the bed-pillow ticking. Because of the lining, the stripes underneath would not show through, and the pillows would look whiter. When Mrs. Eisenhower saw this, she had me cover her pillows for Gettysburg too.

Not a feather is wasted. President Eisenhower wanted small pillows to fit under his neck when he was sleeping, and I made two of old feathers, one for the White House and one for the farm.

Old uniforms are repaired and set aside for extra help who are brought in to work on dinners. The white coats that the housemen wear are fixed up for the busboys who help at garden parties. They are soon ruined anyway, because a lot of punch is spilled on them on such occasions. Odds and ends of cloth became pot-holders.

When Mrs. Truman first arrived at the White House, I was afraid she didn't like me, because she acted peculiarly in my presence. Finally, she told me that she thought I was giving her the worst linens. I explained that we practiced economy at the White House, and that it wasn't just her towels that were repaired. We became good friends then, and I tried to be sure she got the new-looking towels.

In thirty years, I've done a lot of odd jobs, you can bet. I've even made some emergency doll clothes for a tearful, motherless Diana Hopkins, who had come to the White House to live with her father, advisor to FDR.

And I can recall rushing out of the White House, after all department stores were closed at six o'clock, in search of "six large casserole dishes, which must all be alike" for corn pudding for President Ike's old West Point cronies, who were coming for dinner at eight. Around the downtown area, I made a quick survey from my chauffeur-driven car, and saw the situation was hopeless. And then I remembered a dime store that stays open late on upper 14th Street.

Into the dime store I went, and found they had only two suitable casseroles. They "might have more in the storeroom," but they didn't know. They acted as if I shouldn't need so many. Why did I want them, they wanted to know. I didn't dare say I was shopping for the White House at the dime store, and said I was having company in an hour.

Finally, looking at me as if I were slightly demented, and muttering that I couldn't possibly cook that much in an hour, and that I probably didn't know how many I could feed out of a casserole, one of the clerks shuffled back to see if there were four more casseroles. There were, and I felt pretty good as I bore them back in triumph to the White House.

And then there was the time Queen Elizabeth, the Queen Mother, was coming, and no one could find the menu of the dinner she had been served when she had been a guest of the Roosevelts in 1939. It was important to have the menu so that the White House would *not* serve her the same things again. Mrs. Walker finally came to me as the last resort, since I had been there so long and was known to collect and save almost every type of souvenir.

"I think I have that menu at home," I said, "but I'll have to dig around."

"I certainly hope you do," she said worriedly.

I hunted almost all night, but finally found it buried away in one of my many White House "treasure chests." Probably, when she reads this, Mrs. Eisenhower will learn for the first time why she was able to serve cream almond soup, Norfolk oysters, and roast Long Island duck with perfect assurance— she knew that back in 1939, the Queen ate calves' head soup, Maryland terrapin, and boned capon.

Ah yes, I enjoyed my odd jobs around the White House, and waited eagerly for my next one. One of the oddest, I think you will agree, was pleasing Mme. Chiang Kai-shek in the much-publicized matter of selecting her bed linen. I tell this story now, because it is part of history, and I want to set the record straight. Many erroneous accounts were written, which said that Madame Chiang "demanded silk sheets and blankets."

She did not demand them; she brought her own. I was chosen to look after her in this matter for the twelve days of her visit. As a result, I still have a souvenir of her visit, a cuff from her bedjacket that she wanted cut off. My mother, who had been retired from the White House for five years, was brought back by Mrs. Roosevelt to serve Madame Chiang too.

But to get back to the wife of the Generalissimo and her sheets, she wanted them attached to her woolen blankets in a certain way, because she was allergic to wool. This job couldn't be done on a table. I had to put a large sheet on the floor in the third-floor hall to keep the silk sheets clean, and crawl around the floor, folding and sewing the silk sheets over the blanket.

Maids, housemen, and butlers would trail past me as I worked, making funny comments under their breath, especially when I was working with a coverlet that had a huge black dragon embroidered on it. With everyone talking about my project around the house, no wonder it reached the ears of the reporters and got into the papers!

What Madame Chiang actually had me do was make a coverlet out of a blanket. It wasn't easy, and it had to be done every day. I would put a silk sheet on my percale work base, then place the wool blanket so that it was centered on the sheet. Then I would fold the silk sheet up and over the blanket on all sides, carefully mitering the four corners. Finally, I would baste the three pieces together so that there would be a six-inch border with mitered corners all the way round. Fortunately, the embroidered sheet, which was on top, was the exact size of the blanket she had brought, or I would have lost my mind.

Every day the maids, Wilma and Julia, would launder the silk sheet that was next to her skin, but the embroidered sheet on top was not laundered. Fortunately, Madame Chiang had brought four of them (I remember one with unbelievably realistic red roses— it was my favorite), and I simply alternated them so that each was used only three times. For this I received a handsome tip of $15 when Madame Chiang left.

Everyone used to leave tips, and backstairs at the White House we were shocked to the core when Mrs. Eisenhower decreed that there would be no more tipping. Even the First Families would tip when they had entertained a large group, and we had worked especially hard and long. Mrs. Roosevelt was particularly thoughtful that way. Mrs. Truman would check on whether her house guests had left anything for us, and if they had overlooked tips, she would take care of it herself.

But the new rule under the Eisenhowers was that the ushers had to tell the guests, when asked, that tipping was not permitted. Many of the White House help had to do outside work evenings to afford the honor of working in the White House.

When I left, after thirty years, my "take-home" pay check every two weeks was $103.60. Before my mother died, I had to have nursing help for her and pay for it myself, because her pension was only $111 a month. If I hadn't earned extra money sewing for the First Ladies, I'd never have made ends meet.

I know one kitchen worker at the White House who is widowed and supporting two children on about $48 a week before taxes. Losing the tips was hard for her and others like her.

Many people think working at the White House is easy, because the work is divided among so many people, and those who work there have soft prestige jobs. Let me tell you that more people have ruined their health under the grueling strain of working at the White House than you would believe.

True, there is prestige and glamor in working at the Executive Mansion, and people I met were sometimes over-awed to find I worked there. And true, I feel it is a privilege and an honor to work with and for the most important couple in the world, and to see the inner workings of the most important household in the world.

Nowhere do household help have to work with such split-second timing— a State dinner must go on, no matter what; a reception begins precisely when scheduled, period. We are so regulated that we even adjust our expressions for various occasions. Even when a butler serves the family alone, he must pretend that he hears nothing. The best joke, which he may be recording mentally to tell sometime, is received with a poker face.

Incidentally, you may be interested to know that whenever there was a State dinner, I had to stand by with needle and thread to fix any tiny flaws in the tablecloth while it was being ironed right on the table. People are always surprised to hear that we would iron out the creases in the tablecloth while it was on the dining table. Sometimes a girl would be working on one end of the table, ironing, and I would be mending at the other end of it. Napkins too sometimes needed delicate work around the embroidered initials "U.S.," where the material breaks first.

My mother worked so hard when helping Mrs. Hoover pack up to leave the White House, that she blacked out. Two valets ruined their health working for FDR, and his secretary, Miss LeHand, worked so hard that her health broke, and she eventually died. That's just to mention a few Roosevelt casualties.

A cook retired on disability under Truman, because of the strain of hard work. A houseman retired on disability under Eisenhower. I, myself, suffered a small heart attack right at the White House after struggling with 125 sheets and packing boxes of things scheduled to go to the Eisenhower farm at Gettysburg. The White House doctors were excellent, and I was back at work in a few days.

World rulers in general are not easy to work for. I was

at the White House when Churchill's valet fainted from rushing so much.

No, working at the White House is not an easy way to make a living. I hope that Mrs. Kennedy will realize that and provide, as Mrs. Roosevelt did, a place where female help can lie down to rest if they feel badly.

I hope that she will suggest now and then, as Mrs. Truman did, that someone quit working and rest a little. I hope that she will not ignore her household staff, or stand over its members, watching them work. I hope she will give them the feeling she has confidence in them. And I hope she will remember to praise a job well done, as Mrs. Eisenhower did. Praise is still the greatest reward.

I hope she will realize that her staff loves, yes, literally *loves* working for her, and would do anything at all to please her and to protect her. I hope she will return that love with faith.

I won't be one of the seventy-two employees of the household staff, but I hope she will enjoy her fifty-four-room family quarters and some of my touches, which she will find in almost every room. I won't be there, but I'll be thinking of her, and I'll be watching her and the White House as usual, through the eye of my needle . . .

PART TWO

———◆◆◆———

MAMA'S BIG FIVE

———◆◆◆———

Mrs. Taft

The two Mrs. Wilsons

Mrs. Harding

Mrs. Coolidge

MAMA OF THE WHITE HOUSE

Four days before Mama was scheduled to work at the White House, we watched the Inaugural Parade. March 4, 1909, was a cold day, a snowy day. We had had one of the worst snow storms in Washington history, but fortunately it had stopped in time for the parade to be as large and as long as usual.

We stood on the curb on Pennsylvania Avenue— Mama and my brother Emmett and I— and watched Mrs. Taft ride by in a horse-drawn carriage with the President. I remember that she was wearing purple satin. I did not know it then, but Mrs. Taft was making history. This was the first time a President's wife rode from the Capitol swearing-in ceremony to the White House in the same carriage with her husband.

Later, I learned that eleven-year-old Charlie Taft, the youngest of the Taft children, had taken a copy of *Treasure Island* with him to read during the ceremony, so he wouldn't have to listen to his father's speech.

Mama told me about it one night after she'd gone to work for the Tafts, and I liked Charlie more because of it. I liked him still more when a pair of his knickerbocker pants were brought home by Mama for Emmett to wear. Mrs. Taft had told Mama that they no longer fitted Charlie. Emmett and Charlie were the same size, though my brother was a year younger.

Charlie was not above taking off his shoes and wading in the fountain. Emmett, who had a White House job as yard boy, showed he was no sissy either when he played hooky from work, and ran off to the Washington Monument grounds to play baseball. It was his day of dire disgrace when Mr. Brown, his foreman, found him on the Monument grounds in back of the White House, and brought him back, all sand and grime, to Mama.

"I won't report it," Mr. Brown assured Mama. "We'll just give him another chance." Emmett hung his head and said nothing. He knew he'd have some explaining to do to Mama later.

Emmett grumbled to me about it. I was one year older and thus more sophisticated, so he could tell me things. If only Mama knew the things Charlie Taft got away with, he would complain, she'd *really* be surprised!

When his father was Secretary of War, Charlie had had the run of the White House with the children of Teddy Roosevelt, and they had enjoyed wonderful times. They had tied people's shoelaces together under the table. They had lured President Teddy up into the attic, and then turned the light out on him, and the President had almost had his eye poked out on a nail.

Oh, they had had some wild times!

So why was Mama all excited about Emmett's game of hooky? After all, he had finished picking up all the trash from Mrs. Taft's lawn party of the night before. But Mama didn't see it that way. She had gone to great pains to get him that job— she even had to obtain a special concession for him to work because he was only eleven.

Then there was the principle of the thing. Mama was a great one for principles.

"Emmett, never forget that this is the White House," she said. "It is the greatest honor that you can have to set foot here."

At this point, Emmett told me that the only thing that kept him from envying Charlie Taft was that Charlie had to wear a tuxedo to dine with the family. But he did envy him, he admitted, for having an automobile to ride in, even though Emmett had heard the President kid his son by telling him not to get too comfortable in the car, because it would be only a few years before they'd all be walking again.

"We only have a four-year lease on this car," President Taft said. It was the first horseless carriage to be used at the White House.

That was just over half a century ago. I see it all as if it were the day before yesterday— Mama and Emmett and I. Emmett grew to be six feet, two, and has spent a lifetime in military service. Today he is a Government guard, stationed at the San Diego Naval Base, and is looking forward to retirement.

Today, Mama is gone. But, as I now write, I am looking at her account, in her own handwriting, of how she took the job at the White House. Oh time, oh fate! Little did she know then that fifty-one years later I would be copying her description of that terrifying moment when she was to report for duty:

"March 8, 1909: Perhaps nothing ever again will be the same. I received word to report to the White House for duty. I arose early and dressed with care so that I might make a good appearance. While doing this, many thoughts raced through my mind. Would I please them? Was it wise for me to give up my trade, and to start where I was unknown? I walked up and down about twenty minutes in front of the White House, trying to make up my mind whether to go in or not. Finally, I got enough courage to enter the large gate and go up the walk and enter the stately mansion. The door closed behind me. I was escorted to Major Brook's office, the Custodian. He in turn took me to Mrs. Jaffray, the housekeeper. And finally, I found myself, all humble and shaken, in front of the First Lady, herself. She had gentle eyes, and I felt less afraid. I noticed her lovely clothes and the violets she wore. Soon, I would learn that violets were her trademark."

If there is a heaven, and I meet Mama there, I know the first thing she will ask is, "Lillian, did you finish the job? Did you use my notes?" I could hardly face her if I didn't make use of the material she had spent a lifetime gathering.

Before Mama had gone to work at the White House, she had been a beautician. She made her visits to the homes of the wealthy, carrying her own little case of curling irons, lotions, and manicuring equipment.

She met my father, Emmett Rogers, who was the youngest headwaiter in Washington, and they were married. His work seemed to keep taking him away, and among my earliest memories, I was always on the go with him. Then Mama refused to travel so much, and he started going without us. He would send money from wherever he was, but Mama had to keep working to support Emmett and me.

When I was six, I had polio and was left with a crippled leg. I had to wear a heavy brace until I had an operation.

My last memory of my father is associated with the last time I ever saw him. I was nine years old, and Mama had just come to get us from our grandmother's in Virginia, and had taken us back to Washington. When we pulled into the station that evening, Father was there to greet us. Emmett and I had been staying with Grandmother, because there was no one to take care of us with both parents working. Some of the time, I had stayed at a Catholic school too, though I was an Episcopalian. So I wasn't very excited about traveling. I was glad to see Mama and Papa together. But then, they took us from the station to a friend's home and put us to bed. Mama said, "Kiss your father goodnight," and I saw tears in her eyes.

I did not know that when I awoke, he would be gone forever. He went to Kentucky to work, and he never returned. All I can remember of him are happy memories of childhood, when I made him laugh by putting my shoes on backward; standing between his legs as he sat at the table shaving; and peeping into the mirror with him.

My mother did not try to spoil my happy memories, and not until years later, did I learn that he had become an alcoholic and unable to hold a job. She had despaired of ever having a home for us. But when he was working, he was one of the best and highest-paid waiters. Mama never got a divorce, or had any interest in remarrying. She used to say that she never wanted a stepfather for her children. But it was a terrible life for us children, shuffling from relative to relative.

Then, one day, a friend of Mama's told her there would be an opening at the White House. Mama saw in it a chance for steady work, a chance to buy a house, and to keep us all together in a place where she could look after us herself. Half-frightened, half-thrilled, she got together the references that the White House requested. Evidently, she made the grade, because she had worked for many fine people in town, and was in much demand as a hairdresser.

She was called to the White House, and Col. Arthur Brooks, the custodian, asked her if she would be interested in the position of second maid. She said she would, and only a day or two went by before she was called to duty.

Housekeeper Elizabeth Jaffray must have been pleased with Mama's work as a beautician too, because one of Mama's duties was to give her a weekly manicure. Mrs. Jaffray, who was Mama's boss, was a very interesting woman. She had come from Canada, and she was very formal. She served as housekeeper at the White House for seventeen years. She lived at the White House, and her suite was on the same floor as that of the Presidential family in what we call the Center Blue Room, next to which was a small room that served as an office.

Every morning, the head of each department of the household staff would enter her office door and stand there formally, receiving orders, and discussing the coming activities of the day.

Every morning, she would put on her hat and veil and journey to the Center Market, using the carriage and horses of the White House. When everyone else was using automobiles, she refused to set foot in one, and continued using the carriage and horses.

Mrs. Taft always had Irish cooks. She preferred them. However, she brought in a special cook before State dinners to make the terrapin soup— and nothing else. I think the cook was given $5 each time.

Mrs. Taft was very particular about the terrapin soup, and would always come to the kitchen to taste it, and make sure it had reached the peak of perfection. She was one of the few First Ladies who ever came into the kitchen. Mrs. Truman, years later, was another. Mama was always talking about Mrs. Taft and her terrapin soup, and outside, I would look at a turtle and be glad I didn't have to eat it.

Almost every night, Mama had a White House story for us. But there was one rule to the game. We were never to talk about anything Mama had told us outside of the house. Anything she told us was just for the three of us to enjoy, and if Emmett or I ever had repeated a story, that would have been the end of the stories. So we never told, and we waited eagerly each night for Mama to come home and tell us of her wonderful adventures in the White House.

There were stories about eighteen-year-old Helen Taft, who was going to have her coming-out party in the White House, and Mama was very busy about that. Naturally, I lived it with Helen Taft— unknown to her, I'm sure. There was I, the little crippled girl in the gocart, living the thrilling life of "Miss Helen" at second hand, as told to me each night by Mama. We counted once, keeping track of how many nights in a row she had been invited out to dinner, and it was thirty-one consecutive times.

Inspired perhaps by her dazzling example, I determined that I too would walk some day without a brace, and even dance in a "Helen Pink" dress, when I grew up.

Then there were the hilarious stories about Mrs. Taft's troubles with the servants. She decreed that all waiters at the White House must have hair, and that no bald-headed butlers would be permitted in the dining room. She further ordered that all White House employees must be clean-shaven. Everyone shaved off their beards but one old man. He kept shortening it instead, but she would not settle for that, and eventually he had to shave off the whole thing.

Mama would keep us posted on the condition of his beard . . . shorter, shorter— gone.

There were stories about Mrs. Taft, and her outdoor parties, which were forever being rained out like a ball game. All the servants had to rush around and get everything under cover. Mama used to laugh and say that the good Lord must frown on outdoor parties at the White House, because He was forever sending rain.

Eventually, a little tent affair was set up, to help the First Lady fight the elements. Crowds would gather to watch the outdoor entertainment all around the White

House fence, and Mama said she felt like a monkey in a zoo. She hated to be conspicuous.

I hated to be conspicuous too, and I could have died the day I got caught in the White House by the President himself. We had moved into a house near the White House, and Mama was afraid to leave me alone when she went back to turn down the President's covers every evening at twilight. So she would sometimes take me with her.

She would arrange the bed linen, and leave me in the President's bedroom while she went to turn on the electric lights in the other family rooms. Turning on the lights was a momentous thing in those days, because electricity was still new, and there were servants in the White House who refused to touch the switches. Not for love nor money would they turn on electric lights, so Mama was the one who had that job.

"Don't you make a move, and don't touch the bed, and I'll be right back to get you," she would say as she hurried out.

One time, before she returned for me, a very stout man came into the room. I wasn't afraid of him, because he looked so big and jolly, and he beamed down at me. "Well, well, what have we here?" he said. "Are you the little ghost of the White House I've been hearing about?"

"No, I'm not a ghost," I assured him. "I'm Maggie's little girl, and I'm not supposed to be here."

The big, friendly man laughed. "Then let's pretend you're not here."

"All right," I said, relieved. "Just don't tell Mama you saw me."

So he didn't, and I didn't, and that was my first meeting with any President.

Mama brought home many ghost stories that were circulating around the White House, and once she told one about a child in white who sounded a lot like me. I just kept quiet. I had been wearing white when I had my little talk with the President.

But the stories she told about the ghost of Abigail Adams walking through closed doors around the White House still got a rise out of me. Those I believed. And the ghost stories about the Presidents who still haunted the White House I believed too, but they didn't interest me. Mine was a feminine world.

Mama told me that several days a week, Mrs. Taft would talk to all kinds of ladies in the Red Room. All that any lady had to do was send a letter, and she could come. She would like to have a fire going in the fireplace if there was the slightest excuse for one, because it made the room look so good. Mama called it "holding court," and said that Mrs. Taft loved to sit in the firelight and "hold court."

Mama said that the servants were calling the White House "Malacañan Palace," because there is where the First Lady had lived once when her husband had been Governor of the Philippines, and she was trying to make the White House look the same. She brought in Oriental furniture, and Oriental tapestries, and floormats called *petates*. Huge Oriental screens stood in strategic places, and the maids were busy polishing teakwood.

To make the rooms look more like the Islands, Mrs. Taft, during her "reign," filled the White House to over-flowing with greenery. She had plants and ferns and exotic flowers on every ledge and surface, and even in the fireplace. No one around the White House was more important than the horticulturist in those days. Mrs. Taft held long conversations with him on the house plants, their arrangement, their care, and their growth.

It was she who ordered the White House nursery men to round up all the Japanese cherry trees they could find, because she had loved them when she saw them in Japan.

This project of hers had such far-reaching results that it still influences Washington society today in the form of the Cherry Blossom Festival. But, at the time, the First Lady was only interested in copying the *luneta* in Manila, where public concerts were held in the park.

After the Japanese cherry trees had been planted, the Mayor of Tokyo received a report of it from the Japanese Embassy in Washington, and was so pleased that he sent a gift of 2,000 more Japanese cherry trees to the City of Washington.

Many readers will already know that the shipment had to be destroyed, because the trees were found to be diseased. But soon another batch arrived— 3,000 this time. The trees still flourish, and every spring they come alive in glorious color, and form an excuse for the cherry blossom extravaganza that Mrs. Taft would have loved— the selection of a queen to reign over the congregation of dignitaries, and tourists from every state of the Union. Probably Mrs. Taft herself would have picked the queen. She loved pageantry.

As it turned out, the First Lady was a sensation at the opening of Washington's version of the *luneta*. About 10,000 people showed up to watch Mrs. Taft tour up and down the Potomac Drive, and greet her friends in a Landaulette motor car, to the strains of the Marine Band. The concerts continued to be held on Wednesdays and Saturdays, from 5:00 until 7:00, for many years.

One night, the "White House bedtime story" had special significance, because, seated on Mama's lap as she told it, was a kitten that had followed her home from the White House. Mama had worked late that evening, because Admiral Togo of Japan had arrived, and so what could be more appropriate than that we name the kitten "Admiral Togo"?

Not so long after that, the "Admiral" surprised us by marching into the house with a retinue of four kittens, which he— she— had brought out of hiding. Mama didn't want to change the Admiral's name. She said we'd just let her be the first female admiral.

How wonderful those days were! We loved the little house we lived in, and the exciting White House life we shared in a strange way.

One of my favorite stories, which Mama brought home, was how the President and First Lady had met. It was at a coasting party when he was a law student in Cincinnati. He had offered her a ride on his sled.

Mama said that when the First Lady told this story to friends, the President would add, with a wink, "And Nellie and I have been sliding downhill ever since." Her name was Helen, but he called her "Nellie." Mrs. Taft would tell him to behave, or she would tell how he had played "Sleeping Beauty" at his men's club show.

Easter Mondays, Emmett and I would go to roll eggs on the White House lawn, and a neighbor would take us, because we had to be with an adult. Mama would come out on the roof to wave to us. I would be so proud in my "Helen Pink" dress as I waved back, and all the people would look on curiously.

It was a big day when I was invited to lunch with Mama at the White House and take my grandmother sightseeing. A storm came up, and as we crossed Pennsylvania Avenue, I got thoroughly splashed by a passing car. When I got inside, Mama was so shocked, that she took me to the laundry room and washed and ironed my dress before I could have a bite of food or see the White House with Grandmother. Mama said I would disgrace her if I went through the house sight-seeing like that.

I didn't know that eventually I would be working in those very rooms where Mama got me cleaned and primped for my visit. I remember standing and looking in curiously through the sewing room door.

In the summer, the First Family would move to Beverly, Massachusetts, and open up the summer White House. Mrs. Taft would take the first and third maid, the first and third cook and the head and third butler. Mama, the second maid, was left to take care of the President and his guests. The second butler and the second cook would also stay in Washington, and the President would remain at work until Congress adjourned. He would take week-end trips to be with his family.

The President had a strange habit of falling asleep when the First Lady was not there to keep after him. The butler was afraid to disturb him, and would leave the last few courses right on the table rather than wake him. The butler had an agreement with the doorman to finish the job, since the doorman would be the last one to leave.

Mama never got to see much of son Robert, who would one day almost receive the nomination for the Presidency. He was already at Yale when she went to work for the Tafts.

Just once, Mama got to travel with Mrs. Taft. She went to Hot Springs, Virginia, with the First Lady, and they stayed for nine days. Part of the time that she was at the White House, she was a personal maid to the First Lady.

The White House had quite an effect on Mama. She wanted everything in our house to be as elegant as possible, and, as she saved enough money, she would buy additional pieces of furniture. These additions may have come from the second-hand store, but they were always in such good taste, that they looked as if they might have come from that wonderful White House— at least to my eye.

Our yard too was so pretty and full of flowers, that people walking by would stop to look. Mama would laugh when she'd see them out there and say, "Wouldn't they really stare if they knew that the person who lives here is 'Maggie of the White House.' "

I said, "No, you're not; you're *'Mama* of the White House.' "

And so she was to me.

MRS. TAFT AND HER JINX

Little by little, Mama became convinced that a jinx was following Mrs. Taft around. True, it was great luck that she was in the White House and all that. However, everything was always so complicated for her— like the first batch of Japanese cherry trees that embarrassed Mrs. Taft no end.

Mama claimed that the jinx must have arrived at the White House with Mrs. Taft on the very day of the inauguration. It wasn't only that the weather had broken all records for nastiness— freezing cold and nine inches of snow in March— but there was the matter of the missing inaugural gown.

When Mama went to work at the White House, the help was still discussing Mrs. Taft's close call with the dress she wore to her Inaugural Ball. The dress was being made in New York, and was to be hand-delivered to the White House. Transportation was disrupted by the storm, and the messenger had not arrived. Mrs. Taft was frantic. To make matters worse, instead of sympathizing with her, the President calmly sat down and took a nap.

Finally it was time for Mrs. Taft to start dressing, and

she picked out a substitute dress. Her maid was so upset waiting for the gown, that she put up Mrs. Taft's hair three times, trying to get it right for the ball. She was about to try a fourth time, but Mrs. Taft thought that would be bad luck, and started putting on the old gown, feeling that she was not looking her best.

Then the messenger arrived with the dress— white satin embroidered with goldenrods— but it was too late to make Mrs. Taft feel relaxed and happy, as she should have been on this occasion.

It just wasn't her day. Before she had gone to the Capitol, she had had a bit of bad luck with another garment— the aigrette feather on her hat had gotten singed, and it had to be cut almost in half to make it look right.

There was all the gossip about whether Mrs. Taft had pushed her husband into the Presidency. Other servants told Mama that they had heard President Teddy Roosevelt discuss the fact that Mrs. Taft had asked him not to appoint her husband to the Supreme Court, because it would ruin his chances for the Presidency. And they had heard Teddy Roosevelt assure her that her husband was his personal choice as his successor. She had even come to the White House secretly to ask the President not to appoint her husband to the vacancy on the Supreme Court, the third which occurred during his administration.

The servants all said there were no White House secrets under Teddy Roosevelt, because he talked so loud and never closed a door. But Mrs. Taft knew people were talking about her part in her husband's career, and she was hurt because it made her sound "pushy."

To add to the evidence, the servants heard President Taft tell Mrs. Taft, while she was nervous and upset about the missing dress, "Well, now I'm in the White House, and I'm not going to be pushed any more."

And he wasn't. His solution to problems seemed to be to turn on a Caruso record good and loud and fall asleep.

Her problems grew more tense and so did the help. When she was worried, Mrs. Taft would get intensely interested in housekeeping. You could hardly turn around in the kitchens or on the stairs of the White House without running into Mrs. "T." She checked up on everybody to see if the pots and pans were smiling, the glasses sparkled, all the cushions were plumped up, and the floors were shiny. She ran her fingers along things to find dust; when she wanted to, she found it.

Mama felt sorry for her, because she understood it was just her nerves. Mama's own day at the White House was pretty busy too. She began by washing down the grand staircase every morning before breakfast, so Mama knew all about nerves.

Mrs. Taft seemed to feel responsible for everything— her household and her husband's success. The first thing that the household staff noticed upon her arrival as First Lady was that she sat in on her husband's important conferences. None of the old-timers had ever seen this before in previous administrations. Mrs. Taft also entered into political discussions at White House parties with the men who surrounded her husband, and seemed to enjoy that more than talking with the ladies.

It didn't help her popularity to mix into "men's business" though, and then the jinx paid another visit in the matter of a "harmless" letter. It was merely a letter from some women in the Balkan States who had formed an organization for political and social reform work in their country. They suggested that she form a similar organization in the United States.

Mrs. Taft sent a friendly letter, declining the proposition, but somehow they took it to mean that she was encouraging the ladies in their work. American papers claimed that she was "meddling" in international affairs, and it became an international situation in which our State Department had to exchange diplomatic notes with the Balkan government to get it all straightened out.

Mrs. Taft naturally felt very upset, because she had not meant to start an international incident, and Mama felt very sorry for her. "It is hard for a First Lady to say anything that will not be misunderstood," Mama told me.

Taft was the first President to receive a salary of $75,000, and Mrs. Taft seemed to feel that this called for her to make a display of economy in order to show she wasn't affected by it. Mama felt that the First Lady was trying too hard to set a good example for the ladies of the United States, because she did it by keeping a cow right on the White House grounds. Of course, everyone was shocked, even the White House staff, who were used to many innovations, but hadn't seen a cow around since the days of Andrew Johnson, ten Presidents before.

Mama and all the rest of the staff called the cow "Mooly-Wooly." In strange contrast to the cow, there was a white poodle, who gave the White House a very fashionable air. Poor Mrs. Taft had to take some ribbing about her "economical" cow, but she stood fast and even changed Mooly-Wooly for another cow, who gave more milk.

She also took some other steps in her economy drive. Mrs. Taft ordered all foods bought in wholesale lots, to obtain them more cheaply, and laid down the rule that out-of-season food would not be served at the White House.

Meanwhile, Mama had her own economy problems, and took her own steps toward their solution. Whenever there was a reception, she took the wraps in the cloakroom. She did not get overtime for working at social functions, but received tips from the guests, and this helped pad out the $20-a-month salary.

At Christmas, everyone who worked at the White House would receive a turkey and cranberries to take home. When they were passing out the turkeys, they would always say, "Give Maggie the biggest one, because she has two young ones." In our little house, we made that turkey last as long as possible.

Though I was listening to many gay and happy stories of the White House, Mama also told me how tension mounted on tension. Once, a U.S. Senator who had been invited to dinner, did not show up, and didn't even send his regrets before— or after— the dinner. Mrs. Taft took it badly.

It was no wonder that not too long after she had arrived at the White House, the First Lady suffered a stroke, and had to be in bed for some time. The incident revealed to us all the depth of the President's love for his wife. He sat with her for hours, reading to her, and helping her practice to regain her speech. He was tenderness itself, and he didn't fall asleep.

He would always try to make her laugh. He would bring her flowers from the White House gardens and say, "I stole these for you." This running gag began when he picked the flowers for the first time— he was discovered by the gardener, who thought he was a thief.

As soon as Mrs. Taft was well enough, the President was up to his old tricks again, even falling asleep over his dinner. She was back at his political conferences too. But Mama understood why. It was to protect her husband from ridicule over his sleeping habits.

Backstairs, the servants knew that she was trying to keep the President awake by prodding him when she saw him drifting off— something that no one else would dare do. They felt sorry for her. Sometimes she would carry on the conversation for him, for she was a brilliant woman, and she did know his views.

He fell asleep at the most peculiar times, even once at a funeral. Guests would be embarrassed when he would fall asleep in the middle of their stories, and poor Mrs. Taft would have to cover for him.

Sometimes, when they were alone, she would scold him for this bad habit, and would bring up the fact that in Manila, when she needed him most during a typhoon, he had gone to sleep in a chair, leaving her alone to cope with the terrified family and staff. "The chair was shaking— how could you sleep?" she would ask him.

"Now, Nellie, you know it is just my way," he would reply. "I knew you could handle it."

About the only time he wouldn't fall asleep was when he was talking to a pretty girl, and those were the times when Mrs. Taft wished he would. Backstairs, the help joked about the way the President loved to talk to pretty women. He would bore them to death with his long legal explanations, and they would try to look bright and interested. Whenever the President singled out the most beautiful woman at any party, Mrs. Taft, always the perfect lady on the surface, did not fool the staff, who knew she was boiling inside.

Taft had trouble with time too, and seldom kept an appointment at the specified hour. He would stash different callers in different rooms, and forget which room to go to next. It was fortunate that he had Mrs. Taft as his "helper without portfolio."

Mama said that the people did not realize the importance of Mrs. Taft's diligence and absolute dedication. She stood up at receptions again, and wore herself out at them. Her only concession to health was to wear low heels, which further distressed her, because she was style-conscious and dressed beautifully.

She was also weight-conscious— especially her husband's

weight— and somehow she seemed to feel she was responsible for the fact that he weighed a horrible 322 pounds.

Mama copied and brought home a poem that was making the rounds among the domestics; it was on the subject of the President's bulk. It had come to the White House by way of guests, who said it dated from the days of Malacañan Palace:

> "As butterflies fly sipping,
>   There's a waltzer who is ripping.
>   'Tis a sight to see Taft tripping
>   On the light, fantastic toe."

On this score— his weight— even the President was self-conscious. The nation thought that Taft was not at all sensitive about his poundage, but he really was.

A special bathtub had to be installed in the White House, because he would get stuck in a normal tub, and it would take two men to pull him out. When the newspapers made much of the rumor that he needed a special bathtub to hold his 322 pounds, he tried to deny it, but it was true just the same.

I have a picture of that bathtub, with four workmen, fully dressed, sitting in it, but the President hated to think that the country knew he was too fat to sit in a normal tub.

He talked about it in Provincetown, Massachusetts, in August of 1910, when he dedicated the monument that marked the place where the Pilgrims had first set foot in this country. He said, "There are certain stories that I'd like to deny. We have no special bathtubs made for any Executive of any particular size." As the crowd laughed, he added that he too had arrived in a ship named the *Mayflower,* and he brought more laughter and applause when he ended with the punch line, "It did not happen from any particular arrangement, only that the vessel was the most suitable, leaving out the question of bathtubs."

The little meal he enjoyed that day consisted merely of lobster stew, salmon cutlets with peas, cold roast tenderloin with vegetable salad, roast turkey with potato salad, cold tongue and ham, frozen pudding, cake, fruit, and coffee. It did tend to put on weight.

Mrs. Taft worried constantly about his weight, and at first, wondered why the diets she put him on did no good. But we *knew* why.

The President could eat everything and anything— and he did. He had pains in his toes, and Mrs. Taft told him that this meant the gout, but he denied it, and refused to see a doctor. When he finally did see a doctor, that was what he had, and he was placed on a strict diet.

Mrs. Taft hovered over him, and supervised the diet at the White House, but the President was not always at home. When he didn't lose weight, and didn't lose weight, she found out that he was gorging himself elsewhere. Any time he went on his private train, he would have it well-stocked with all the foods he wasn't supposed to eat. All his friends seemed to cooperate with *him* in beating his diet, rather than with *her* in keeping him on his diet.

The person for whom the staff felt sorriest was Helen, who was at that painful college age when it hurt to have a daddy whom people said looked like Santa Claus.

Mama and the other maids felt the shadow of Mrs. Taft's jinx too. Every outdoor party was marred by some act of fate, including stinging mosquitos and flies that flew into the punch.

Mrs. Taft's favorite cook married suddenly, and Mrs. Taft took it as a personal blow dealt by the same unremitting fate. No cook would stay. No wonder: the President was forever keeping the kitchen off balance by bringing any number of guests home with him without advance warning. This, coupled with Mrs. Taft's habit of looking into their pots and pans, made them decide that the honor of working in the White House wasn't worth the strain on their nervous systems.

Even the cooks who cooked for the help wouldn't stay. Mama once filled in, in an emergency, and the servants complained that she cooked "scrambled food."

Finally, Mrs. Taft became so desperate, that she lured back the cook, who had left to get married. But the jinx struck again— it was discovered that the cook's husband had TB. Then the situation became further complicated by the cook's baby, and Mrs. Taft even had to arrange for the care of the baby so its mother could cook at the White House.

I asked Mama if Mrs. Taft's jinx had gone along to the Malacañan Palace, and Mama said, "Of course. It travels everywhere." Mrs. Taft had told her that almost upon her arrival, there had been such a terrible tropical storm, that the palace entrance hall had been inundated under several feet of water.

And once in London, traveling with her children, when she was the wife of the Secretary of War, she lost her luggage, and the boat train was held up until they could find it. Her credentials got her nowhere, and the only way in which she was able to hold the train was to explain that she was the wife of "the man who is travelling with Miss Alice Roosevelt." Even in London, they had heard about that much-publicized official junket of the President's daughter, and a Congressional committee, to the Philippines.

Although Mrs. Taft often told this story, always with a genteel laugh, Mama always felt that the First Lady was envious of Alice Roosevelt Longworth, the young matron who continued to hold the public's attention and affection, even throughout Taft's administration.

And, another time, when she went to Cuba to join her

husband, hadn't the jinx gone right along? A rebellion broke out, and she needed the Marines to protect her. "But," she used to add proudly, "as a result, I was mistress of the palace at Havana for three days."

There was no doubt about it, the First Lady would have made a happy queen, had the Americans chosen a monarchy. The servants agreed on that. They would look at Mrs. Taft's treasured photos of herself in native Philippine dress, and chuckle, trying to imitate her voice: "They don't do things at the White House the way we used to do them at the Malacañan Palace."

But if she didn't succeed, it wasn't for not trying. She decreed that all the staff would have fancy uniforms, and the houseboys were to wear full-dress uniforms while they worked. They were saved from this fate when one boy said to another in her hearing, "Won't we look fine cleaning windows in tails?" They heard no more about it.

Then there was the tragedy of Captain Archie Butt. He was the military aide appointed by Teddy Roosevelt, and was one of President Taft's closest friends. He spent much of his time at the White House and frequently stayed overnight, because his conferences with the President would last so late. Eventually, the strain made him ill, and he went to Italy for his health.

He had a strange premonition before he left. Mama knew about his feeling, because he told her, "Maggie, I can't sleep. I feel so restless. Something is hanging over me." Mama moved him from room to room to try to get him to rest, because he was then staying at the White House.

He even quit teasing Alice, the second cook. Alice specialized in making waffles and griddle cakes, and waffles were Captain Butt's favorite food. No matter how many times he would pass the kitchen on the way to the President's office, he would put his head in the door and call to Alice, "Say, Alice, when are we going to have some waffles?"

Alice had a stock answer. She always replied, "Tomorrow," even though he had just finished eating some.

But suddenly he wasn't even interested in waffles or teasing Alice any more. Captain Butt went to Italy and never returned. On his way back to the States, he went down with the *Titanic,* in April, 1912.

The jinx seemed to have affected the President's disposition too. He had practically lived at the White House when Teddy Roosevelt was there. He came to lunch almost every day, and was welcomed by the servants as the best-tempered man they knew. Now, as President, they classified him as a "sourpuss."

The public also grumbled, saying that as a President, Taft would make a better judge. He spent so much time deliberating, that he never got around to action till the crisis was over, and he became known as a "do nothing" President.

He was the first golfing President, and his administration was ideally suited to the growth of private enterprise and individual initiative. The only *unpleasant* thing that happened was the 16th Amendment, which meant that everyone would have to pay an income tax, and *no one was happy over that!*

When it was time for the nominations again, the special Taft jinx really struck when the former President, Teddy Roosevelt, actually ran against the man he had hand-picked to succeed him. That was really bad luck.

When I grew older, I asked Mama why President Roosevelt had turned against President Taft, and why they hadn't even ridden together in the same car that inauguration day in 1909. Mama said that all the help had agreed that President Roosevelt owed favors to various people and had wanted President Taft to promise to appoint these people to his Cabinet, which he wouldn't do.

President Roosevelt took this failure of Taft's to do his bidding for ingratitude, and once started downhill, the friendship fell apart. Half the servants were for Taft; half were for T.R.; but they were careful that the family heard no part of their arguments.

Mother was definitely on the side of Taft, and she thought it shocking that a man would relinquish an office without a fight, and then, four years later, try to regain it from his successor, especially since they had once been friends. The servants had taken sides on that issue too— did T.R. have the right to be angry with Taft?

Half the staff thought that Taft had erred and deserved the enmity of T.R., because "a promise is a promise, and must be kept," but again Mama was loyal to her boss, and she claimed a President was chosen to lead the people, because the public had faith in him. Therefore, they wanted his choice of officials, and not the choice of someone else whom they had not elected.

Mrs. Taft was sure that her husband would win in his fight for re-election. She was so indignant when she saw critical stories about her husband during the Presidential race, that she stopped reading the newspapers.

Mama was very sad when Taft failed to make it, and Woodrow Wilson, a Democrat, won out over the Republican party and the Bull Moose, Teddy Roosevelt. Still, she remembered that her duty lay with the White House, no matter who was in it, and that carried her through the bleak days when she was helping an embittered Mrs. Taft to pack up.

When it came time to go, Mrs. Taft left the White House without saying good-by to Mama, and Mama was hurt, because she had grown so fond of the First Lady. She couldn't believe that Mrs. Taft would fail to say good-by to her. But Mama felt better when she found out that she was not the only one who hadn't received a personal fare-well.

One day, years later, when I was inspecting the packages and cameras of the tourists as they came through the White House, I noticed a pretty blonde girl who came in alone. She was about fifteen or sixteen, I think. She didn't hurry on with the rest, but lagged behind, looking around. Finally she said wistfully, "I wish I could see more. I'd like to see the parlor, because my grandfather was here once."

I thought her grandfather might have been a guest at some time, and I asked who he was.

"President Taft," she said.

"What is your father's name?" I asked.

"Charlie Taft," she said.

I thought of the little boy who had waded in the fountain, who had grabbed phones when he shouldn't have, who had held long discussions with reporters, and whose pants had been worn by my brother.

Charlie Taft's daughter was escorted through the whole White House. As I walked with this sedate little girl, I thought of how unlike her father she seemed to be, and I remembered the Charlie Taft whom Mama and Emmett knew, the Charlie Taft who had tied shoe laces together under the table, and who bragged how he had helped Quentin Roosevelt stick spitballs that looked like warts on a picture of Andy Jackson that hung in the White House.

It was hard to realize that the mischievous little boy, who had made White House history for me, was now the dignified father of this dignified little girl. Somehow I wished she could have known the other Charlie too.

I don't know how you feel about jinxes, but even after

Mrs. Taft left, her jinx seemed to remain with the bed she had slept in.

Mrs. Taft had been the first President's wife to introduce twin beds in the White House. It was on one of these that she suffered such a breakdown of health, that she even lost her power of speech. It was on this bed that the next First Lady, Ellen Louise Wilson, died. It was on this bed that Coolidge's son lay in pain with blood poisoning before he was carried to the hospital to die. And it was on this bed that Mrs. Harding would lie at death's door.

The happy ending to this chapter belongs to President Taft himself. He finally got what he really wanted all along— a seat on the Supreme Court. He was Chief Justice for nine blissful years, from 1921 to 1930. Mama said Mrs. Taft's jinx was non-transferable *out* of the White House.

AN ANGEL IN
THE WHITE HOUSE

Mama came home saying it was just too good to be true—there was an angel in the White House, the new President's wife.

I had seen her, of course, in the Inaugural Parade, when the Democrats celebrated the return of their party to power and really whooped it up. The line was long, and the watchers jubilant. Mama was a little worried, because the President looked so stern with his long, lean face, so different from the Santa Claus features of Taft. Why, this man did not even have a mustache to soften his features!

I could hardly wait to hear what kind of people these were. It didn't take long to find out.

"Lillian," Mama said, "I hardly can believe my ears. I think we have an angel in the White House. She is talking about helping the poor and improving the housing." I had to admit that much as we were proud of our house, it could use some improvement; we had gas lights, and not even a furnace— we hovered around a small coal stove.

The next night, she told me, "Lillian, would you be-

lieve it, today the First Lady asked me all about you and
Emmett, and she wants to come to see you."

I remembered how I'd felt when I saw Mrs. Wilson go
by in the Inaugural Parade, in a big hat and elegant dress.
Her hair was dark brown, and her eyes were soft and
luminous. I had held my breath a moment because it
seemed, for an instant, that she was looking straight at me.

Mama told me she had seen the President wandering
around the hall with a Bible under his arm. He was, from
all that Mama could gather, a very religious man, but
one who did not make a show of it. He was the son of a
minister, and Mrs. Wilson was the daughter and granddaughter of ministers.

When Mrs. Wilson's maid was away, Maggie would
serve her, and she always came home shaking her head in
amazement because a woman of such importance and
such high rank could be so gentle. It was as if Mrs. Wilson
wanted to make the world around her a little better place
to live in.

One night, Mama came home with a box full of clothes,
to be cut down for me. They were clothes from the Wilsons' girls, Margaret, Jessie, and Eleanor, reading from
oldest to youngest. Our house was always clean, but for the
impending visit of the First Lady, we polished and polished everything in sight. The White House, I'm sure,
could never have been cleaner, even before any official reception.

Mrs. Wilson did come to visit quite unexpectedly, just
as if it were the most usual thing in the world, and Mama
showed her with simple pride the pieces of furniture she
was buying one by one. Mrs. Wilson expressed admiration,
and even made a few suggestions as to what would "look
nice in that corner." Then, in the flicker of an eyelid, she
was gone.

Mama explained that Mrs. Wilson was not only visiting

our place, but hundreds of places all over the Capital, to see how the poor people lived, and that she was going to do something to improve their slum conditions. Mama said that Congress was not pleased that a First Lady was getting involved in things that were men's business— and more openly than Mrs. Taft too. Mrs. Wilson was calling for legislation to clean up the slums of the Capital, and Congress was appointing a committee to look into her investigation to see what should be done.

Meanwhile, life at the White House was idyllic for Mama, and even the President had taken a kindly interest in her. Mrs. Wilson had told the President that Maggie was raising a crippled daughter. One day, the President saw Mama washing down the grand stairway. He said to an usher, "I don't ever want to see Maggie on her knees again." Thus Mama was relieved of one of her hardest jobs.

A strangely gentle way of life set the tone at the White House, so in contrast to life there with the Tafts.

Mrs. Wilson planted box bushes, rose bushes, and rose trees, making a garden between the White House and the President's office on the South Lawn. At one end of the garden was a marble bench with an awning over it. Here she had a telephone installed for the President, so he could keep her company while still remaining in touch with the Government.

A statue of a little boy overlooked the garden. Mama said that perhaps he was the little boy Mrs. Wilson wished she could have given the President to carry on his name. The President was very tender with his wife, and very attentive in the Rose Garden.

The servants considered Mrs. Wilson a beautiful woman, and they especially liked her soft voice, a contrast to Mrs. Taft's more authoritarian tones. She had hair and eyes that matched her voice in softness.

Backstairs, they called the President and his wife "the Professor and His Lady." If someone said, "The Lady wants her tray," that meant, in the mind of the person spoken to, "the Great and Good Lady," and I don't think a single servant disliked her. She laughed off mistakes, and always gave someone another chance.

But the Wilson girls were another matter— Margaret, Jessie, and Eleanor. It wasn't that they were disliked; it was just that they were full of girlish pranks and surprises, and no one knew what trick would be played on them next. They liked to confuse the servants by pretending they had asked for something they hadn't, or by popping out from dark corners to frighten them into dropping things. Their favorite trick was to pretend to be tourists and march through the White House with the other tourists, making nasty remarks about themselves.

Once, they did the same thing in the sight-seeing bus, and they came back howling with laughter, because they had gotten the driver to promise he would do everything in his power to get them in to see the whole White House.

Why they were not recognized I do not know, except that they were not beautiful girls, or the kind who especially draw attention. Mama said they really looked better than the newspaper pictures I saw of them. Eventually, I sewed for the youngest one when she was the wife of the Secretary of the Treasury (this was before I ever went to the White House to work), and found her very charming.

As Mama described it, the White House had become a household of women, all hovering around one man— a wife, three daughters, and even an extra woman, Miss Helen Bones, the President's cousin, who came to visit and stayed on, and on, and on. She became a sort of social secretary to the First Lady.

Mama heard the ladies laughing over the possibility that Mrs. Wilson might not have been in the White House if only she had made the right bus connection. Mrs. Wilson was telling Miss Bones how she was trying to escape Woodrow Wilson when he was busy studying political history and teaching, and at the same time courting her. She was a young artist, intent on fame and fortune. He had written that he was coming to marry her, and she had run away. But she had missed her bus connection, and by some quirk of fate, Wilson's bus had pulled in right behind hers.

"I just gave up and married him," she said to Miss Bones with a laugh.

"But you shouldn't have given up your painting," said Miss Bones.

"Well, three daughters take more time than three canvases," said Mrs. Wilson, although she promised that she would get back to painting since the strain of the long years of hard work were over.

She did too. Mama helped her fix up a studio for an artist's workshop, and Mrs. Wilson spent many happy hours there. The pictures that she painted— landscapes— brought a good price because of her high position, and she sold them for every worthy cause— the education of Southern mountaineers and the crippled children of Washington, for example.

Years later, when President Eisenhower was painting, and I would see him at his easel, I wanted desperately to tell him what Mrs. Wilson had done, and to suggest that he too consider selling his paintings for some worthy cause, but I didn't feel that it was my place to do so.

The studio that Mrs. Wilson had fixed was up on the third floor, which was actually the attic of the White House. New stairs had to be put in to replace the attic-like steps. At the same time that the third floor was being done over, Mrs. Wilson added three more guest rooms, and a room I would frequently use in the future— a sewing room.

The Swedish cook, who had worked for Mrs. Taft,

stayed, though it meant a demotion under Mrs. Wilson. She had her own cook, whom she had brought from New Jersey, who ruled the kitchen. What Archie Butt had been to Taft, Col. Edward House was to President Wilson— advisor and constant guest at the White House.

Everyone asked Mama what manner of man Wilson really was— didn't he have any peculiarities? One of his peculiarities had to do with the lights. Mama was still the one who turned on the electricity in the private quarters of the White House every night, and under the Tafts, she was used to turning them on whenever she pleased. But President Wilson made a fetish of not being wasteful, and one night, as she was going around turning on lights, she found that he was right behind her, turning them off.

"Waste not, want not," he said, and after that, Mama made sure it was dark outside before she turned on any electricity.

But the strangest thing about the President was that he was really a frustrated actor. Mama would find him making faces, clowning, and doing a jig with his daughters, or taking a very serious part in a play, and speaking with one arm raised dramatically, as if he were on the stage.

He had a good audience, because all five women of the household adored him. So did the two dogs— Sandy, an Airedale, and Hamish, the English sheep dog, who had come with Miss Bones, and had taken up residence at the White House on a more or less permanent basis too.

His family could always get the President to go to a play, and no matter how tired he was, he was never too tired for the theatre. Once in a while, though, he would reach the saturation point of feminine company, and escape and play a game of solitaire. If the women wanted him then, he would tell Mama to tell them he was busy and would see them later. He would also escape to the golf course, and he was called the second golfing President. Mr. Taft was the first.

Mrs. Jaffray was still in charge of the house, and in the servants' area, there was comment that sometimes she acted as if it were *her* White House alone, and then she would lord it over Mama and the other servants. But she proved she did have a heart when *Maggie* got sick with pneumonia after staying up very late at the White House, checking the wraps of the guests. She came to visit Mama, wearing her stately Queen Mary hat with veil, black kid gloves, and full regalia. Miss Helen Bones visited us too, and between them, they kept bringing every kind of food from calf's-foot jelly to spinach, in the hope that it would help Maggie get well fast.

And then suddenly things started to change at the White House. We didn't know it then, but it would never be the same. It began with the weddings of two daughters, Jessie and Eleanor. People did not know it, but Mrs. Wilson was already ill while she was in the thick of preparations for the wedding of her daughter Jessie to Francis B. Sayre.

Everyone in the kitchen held their breath to keep from disturbing the cake, which was being baked by the same woman who had made the wedding cake for Alice Roosevelt when she married Representative Nicholas Longworth. Her name was Mme. Blanche Rales, and she came from New York just to bake the cake in the White House kitchen. The cake stood thirty inches high, and was three feet across, and weighed 130 pounds. All the servants tiptoed by, afraid it would collapse.

Jessie's wedding took place in the East Room, November 25, 1913, at 4:30. I still have the invitation that Mama received. Mama and all the help shook their heads, because Miss Jessie's would be the thirteenth wedding in the White House. Someone mentioned it to her, but she only laughed and said *she* felt lucky. She was too for twenty years, until her untimely death at the age of forty-five.

She was married standing on a white vicuña rug, a fur which had not yet come into disrepute in the White House and did not until the Sherman Adams vicuña coat incident. This rug was a gift of the Peruvian Ambassador, and was supposed to bring good luck to a bride.

Maybe the bad luck that Jessie did not have was passed with the wedding bouquet to Miss Margaret, because Margaret was not the next bride. Instead, Eleanor, the baby of the three, became the fourteenth bride of the White House. Everyone was more startled than thrilled when her engagement was announced to the Secretary of the Treasury, William Gibbs McAdoo, a widower who had grown children, some of them older than the bride-to-be.

The backstairs help talked of little else when the frivolous and light-hearted Eleanor, who was just in her early twenties, started seeing the middle-aged Secretary of the Treasury. "He's too old for her," some said. "She'll have trouble with his children," said others.

Mama didn't give her opinion at the White House, but when she got home, she ventured the theory that Eleanor was marrying in desperation, because she wanted to do everything her big sister did, and could not stand waiting. She could not believe that life was anything but a lark, because she had grown up in a happy atmosphere, with contented parents who showed deep love for each other. Weren't all marriages like that?

Some said that Mr. McAdoo was using her position to improve his own, because he had his eye on the White House too. One of the servants reported how shocked the President had looked the first night when the usher announced that the Secretary of the Treasury had come to see "Miss Eleanor." Typical of her, as the romance progressed, Eleanor was heard teasing the Secretary; she said that she would not have anything to do with him unless he learned the new dance steps, and the Secretary, entering into the spirit of her challenge, permitted her to teach him to the music of the Gramophone.

The best story about the wedding ceremony was that Ike Hoover, chief White House usher, saved the day and the bride's dignity by rushing out and turning the bride's train when it looked as though she would get tangled and fall down in it.

She too stood on the vicuña rug to be married, but the luck of the rug did not hold out; eventually, she was divorced, and she never remarried.

In the beginning of the marriage, everything seemed sublimely happy. She had two children— Ellen, named for her mother, and Mary Faith. Margaret was now alone, and she had suitors by the score, but she was not interested in them. She was one of those newfangled career girls, and, like another famous White House daughter, Margaret Truman, she began a singing career while still in the White House.

It was as if Mrs. Wilson knew she had finished her work on earth, and could rest at last. She was very tired. She had seen two daughters happily married. Maybe she knew that the third daughter was too independent ever to marry.

But even in the last moments of life, her thoughts were with others. The President was with her when she died on August 6, 1914, and he came out of the room saying that her last words had been for the slum-dwellers of Washington, asking that something be done for them.

Until her body was taken to her home in Rome, Georgia, for burial, the family spent all their time in the hall outside her door. Sometimes they read; sometimes they just sat, so that they could be near her throughout the last possible moments.

Once, Mama heard the President talking to his dead

wife as he stood beside her body. She happened to be in the room at twilight when the President came in and stood looking at his wife's face. He picked at the lace on her dress, and Mama could hardly keep from crying at this wistful, hopeless scene. The President spoke aloud, brokenly, "Never, never, never." Then he walked out.

We tried to decide what he had meant as we sat in the kitchen of our little house, talking about the sad event at the White House, and shedding a few tears ourselves. Mama thought that maybe he meant he would never remarry.

If that were the meaning, even a President can change his mind, because life did go on, and new lives were born in the White House, and the President did remarry— perhaps even too soon. But don't let me get ahead of the story . . .

There came a day when the thought of Mrs. Wilson, though unspoken, was in the minds of everyone. That was the day when a new life came to the White House. Miss Jessie had come back to her White House home with her husband, to spend the first Christmas since the death of her mother, and here her first baby was born, Francis B. Sayre, Jr. Mama was called to the Small Rose Room, where the birth was taking place, and several nurses were standing by. Dr. Cary Grayson handed the baby to Maggie and said, "Take him to the fireplace in the Large Rose Room, and keep him warm."

Mama was walking out with the baby when the President arrived. He looked at the baby and then away, as if into the past, and tears filled his eyes. He didn't say anything.

It was the moment he could not share.

WHEN LOVE COMES TO
THE WHITE HOUSE

The White House was in an uproar. The servants were upset. Some of the more dignified and conservative ones were saying it was too soon, it was almost indecent for a man to be courting a woman before his wife had been dead for a year.

It had happened so suddenly, so naturally, so innocently. The doctor who had taken care of Mrs. Wilson during her illness, Dr. Grayson, was in love with a Miss Gertrude Gordon, and the mood must have been contagious. Suffice it to say that an aura of love and romance hung over the White House, though at first, Dr. Grayson was the sole beneficiary.

Then, one day, Dr. Grayson came to tea with Gertrude and a lovely stranger. She was a widow, looked somewhat like the first Mrs. Wilson, and was dressed with quiet elegance. The servants noticed that the President did not send her home with Dr. Grayson, but took her home himself.

That was a day in March, 1915, just seven months after

he had become a widower. Still the staff wasn't too disturbed until they saw Mrs. Edith Galt arrive at the White House for lunch again and again.

Suddenly the President was effervescent and full of jokes. The happier he became, the sadder the servants were.

"He couldn't," said some.

"Wait and see," others predicted.

"She's a dozen years younger than his wife was," most everyone noted.

Almost everyone agreed that Dr. Grayson must have had something in mind, when he brought her over, beside his avowed purpose of finding someone to be a companion to his fiancée. Who was this woman? Mama explained that she was the widow of a man who had owned a jewelry store downtown— and that she wasn't poor.

As I waited each night for the next exciting chapter in the great romance of the century, I determined that as soon as possible, I too would work in the White House, because nowhere was life more exciting or the surroundings more beautiful.

I was growing up, and already in my teens. I was doing the cooking and cleaning, but I was still on crutches. Clearly, I would not be dancing in the near future. But even a cat may look at a queen, as Mama always said, and even I could dream of high romance. If I couldn't have it for myself, I assured myself, as a sort of promise, that I would put myself in a place where I could take part in other peoples' lives, and life would be as exciting as though it were happening to me.

"The Professor is writing love notes," Mama reported to my eager ears. "And I hear that he has sent over to the library to get all kinds of quotations about love so that he will know what Anthony said to Cleopatra and people like that."

"Have you seen any of the letters?" I asked.

"Heavens no, child, do you think I'm a snooper?" she said indignantly.

Frankly, I was disappointed. I wished heartily she had been a snooper, and I would have given my last penny to have taken a peek at the love letters that matched those of history and told what Anthony said to Cleopatra.

Evidently, the recipient of those letters was concerned, because a lot of other people were interested in them too; and years later, I heard that she had destroyed them all.

Mama reported that there was a rumor that Congress was angry because the President was spending too much time writing love letters when he should have been writing reports on the grave war situation in Europe. The question, said one angry Congressman, was not whether Mrs. Edith Galt loved Mr. Woodrow Wilson, but whether we were going to get into a war or weren't going to get into a war.

For a brief moment, Miss Margaret Wilson was able to grab the spotlight for herself by giving her first big concert. It was at Syracuse, and a record crowd of over six thousand people came to *see* the daughter of a President sing. For this she got $1,000.

I waited to see what she would do with that money. New clothes? A trip around the world? No, she was a chip off the old block. She gave the money she had earned to two institutions for the blind in Washington. Mama's eyes were filled with tears when she told us this.

"She has the goodness of her mother," said Mama, "and it makes me feel that Mrs. Wilson is not really dead." Mama was in one of her philosophic moods. "That is the real reason for having children," she said, "and why I am glad I have you two. As long as I have you, I will always live."

I got her back to the subject of Edith Galt as soon as possible, because I was not in the mood for lectures. Matters of life and death seem very far away when you are young.

Mother told me she was going to go on the Presidential yacht, the *Mayflower,* with the President and Mrs. Galt for a short cruise, and that they would see a big naval parade.

"Are you going all alone with them?" I asked.

"Of course not," Mama assured me. "There will be many chaperones— Miss Margaret, Miss Bones, Dr. Grayson, Miss Gordon, the President's secretary, and several others." Mama's job was to take care of all the ladies, especially if they should get seasick, and to help them dress and fix their hair.

They started for New York, but soon ran into a big storm on Chesapeake Bay. Everyone except President Wilson and one sailor got sick. Mama couldn't help any of the ladies, because she was the sickest of them all.

After they had reached New York, and the ground steadied under foot, Mama had a magnificent time as part of the Presidential party. But the curious crowd pushed them so, that she was frequently in danger of being lost from the group. Miss Bones, who took charge of Mama, said to her, "Hold on to me, Maggie, and I'll get you through."

The engagement of the President and Mrs. Galt was announced on October 7, 1915, but by this time the White House crowd had adjusted to the idea of a new First Lady. The wedding was set for December 18, and officials had a "let's-get-it-over-with-and-back-to-work" attitude.

One person who didn't approve of the marriage was Colonel House, who had come down from New York to warn the President that if he were to marry so soon, he would lose the election the following year. This just made the President, who was a real fighter, determined to get married right away.

The Colonel was the only person from whom the President would take advice, but Mama said that in this case he had used the wrong tactic. Wilson wasn't the kind of man to let public opinion scare him.

I waited eagerly each night to hear what new presents had arrived for the bride-to-be. There were crates of candy— Mama brought me home a sample— a great number of cakes, which were slowly getting stale, enough soap and toilet preparations to keep an elephant spanking-sweet for a lifetime, and, oddly enough, one barrel of popcorn. That was my favorite gift. Mama, being furniture-conscious, was more interested in the gorgeous rugs, table linens, clocks, silverware, delicate glass, and even a sixteenth century Chinese Ming bowl. I still treasure the invitation that she received to the wedding.

Little did we know when the happy couple made their vows in Mrs. Galt's tiny living room off Dupont Circle, and went to Hot Springs, Virginia, for two weeks' vacation, that this would be a most unusual marriage.

At first, it was everything a marriage should be— a wedding out of a story book. The President and Mrs. Wilson had breakfast together in the family dining room, and the bride walked to the office with her husband through the Rose Garden. If the new Mrs. Wilson knew that the roses had been planted by another Mrs. Wilson, she did not let on. But sometimes, when Mama saw the President stop and stoop to smell a rose, she would wonder, and the servants sometimes commented that they wished the new Mrs. Wilson would use a different route.

The first social season under Edith Galt Wilson was a brilliant one, starting off with a diplomatic reception in January, 1916. Mrs. Wilson stood tall and beautiful in a white gown, brocaded with silver, and draped with white tulle. Then came a ball at the new Pan American Union, which Mama always claimed was the most elaborate affair she had ever seen. Mrs. Wilson stood out from all the

dazzling colors by wearing a black velvet gown and carrying a grey feathered fan. Mama was sent over to the Pan
American Union simply to check Mrs. Wilson's evening
wrap when she arrived.

The new Mrs. Wilson was certainly different from the
first Mrs. Wilson, who had not even held an Inaugural
Ball when she first came to the White House.

It was a gay life at the White House, but Mrs. Wilson
danced on the brink of war. On May 24, 1916, there were
more festivities when Dr. Grayson married his fiancée in
New York, and the President and his bride attended.

But by the next month, war clouds hovered over our
shores, and there was talk of little else. President Wilson
led a preparedness parade from the Peace Monument, at
the foot of the Capitol grounds, to the White House. And
then he started making trips around the country, deliver-
ing campaign speeches in which he talked of preparedness.

The President wanted another term in office. In the
kitchen and sewing room, and in the halls of the White
House, the servants wondered whether the marriage of the
President so soon after he had been widowed would lose
him the election. That there was another issue— turned
into the slogan "He kept us out of war"— did not seem as
important to us as his personal life, probably because he
had given himself over so completely to his romance.

Election day came and went, and it looked as if he had
lost. At home, we all went to bed on election night with
the report that Charles Evans Hughes had been elected.
Mama felt terribly sorry for Mrs. Wilson, who might have
been blaming herself. She also felt pretty sorry for herself,
because she had been assigned to help Margaret, and liked
that position very much.

When Margaret asked for her, Mama was a little afraid
to accept, because that would mean that if Wilson had lost
the election, she, as the personal maid to the family, would

be out of a job too. But Wilson had told Mama not to worry, that she would always have a job.

After several days of great anxiety, it became apparent that Wilson had won after all, and Mama still had a job at the White House. We were as happy as the President.

Since March 4 was a Sunday, for the fifth time in history the inauguration ceremony was on a Monday, and, as a spectator, I saw that the second Mrs. Wilson looked positively radiant in a Lillian Russell hat and black velvet suit, highlighted with violets. Violets seem to have been a tradition for inaugurations, for Mrs. Taft had worn them at the first inauguration I ever saw. Soon, the second Mrs. Wilson switched to orchids, and they became a fad and then a fashion for those who could afford them. The fashion is still with us today.

The second Mrs. Wilson liked to show friends the Lincoln bed, which she had installed in her suite rather than the President's. When she used it, it still had the original canopy, which was removed by the time I went to work at the White House. I once saw the original record of the purchase of the bed. It cost $375.50, including the "canopy and curtains." It was dated December 21, 1864, and was approved January 3, 1865, by "Mary Lincoln." The dimensions of what is probably the world's most famous bed are as follows: length, 8 feet; width, 5½ feet; headboard, 9 feet tall.

I was queen for a night when Mama smuggled me into the White House to see how a State dinner takes place. I watched from behind potted palms as the guests arrived in their furs and finery, and later, she changed my position, so I could see how President Wilson and the First Lady marched in to dinner with their guests.

Margaret Wilson had her own piano in her room and practiced religiously, making big plans for her career. We wished she were prettier, so that her chances of success would be increased; we hoped she would realize a career on her own, without the glamor of her father's name.

"The trouble with Margaret," the staff backstairs agreed, "is that she's the spitting image of her father." There was nothing sweet and girlish about *his* looks. Margaret knew that folks came to see "the daughter of the President" rather than the independent young lady with plans of her own. In talking her father into letting her appear in public, she pointed to the precedent set by President McKinley's niece, who started her career with White House backing also. Though Mabel McKinley was crippled, she had sung in vaudeville.

As I sat at home, listening to the story of how President McKinley's niece had used crutches to walk on the stage, because she had been crushed by some falling lumber when she was a child, it gave me new hope for my own future. I looked at my own crutches leaning against the wall, and vowed again that somehow I would be a part of the White House life. There must be some way I could go to work there, crutches or no crutches.

Though Margaret Wilson frequently sang at the White House, Mama said that the guests did not consider this a treat; it was simply the price of being invited. Mama wished she could design a new hairdo for her, but didn't feel that it was "her place" to tell a President's daughter what to do.

McKinley's niece, Mabel, had sung at the White House too, but it was said that she had had a beautiful face. Mabel had even succeeded in catching a husband, in spite of her crutches— a doctor, Hermanus Baer— and McKinley had attended the ceremony.

But Margaret Wilson never did marry. Instead, her story has a sad ending. She went to India, to live in a religious Hindu colony in Pondicherry, and died of uremia. Before she departed, to study the doctrines of Sri Aurobindo, she vowed never to return to the United States.

What part her father's remarriage played in her disillusionment, I have always wondered. But when she was at the White House, with Maggie looking after her, she felt deserted by everyone, what with two married sisters, and a father busy with a new bride. So she threw herself into music, in a search for beauty in her own life. She was as generous with Mama as her mother had been, and sent boxes of clothes and candies home to me with Mama.

A second grandchild was introduced to the White House. A baby girl had been born to Eleanor McAdoo, and soon tiny Ellen McAdoo was wheeling over to the White House in her pony cart, which was large enough to accommodate a nurse and a footman.

As Mama described it, her arrivals at the White House would be quite a sight. Everyone would ask her who lived at the White House, hoping to hear her say "Grandfather," but she would always answer "Mays."

The President laughed and laughed, because his grandchild always gave the doorman, John Mays, top billing. Mays would treat Miss Ellen with great dignity, and, after he had lifted her from her cart, she loved to stand and talk with him about all her adventures instead of rushing in to see the President.

This beautiful child had a tragic life. She grew up and married, but later she destroyed herself.

The President did not seem too happy after the election. It must have hurt him to know he was not popular enough to have won a clear victory— he barely squeaked through.

After the President had remarried, at first a few servants grumbled that they did not want to work for any Indian, regardless of her status. Mrs. Edith Wilson did not deny that she had some Indian blood; in fact, Mama heard her

When Love Comes to the White House 149

tell a guest that she was a direct descendant from Pocahontas. She was a ninth generation descendant of the Indian Princess. Mama used to study her face to see how
much of the Indian ancestry showed, and she decided that
a certain firmness of line and straightness of feature could
have come from the Indians. No one denied that the new
Mrs. Wilson was beautiful, and her knowledge of her own
beauty was visible also, which did not help her win friends,
as the first Mrs. Wilson had done.

The new Mrs. Wilson had only one goal— to please her
husband. She paid attention to very little else, but concentrated on being a complete companion. No outside
hobbies did she have, no painting, no designing of gardens.
She centered her full and complete attention on her husband, and even went golfing with him.

The poor President could not even turn to golf to get
away from the womenfolk. Nor did he have time. He was
busy with his war problems every moment.

Colonel House was at the White House much of the
time, and the President leaned on him heavily— even working out a special code so they could send confidential messages to each other. Mama was pleased that Colonel House
and the new Mrs. Wilson became friends, and Mrs. Wilson
entered into the spirit of things. Mama would often see
her busy at coding and decoding for the President.

His concentration was beginning to show on him, but
so was her concentration on him beginning to tell on
her. She became so exhausted, that several times, she went
to bed for a full day to relax and at least partially unwind.
Cabinet officers and advisors came to the White House at
all hours of the day and night. The President's work hours
started at dawn.

To top it all, as a minor irritation, lady suffragettes
were starting to picket the White House. Strangely enough,
the man who wanted a League of Nations was not equally

interested in rights for women. It was some time before he was convinced that women should vote.

Once, when the Russian delegation was visiting the White House, the suffragettes congregated outside in full force with a streamer that read, "We, the women of America, tell you that America is not a democracy. Twenty million American women are denied the right to vote. President Wilson is the chief opponent of their national enfranchisement. Help us make this nation a really free nation. Tell our government that it must liberate its people before it can claim free Russia as an ally."

I still have the clipping that shows the ladies picketing. But what it doesn't show is how Wilson looked, on the other side of the fence, as he peered out the North windows of the White House at the entrance where the ladies were marching. Mama said he was greatly upset. Someone went out and copied the exact words on the streamer, so that the President would know what the message said.

The President thought about it, then replied, "I don't care what they say, because they have a right to their opinion, but I still think we should invite the ladies in for some hot tea. It's cold out there."

Mrs. Wilson did not want them invited, for she was quite indignant about the whole thing, but the President told Ike Hoover to extend his invitation to the ladies to come and warm themselves in the White House.

Mr. Hoover returned alone. The ladies had refused the hospitality of the White House. Mama said that this seemed to hurt the President most of all. Eventually, several women were arrested for disturbing the peace and sentenced to *fifteen days* in jail. One of the servants spread the word among us that the President wanted to issue a pardon for the ladies, so that they would not have to serve jail sentences, and that the First Lady wanted them to stay in jail so that it would serve as a lesson to them to act with more dignity in the future.

"She probably wants to have them burned at the stake," said one of the staff who was most prejudiced against Indians, and before we knew it, a new nickname had been added. The President and his First Lady were now "the Professor and Pocahontas."

War was declared on April 6, 1917, and the First Lady went with the President up to Capitol Hill when he made the war declaration. Later, the White House staff was shocked when, instead of speaking of all the misery that war would bring, Mrs. Wilson talked about how the galleries had applauded her husband. She just didn't seem to realize the meaning of war.

Mama found out what it meant, because she did not get any letters from Emmett, who was shipped to France with the First Expeditionary Force.

Emmett had gotten into the army the year before, without Mama's help. I remember that he had gone directly to the White House to see Mama in the summer of 1916; he wanted her to sign a note, giving him permission to enlist, because he was not yet eighteen. Mama refused.

When she came home that night, there was Emmett in full uniform. He was big for his age and had gotten in anyway. Mama looked at him and turned pale. Then she said, "Don't ask me to get you out, and never disgrace that uniform."

Emmett had gone to the Mexican border with the American Expeditionary Force, headed by General Pershing, to capture General Francisco "Pancho" Villa, a mission which was never accomplished. Emmett then was assigned to guard duty in the War Department. He was part of the special guard assigned to the missions that came to visit the United States— the British, the French, and the Belgian. Mama was very proud of his position of trust and honor. He had not disgraced her.

During the war, Mama did not know where Emmett was, but gave a package to one of the White House military aides who said he would be seeing him. She waited, but heard nothing from him, and she feared that he had been killed.

There was no sleep for anyone in the White House during the war. The First Lady finally got interested in some activity other than being a companion to her husband; she worked with the Red Cross, rolling bandages and doing other menial tasks.

All the social functions were discontinued at the White House, and Mrs. Wilson inaugurated meatless days, heatless days, Sunday gasless days— meaning no Sunday pleasure drives— and she spent many hours before her own sewing machine making pajamas for the soldiers in the hospital wards, to be distributed by the Red Cross. Her secretary, Edith Benham, and Miss Bones, who was still at the White House, helped.

Conservation was the byword around the White House; eight sheep were soon to be seen gracing the lawns— for a while "Pocahontas" became "Little Bopeep" to the White House help. But her idea was finally applauded by even her worst critics among the staff, when many thousands of dollars were raised for the Red Cross through the auctioning of the wool. Two pounds of wool were sold for each state when the sheep were fleeced of almost a hundred pounds of raw wool.

Another successful money-raising idea of the First Lady's was to have famous movie stars sell liberty bonds on the Treasury steps. It was a great occasion, to my glamor-hungry mind, to see Mary Pickford, "America's Sweetheart," Charlie Chaplin, "America's Clown," the romantic idol, Douglas Fairbanks, and the dignified Marie Dressler in the flesh.

When the President heard that Mama was worried about Emmett's safety, he shook her hand warmly and said that he hoped that her son would return. Emmett did return after the war, but it was the President himself who was the war casualty, for he suffered a series of strokes, one of them on his bathroom floor in the White House, after returning in a state of collapse from a speaking tour.

Of course, it was a delayed action breakdown that took almost a year to come about. Mama said that in one year he had won the war and lost the peace, and his health with it.

What happened is that immediately after the Armistice in 1918, the President, in an exhausted state, went to Paris twice in rapid succession to preside at the Peace Conference, and to set up a League of Nations. Mama was invited to go along to be Mrs. Wilson's personal maid in Paris. She didn't want to leave me, so the Swedish cook, who knew foreign languages, got to go.

I didn't want Mama to miss such a trip for my sake, but she insisted on making the sacrifice anyway. Had she gone, she would have had the thrill of seeing our President hailed as an idol, and streets and avenues named for him. She would have stayed at Buckingham Palace in London, and ridden in the royal train of King Victor Emmanuel in Italy.

As it was, she only got to hear the angry voices of Congress, led by bearded Senator Henry Cabot Lodge (whose name was not to be mentioned in the White House), make fun of "naïve" Wilson and his League. It was after he had returned from France again and made a twenty-five day speaking tour of the country, trying to convince the people of the need for a League of Nations, that he simply could go no further, and collapsed in Pueblo,

Colorado, after mumbling and crying his way through the last incoherent speech. That day of doom was September 26, 1919.

Suddenly the White House became a hospital. Hardly anyone knew what was going on except that the President had returned ill. By October 4, his collapse was almost total. He would never be able to use half his body again. Mrs. Wilson gave up her Red Cross work and lived the life of a nurse.

As the President hovered between life and death, no one dared tell him how grave his condition was, for fear he would lose his will to live. Even as he lay at death's door, word came that the Senate had rejected the Versailles Peace Treaty, because the League participation was part of it. Mrs. Wilson was in continual consultation with the doctor over whether or not the President should resign.

As the crisis passed, the word got around the White House that the First Lady could still not even suggest to the President that he resign, because if he could not work toward the eventual American acceptance of the League of Nations, he would quite possibly lose any hope or will to live. The League was his magnificent obsession, even in his sickbed ramblings.

From then on, the White House saw Mrs. Wilson become more and more involved in the actual workings of the Government. Documents were delivered directly to her, and she stayed up late nights studying. Cabinet officers and Congressmen came to see her. Mama said you could just see the First Lady mature and develop judgment as she became more and more involved in the affairs of the nation.

In the kitchens and back halls of the White House, the regulars were shaking their heads. They were glad that the President had weathered the storm and was improving, but most of them thought he should resign and allow a competent man take over the reins of Government.

A houseman tried to be funny about it when he said, "I always knew it would happen. The Indians have finally taken over Washington, and now we'll all be scalped."

Mama did not think that was too funny. She was all for Mrs. Wilson and what she was doing. In fact, for the first time, Mama seemed to have the same love for the second Mrs. Wilson as she had had for the first. The second First Lady's example was, to Mama's mind, a sign of how capable women could be when given a chance, and she was proud of the way in which Mrs. Wilson had risen to the occasion.

"She will go down in history as a great woman," Mama predicted sagely, nodding her head as she told me how the President's wife was laboring to keep a Government in good working order. The word was that the President was able to think things through and make decisions, and that Mrs. Wilson carried out his orders, and helped him sign his name to the important papers.

But, as months and months rolled by, and the First Lady was still acting as the unofficial President, newspapers showed that the public was greatly disturbed. Once Mama was in the room when Mrs. Wilson, in a very low frame of mind, struggled with some papers. "I just don't know how much more criticism I can take," she said sadly, pointing at the newspapers beside her.

Mama told her then of the sign that Mrs. Taft had ordered printed and put on President Taft's desk. It was a quotation from Lincoln, which Mama had copied for herself, and she showed it to Mrs. Wilson:

"If I were to try to read, much less answer, all the attacks made on me, this shop might as well be closed for any other business. I do the very best I know how— the very best I can, and I mean to keep on doing so until the end. If the end brings me out all right, what is said against me won't amount to anything. If the end brings me out wrong, ten angels swearing I was right would make no difference."

From then on, Mama prayed every day for strength for the First Lady so that she could carry on her work, and for the quick recovery of the President. When Miss Margaret went to New York to live and to continue her vocal studies, Mama chose to stay at the White House rather than accompany her. Mama really felt that Mrs. Wilson needed her and what little she could do to help her.

Various members of royalty came to visit the President while he was ill, including the Prince of Wales, who was later to lose his crown for love just as Wilson almost lost his Presidency in the re-election. What hurt Mrs. Wilson the most was that people were saying the President was insane, and that his guardians had found it necessary to put bars on his bedroom windows. Over and over, she explained that the bars were on the windows of another room, and had been installed long ago for the protection of Teddy Roosevelt's children.

Mrs. Wilson also protested that the President's mind was completely untouched by the paralyzing stroke he had suffered, but, of course, Mama was not able to confirm this. Mama did see that President Wilson was able to receive the King and Queen of Belgium, who brought with them a wonderful thousand-piece set of china, showing historic places in Belgium.

But to show how a little thing could keep things in an uproar, once they were going badly, when the Queen was interviewed downstairs on her way out of the White House, she mentioned that the President had been dressed in a warm wool sweater.

The reporters misunderstood, and the stories came out that the President was wearing a "torn" wool sweater. Indignant ladies from all over the country wrote to tell the

First Lady that they didn't approve of the poor care the ailing President was receiving. Mama didn't know whether to laugh or to cry.

The Congress eventually sent two Senators over to check on the condition of the President's mind, and they came out gasping that they wished their own minds were as sharp and clear. One of them had told the President that they were praying for him, and the President had retorted, "Yes? Which way?"

Mama was also convinced that his mind was clear, but she suffered agonies when he would try to give her a little smile as he was wheeled around the White House in his wheel chair, and the smile would come out twisted because he could use only half his face. For this reason, the Secret Service men would place him in his car, when he was being taken out for fresh air and sunshine, so that people would not see the frozen side.

That was really pathetic, because he was so crushed by the change from his triumphal European tour and the roaring, approving crowds, to his lonely life of invalidism, that the White House staff would go out and cheer him when he would return from his ride. Mama would come home and cry about that. The First Lady would cry a little too when he would say to her, "You see, I'm not too unpopular."

Mama would both laugh and cry about his childish irritability, which had resulted from the breakdown. She told me how he would pout if he didn't have his way; how he would set up rules for everyone; and how one time, when his wife hadn't consulted him about a drive, he refused to ride in a car and ordered a horse and carriage for himself instead.

Congress might think that the world was not ready for the League of Nations, but the White House staff was, and from the lowliest houseboy to the eloquently-dressed ushers, the White House staff felt that Wilson could really have saved the world from future wars, and that he was the man who had the vision to understand what was needed. They had seen him with his Bible enough to know that he was a completely sincere and religious man, who asked the help of God in whatever he did.

When he went to France and attended the Peace Conference, they held their breath. Though it was superstitious, they felt it was bad luck for him to break the unwritten law that an American President does not leave American territorial waters. Wilson was the first President to set foot on foreign soil during his term of office, and his vision of America's joining the League of Nations went down the drain.

Just one funny thing happened on the trip abroad, and it happened to a White House maid. Mama said that maybe she should have gone just to have been there when it happened. When they were staying at Buckingham Palace, Queen Mary graciously asked this maid, when all the White House staff was lined up before her, "Are your quarters satisfactory?"

In spite of all the prior coaching she had received, the maid said with great enthusiasm, "They sure are, Queen! You bet!" She came back in disgrace, and was transferred out of the White House to another job.

When it was time for the Wilsons to leave, a year and a half after his stroke, the President gave Mama two oil paintings for the living room, which his first wife had told him about. Mama didn't have the heart to tell him we had finally had to give up the little house and move to an apartment, because the terribly long hours Mama had been spending at the White House had made it impossible to take care of our home. She also received a hundred-dollar Government savings bond. But, more than the money—which went to pay for new braces for my leg and fillings for my teeth— Mama cherished the gift she got from Margaret, a record of her singing.

Of such things are dreams made— a record that brings back the voice of a girl who once laughed and sang in the White House, and then renounced her country; two wedding invitations, grown a little yellow; and a photograph of a beautiful woman, who married with high hopes and became a scapegoat for a disgruntled nation.

But the White House still looked pretty glamorous to me, and I could hardly wait to fit myself into it somewhere.

Mama helped Mrs. Wilson pack her things to move to a little house in Washington. Mama had a personal interest in reading about the conventions that were being held to see who would be chosen to take the place of Wilson.

When the Republicans had their convention, the papers told about the wife of one of the candidates; she was sitting in the gallery, watching and keeping an eye on everything. She was supposed to be manoeuvering behind the scenes with the party politicians to get the nomination for her husband, in case they couldn't decide on a front-runner. And she did.

That woman was Mrs. Florence Harding. Mrs. Wilson had said sadly to Mama, "If I had done that, think of what they would have said." But it hurt even more when Harding adopted as his slogan "Return to normalcy." Mrs. Wilson took that as a personal insult, as though she had not done her best to keep things normal.

THE HARD-LUCK
MRS. HARDING

Mama had said over and over that this time she would not become personally involved with a First Lady, because it was too hard on her emotions. She had decided finally that the White House just naturally brought sadness to its inhabitants, and this time, whatever would happen, she was not going to care.

"I'm just going to do my work and not pay any attention to what is going on, and I'm not going to listen to the gossiping help," she told me when she came home from work, and I sat at the kitchen table of our roomy apartment, waiting to hear what the new First Lady was like.

"She's just a woman, a very nice woman, and she stands nice and straight and looks very dignified with her grey hair."

Did she like her? What changes was Mrs. Harding going to make? How did she get along with the President?

Mama wasn't telling. I was afraid that the wonderful running story I had been listening to, of the past three First Ladies and their adventures in the White House, was at an end. Mama was only answering in monosyllables. She was painting no more pictures for me. I knew her heart was still at S Street with Mrs. Wilson and an ailing ex-President.

But, fortunately, I had my sewing to keep me busy at this point. I had become a seamstress, and was doing my work at a little shop on Connecticut Avenue for the socially and politically prominent. Mama said I sewed well enough for Presidents' wives. She didn't know it, but that was exactly my goal.

I encouraged her to bring home sewing from the White House for me to do. It wasn't the tiny sums I earned for doing a hem for this person, an edging for another; it was the opportunity to deliver the finished goods to the White House. Mrs. Jaffray too started sending White House mending for me to do on the linens, and I was thrilled.

Several times Mama had gone over to S Street to help Mrs. Wilson and had found, to her surprise, that she was not the only person there from the White House. Mrs. Wilson, it seemed, was still in the hearts of the White House staff.

Especially so since the new First Lady, Mrs. Florence Harding, was openly bragging that she had put her husband in the White House. And the President, himself, freely admitted that he owed it all to "The Duchess." That was his nickname for her.

I didn't hear the story first from Mama. I heard it from the customers at the dress shop where I was sewing, and told Mama about it. The story was all over town.

Mama admitted sadly that the story was true. All the backstairs help, she said, was talking about how Mrs. Harding was proud of her handiwork in helping her husband reach the pinnacle, and she didn't hesitate to say so. What hurt, Mama explained, was that Mrs. Wilson had been accused of having a "lust for power" when she really didn't, and was only trying to protect a sick man and a nation's picture of him, and her successor was a woman who freely admitted she had had a drive to become First Lady, and was being applauded. It was ironic.

Loyalties, loyalties. Mama didn't know how she could do her best for the new woman in the White House when she felt so badly about poor Mrs. Wilson leaving almost in disgrace. Mama was fiercely loyal to her, because she had seen how hard Mrs. Wilson worked to keep things on an even keel.

Although Mama assured me she was not going to get too involved with Mrs. Harding, I should have known it was inevitable that she would. Mrs. Harding heard that Mama had been a hairdresser, and tested her out. Thereafter, Mama had to spend a lot of time around her, keeping her perfectly groomed and her hair in perfect waves— a trick done with a curling iron.

Sure enough, pretty soon Mama was coming home full of stories and praise for Mrs. Harding. As she was having her hair done, Mrs. Harding loved to talk about her early life and troubles with her hardboiled father, and how she had proved to him that Warren Harding would go places, and how she had been a helpmate to the President when they were first married. She was the most outspoken woman in high place Mama had ever known. And the reason, Mama said, was that she had been a newspaper reporter and had learned to express herself forcefully. And she did.

Mrs. Harding had been a widow, teaching music and taking care of her father, when Warren Harding first came to her home town, Marion, Ohio. He bought the town's newspaper, The Marion *Star*, and they met and fell in love. Her father, who was a banker, forbade the marriage, stating flatly that Warren would be a failure.

When she married Mr. Harding anyway, her father did not speak to her for seven years, but she still didn't visit him until he finally came to her house first, after *she* had proved that her husband could climb in state politics with no help from him. All this had taken fifteen years.

Mama said she sounded as though she had spent her whole life proving how wrong her dad had been about her husband. Her father had finally admitted he'd been wrong regarding Harding's qualifications as an in-law when Harding became Lieutenant Governor of Ohio, she said. She didn't mind admitting that she had helped on the business end of the newspaper too, and with her help, her husband had become, for the first time in his life, an influential member of the community and a financial success. But one thing the First Lady did give him credit for was his great speaking ability. Because he could speak so well, he had been called upon by state politicians, and thereafter, he was on his way toward the Presidency.

Mama started defending Mrs. Harding by saying that the First Lady shared honors with (and gave credit to) Attorney General Harry Daugherty for helping her husband to achieve the Presidency. Mrs. Harding said she'd worked with Daugherty, who spent half his time at the White House, as a team when they found out they both knew "what was best for Harding." "At least," said Mama, "she doesn't take *all* the credit."

Mama said that Mrs. Harding treated the White House just as though it were an ordinary home. She would go running down the steps and greet the tourists, who came in to look around, with a big hello. They would be really started! Both the other Presidents Mama had worked for had kept the White House closed to the public except for a few short hours, but the Hardings opened the gates and let everyone in.

Mama was in the presence of the First Lady quite often, and was quite surprised at the way in which the President made her look important. When someone wanted him to do something, he'd say, "I'll have to check with the Duchess," and then turn to her for permission. Part of the time, he seemed a little afraid of her.

It was true that she had a fierce temper. And she was always imagining things. She had a little red book in which she wrote the names of people who, she felt, had "snubbed" her.

Mama said she had to be careful all the time to keep from touching anything. The First Lady was forever putting things some place and forgetting them and thinking a servant must have taken them.

Once she even called in a Secret Service man to find out who had taken a piece of jewelry. It turned out that no one had taken it, but that she had mislaid it. It had become covered with a pile of things, and she just hadn't looked in the right place.

These outbursts did tend to make the servants jumpy.

Mama became very sympathetic with the First Lady when she found out her secret— she was quite a bit older than the President. Mama could never figure out exactly how much older, but it was at least five to eight years. This awareness had a terrible effect on her whole personality, and she was forever driving to keep young. It was pathetic, Mama said, to see her try to get compliments on how nice she looked from Mama and from friends and from the President, who always said something nice whenever she prodded him.

She had a facial almost every day. A specialist would come to the White House to apply the creams and lotions. They would be closeted for a few hours. Then Mama would be called in to marcel her hair.

She had many dresses for evening that were heavily beaded, and her wardrobe for day or night was lavish. She felt the beads distracted attention from too close scrutiny of the lines in her face and made her sparkle a little. Whenever she could, she also wore a ribbon or a dog collar of beads around her neck to hide the lines. I have one that she gave Mama— black velvet, set with rhinestones.

Mama was quite impressed with the way in which Mrs. Harding took care of her clothes. It took two maids to keep the immense wardrobe in perfect condition. Gone were the somber blacks of Mrs. Wilson. Pearl-grey satin was a favorite, and so were rich brocades. What impressed Mama the most was that Mrs. Harding had special shoes to match each dress, and these shoes were kept in glass cases just as though they were in a store.

Glass cases! I couldn't believe my ears! I had never heard of such a thing before, and after Mama had told about them, visions of lovely clothes, and shoes to match, danced in my head like visions of sugar plums.

I had to laugh when Mama came home with the news that the Lincoln bed was on the march again. Mrs. Harding did not want to sleep in the Lincoln bed, left in her bedroom by the second Mrs. Wilson, and back came the twin beds that Mrs. Taft had bought and the first Mrs. Wilson had used.

I did not understand how anyone could fail to want to sleep in the bed Lincoln had slept in. There was a story around the White House that a workman had once wondered what it was like to lie down on Lincoln's bed, and had done so. It felt so good that he had fallen asleep with his shoes on, and had to be roused by a maid, who protected him by not reporting it.

The old order had certainly changed around the White House. Instead of a hushed university classroom, or a hospital room atmosphere, the air around the White House seemed gay and lighthearted. Mrs. Harding loved to play the piano, and her music floated through the rooms as the help scrubbed, cleaned, and dusted and felt that work had become more of a pleasure. Her favorite song was "The

End of a Perfect Day," which the Marine Band always included at every program at the White House as a tribute to her.

A favorite character around the White House was Laddie Boy, an Airedale. The President and Mrs. Harding had a lot of fun with Laddie, putting him through his list of tricks.

"Duchess, has the paper arrived?" the President would ask. The First Lady would say, "I'll see." Then she would roll up a newspaper and give it to Laddie Boy with the command, "Take this to Warren."

The President was just "Warren" to Laddie Boy, and when he heard "Go to Warren," he always ran to the President to deliver something or to get something. Laddie Boy also retrieved golf balls on the White House lawn.

Mama thought Mrs. Harding was overdoing the friendliness a bit when she shook 6,756 hands at a New Year's reception. Her hand was swollen for days. Mama wished she could have scolded her and told her that other First Ladies had never been that friendly, but she hadn't felt it was her place, and Mrs. Harding was so pleased at the newspaper praise she had received for doing it, that it eased the ache.

But there was another ache that was developing in the Harding family. And gradually I knew that Mama was starting to worry about the First Lady.

The President was spending a lot of time away from the White House. Mama knew Mrs. Harding kept worrying about whom he was with. The papers referred to them as "poker-playing cronies." The more he stayed away, the more tense Mrs. Harding would get.

Mrs. Harding's closest friend was Mrs. Evelyn Walsh McLean of the Hope Diamond, which was supposed to bring bad luck. Mrs. McLean would keep her company when the President was away. Mrs. Harding would go to her house too, and the President and she would attend parties there together.

Both ladies dressed to the hilt, Mama said, and liked to impress each other. And both were superstitious too, and were always talking about predictions. Mrs. Harding told Mama that her husband's presidency had been predicted when he was a Senator. She and Mrs. Jaffray, the house-keeper, both believed in fortune tellers and would go to them.

Mrs. Harding asked Mama if she believed in them. Mama said she didn't know. Sometimes, when Mama was fixing her hair, Mrs. Harding would tell her to be careful. "This is a day I have to be careful," she would say.

Mrs. Harding gave Mama an ivory clock which is a replica of the United States Capitol. It still keeps time for me. It was given to the President by the India Ivory Company, which was located, in Providence, Rhode Island. Once, Mama also brought home a small Chinese brass ash tray, which had rested on the President's bedside table. Mrs. Harding had decided another ash tray would look better, and had given the used one to Mama. Harding smoked cigars to please her, but, with the connivance of the help, managed to keep a supply of chewing tobacco stashed away in various rooms.

The President did not pay much attention to the White House servants, but left all arrangements to the First Lady. He did cause a little commotion, however, when he personally called for toothpicks to be kept on the table.

"That's being too much a man of the people," said the butlers, who disapproved of toothpicks in the Executive Mansion. "Doesn't he know this is the White House?" they grumbled. But they conformed, of course, as everyone does when the President or First Lady even "suggests" that something be done. Mama said she bet that was the first and last time in history that toothpicks would be on the White House table.

Mama said that when the President had his card-playing friends in, he also had a standing order for knockwurst and sauerkraut. When FDR, years later, did the same thing with pigs' knuckles, Mama remembered it.

Both men wanted to be known as men of the people. Mama said that President Harding wanted so much to be a man of the people, that he would pop up at parties all over town and act like any other guest. No President had done that. He used to tell friends at the White House to forget he was President and "just relax."

Mama and some other servants were shocked whenever liquor would be served at the White House, for it was against the Prohibition law. Of course, "bathtub gin" was a common expression, but Mama felt that the White House should set the example. No liquor was served at the formal dining table, even when there was a great world conference on armaments, and the representatives of nine nations came to Washington in November, 1921. But after hours, with his friends, the President would call for the setting up of the bar.

Speaking of November, 1921, the big event for me, in the Harding administration, was the dedication in that same month of the Tomb of the Unknown Soldier at Arlington Cemetery. It was a thrilling moment when, with President and Mrs. Harding there, the sentries began the permanent guard duty, which continues to this very day.

Now and then, I still go there to sit quietly, watching a single soldier silently pacing back and forth until he is relieved by the changing of the guard. As I sit, I look across the river to Washington and think of all the events of history I have seen and lived through and pondered over. And I think of all the opportunities for greatness that the

Federal City has given those who had the right qualities, and how sad it was when one failed.

But getting back to Mrs. Harding and Mama, things were getting more and more tense at the White House, and it was making Mama a little nervous too. Mama told me that Mrs. Harding had asked to have a Secret Service man assigned to protect her, and that it was the first time in history this had been done. At night, she kept him sitting in the hall outside her bedroom door.

For the first time in her life, Mama gave me a mysterious order. She said she didn't want me to go past a certain house on K Street— 1625. I thought she was out of her mind. Why couldn't I go past 1625 K Street, I demanded. I was an adult and earning my own living, wasn't I? Mama said that a lot of things were going on there and to just stay away, and she meant it. She called it the "little green house."

Naturally, with that incentive, I did walk past the "little green house," and nothing happened. Later, when I went to the White House to work, the help was still talking about that house and of certain rumors of politicians who brought girls there. Once, two girls were supposed to have had a fight there with broken bottles. I suppose my mother was trying to make sure that I would not be dragged off the sidewalk into that "den of iniquity," but I doubt that they were dragging girls off the sidewalk, especially girls on crutches, like me.

But her warning showed the state of Mama's nerves. And in September of 1922, the First Lady's health broke down. She was sick for many weeks, and again the White House was like a hospital. There were times when the servants whispered that she was not expected to live. She had only one kidney, and it was infected.

The First Lady had grown to depend so much on Mama, that although she had every attention from the nurses, she insisted on Mama being near her all the time. For weeks, I hardly saw my mother. She would not come home until the First Lady had fallen asleep, secure in the knowledge that "Maggie is near."

In the morning, Mama would hurry to the White House to be on hand when Mrs. Harding's tray appeared, and to cajole and scold her into eating. Some of the time, Mama just slept on a cot in the White House, to be near if the First Lady should call. For a while, Mama was on the verge of a nervous breakdown herself.

Mrs. Harding did recover, but the happy atmosphere that had first been there, with the happy tinkling of the piano, never did return to the White House, for "The Duchess." The President looked worried, but stayed away even more, and Mrs. Harding used to murmur, "I wish he would listen to me. I wish he would pay attention to me."

She would try to keep him home, and once Mama was very shocked when Mrs. Harding shouted at him over the banister, "You are not leaving this house tonight!"

But the President pretended he didn't even hear and walked out.

It broke Mama's heart to see the couple who had lived so closely together drifting apart. Mrs. Harding spoke of ingratitude, and said that she could see now that her happiest times had not been at the White House, but when they had worked shoulder to shoulder at the newspaper. She said *he* thought he didn't need her any more, but he *did,* and *if only* he would listen to her.

Suddenly there was a shocking rash of resignations and suicides among the men to whom Harding had given high office. It was rumored that graft was rampant in the handling of contracts by the Veterans Administration, and the head of the Veterans Bureau, Charles Forbes, went abroad and sent in his resignation from the other side. His legal advisor, Charles Cramer, committed suicide. The Secretary of the Interior, Albert Bacon Fall, also resigned. And then Jesse Smith, who was the confidant and housemate of the President's top advisor, Attorney General Daugherty, committed suicide. That was May 30, 1923.

It was not a happy time at the White House when President Harding decided to take a trip to Alaska. But he was taking "The Duchess," and Mama hoped that this would bring back the old feeling between them, and that they would return with the old comradeship they had known when they first came to the White House.

They left in July, 1923. On August 2nd, the message came that the President had collapsed on a train and died in a San Francisco hotel. They had been returning from Alaska, and the President had been stricken by what was first diagnosed as food-poisoning. Later, doctors said that it had been a blood clot in the brain, complicated by pneumonia. Just before he died, there had been a report that he was getting better and that the danger had passed. Mrs. Harding refused to allow an autopsy.

Mama was devastated. "Oh, I knew it, I knew it," she said. "The White House brings tragedy." The White House had five days to get ready for the arrival of the President's body. The train was nine hours late, and came in at 10:30 at night. Mrs. Harding received friends and officials until one in the morning, and Mama was shocked at how calm the First Lady was. "She has turned to ice," Mama said.

After everyone had left at 1:00 A.M., Mrs. Harding went into the East Room, where the body of her husband was, and selected a few small floral wreaths to place near the casket. "The ones Warren would like," she remarked coolly and with poise, as if the funeral had to do with someone else she hardly knew.

The next morning, the house was crowded with the

diplomatic corps and members of Congress, waiting for the body to be taken to the Capitol.

Services were held for the President, and the body was taken to Marion, Ohio, for burial. Mrs. Harding returned on the 11th of August in the private railway car of her friend, Mrs. McLean, and when Mrs. Harding left the White House on August 17, she went first to rest at the McLean home.

After she had returned to the White House alone, Mrs. Harding acted like an entirely different person, and Mama could not understand it. She was hurt by Mrs. Harding's coolness toward her. But Mrs. Harding was cool toward everyone, and a little irritable and suspicious.

Mrs. Harding had a notion that the new President was trying to push her out of the White House when, actually, she was the one who lagged around the mansion for a week, while President and Mrs. Coolidge were waiting at the Willard Hotel. Mrs. Harding could not be placated. She claimed that the Coolidges were responsible for some mix-up about precedence in the order of the automobiles in the funeral cortege. The Coolidges had had nothing to do with it, and tried their best to be friendly and kind toward the First Lady in her grief. They had dinner with her the night of the funeral and again on the night she left the White House.

Mama said that the Coolidges were bending over backward to do the right thing, and they even continued to fly the flag at half-mast beyond the mourning period, to try to make Mrs. Harding feel better. But the thing that Mama could never get over was that a President had died, and she, who had been so close to the First Lady, had not seen her shed a tear.

About the last thing Mrs. Harding did before leaving the White House was to give Mama her beautiful canary.

Mama thought Mrs. Harding would break down and cry, but she didn't. It almost seemed as if she wanted to get rid of the bird, but Mama knew how much Bob, the canary, had meant to her. She also gave Laddie Boy to a servant. Perhaps she didn't want to see any pet that would remind her of those happier times at the White House.

For five years Bob was the life of our household, chiming in whenever we put on a record, and carrying a tune by himself when we didn't. I say five years, because we had a fire then that took Bob's life, and ruined the two oil paintings that President Wilson had given Mama.

It was so strange to realize that President Wilson, who had suffered a stroke while in the White House, had outlived his successor. But not for long. Wilson died a half year after Harding's funeral, which he and another ex-President, Taft, attended.

Mama said that President Harding didn't really start to make news until he was dead. Then everything came out. It was during the Coolidge administration that people were rocked to their heels to learn what had really been going on in Harding's time.

Everyone has heard about the Teapot Dome scandals. Day after day, in court, shocking things came out that resulted in the conviction of Interior Secretary Fall for accepting $100,000— delivered in a little black bag— for leasing Government-owned oil reserves to private companies. Gaston B. Means of the Justice Department and Thomas W. Miller, Custodian of Alien Property, also went to prison for their part in corrupting Government.

Mrs. Harding did not live to see justice meted out to the men who had come between her and her husband. A strange thing happened. Just a year after the President's death, she went home to Marion to visit, and had dinner at the home of her old doctor, Charles Sawyer, who had been made a general and brought from Marion to be

the doctor at the White House. They had eaten dinner—
Mrs. Harding and the doctor and his family— and after
dinner, he retired to another room to rest, and was found
dead by his son.

The shock of this death, so similar to that of her husband,
was the final blow to her own health. It probably brought
on her own final illness, and she never rose from her sick
bed. She died just one year and 100 days after her husband.

Fortunately, she did not live to experience the humilia-
tion attendant upon the publication of the only major
literary effort of a former Marion school girl reporter.
When Nan Britton's book came out, I asked Mama if any
of it were true, and she gave me the best answer in the
world, "I don't know. I wasn't there."

But I had to agree with Mama. Mrs. Harding was
certainly one hard-luck Lady.

A FIRST LADY PROVES THAT
OPPOSITES ATTRACT

Since Mama felt that Mrs. Coolidge had not received a friendly greeting at the White House from Mrs. Harding in those sad last days, she was all set to make it up to her personally.

Mama was always on the side of the underdog, and the fact that the Coolidges had waited timidly at the Willard Hotel for three days, while the White House stood empty, definitely placed them in the role of underdogs. So Mama was ready to give her all to the mistreated First Lady.

It was a relief, according to Mama, to have the Coolidges move in and hear the soft, gentle voice of Mrs. Coolidge after the harsher sound of Mrs. Harding's voice. For the first time, a First Lady did not bring any servants with her, and the story went around backstairs that Mrs. Coolidge was used to doing all her own housework.

Mrs. Coolidge smiled so much that she seemed to bring a ray of happiness wherever she went. This quickly earned her the nickname of "Sunshine" backstairs. But the President was another matter. Whenever anyone saw him smile, it was big news, and the word would be passed among the servants, "I saw Smiley smile today."

That was his nickname in no time at all— "Smiley." It was spoken in jest, with a slight edge of sarcasm, but the nickname of the First Lady, "Sunshine," was meant earnestly, because she really did spread sunshine wherever she went. The word was that she had to make up for the President's sour countenance, because without her there, he would frighten people away.

Mama noticed that the First Lady was always quick to explain what the President had meant, so that people wouldn't take offense. She was a buffer between the President and the public.

The first interesting tidbit that Mama brought home was that the restless Lincoln bed was on the move again. She reported that Mrs. Coolidge had ordered the Lincoln bed into her room, and another double bed for the President's room. The beds that the Hardings had slept in became the boys' beds across the hall.

Another story Mama brought home was about one of the boys, who had been on his grandfather's farm in Vermont, doing farm work, when the news arrived that his father had become President. Some of the hired help told his son, "I wouldn't be doing the work you're doing if my father was President," and Calvin had answered, "Oh, yes you would, if *your* father was *my* father."

Nor did the boys rush to the White House as soon as their father was President. Calvin finished helping on the farm, and John finished his summer enlistment at a military training camp before they were permitted to come to their new home. "Cal," Jr., was fifteen and John was seventeen when the White House became their home.

It didn't take long before Mama was completely wrapped up in the life of Mrs. Coolidge and the new round of events in the White House. "Lillian, I do believe that this time we have a perfectly normal family in the White House, and I think they're going to break the bad luck spell," she told me as I sat sewing in our living room, which by now had taken on quite a dignified "White House" look.

"Don't get threads on the rug," she warned me, looking proudly at the Oriental rug she had purchased for our parlor at her favorite second-hand store. "I do declare, it does look just like the rug in the back guest room at the White House, even if it is a bit smaller."

I used to kid my mother by telling her she was determined to have me living in the White House, even if she had to build it herself "a stick at a time." But I had caught the bug myself and had bought Mama a present of a beautiful hall runner that was as close to White House style as I could get with practically the first money I had saved. It was fifty feet long, green, with a dignified, inconspicuous border.

I had tried several kinds of work— cashier in a theatre and receptionist to a doctor, but found I really liked sewing the best. Mama was bringing home the towels and tablecloths for me to mend, and, sometimes, if they were too heavy, they would be sent by a White House car.

I was dating, and my mother never objected to my staying out late. "Have fun but don't forget to be a lady" was her only advice.

A short time after the Coolidges came to the White House, they attended a large reception for the dedication of the Pan American Building.

Mama was proud when again she was chosen to go over to the reception to check a First Lady's wrap. Mrs. Coolidge wore a white brocade gown, which had been made in a hurry for the occasion. She had kindly promised the dressmaker, as a reward for her speed, that she would give this dress to the Smithsonian Institution when the time came for it to be placed on the manikin that would represent her in the gallery of the First Ladies. She kept her promise too, but later, when the Smithsonian officials asked for a fancier dress (as all the preceding First Ladies' dresses were more elaborate), she exchanged it for a brilliant gown of American Beauty red velvet.

I used to ask Mama if the President were really as stern and sour-faced as he looked in pictures, and she would assure me that he certainly was not.

"That's just his way, and he has the public fooled," she said, "but he has the best sense of humor and makes more people laugh than any of the other Presidents I've known. He even has nicknames for everybody."

"Who are you?" I asked.

"I'm 'that Maggie gal.'"

The head butler, Thomas, was called "Bug" by the President because of his last name, Roach. John Mays, the doorman, was "Mink," because he looked like a mink to Coolidge's quizzical eye; and Frank Wilkinson, a houseman, was "Frank the Frog" because of his posture.

At the table, Coolidge had fun pretending there was something in the food. Once he claimed he'd found a bug. When the butlers turned, in horror, to investigate, he remarked dryly, "Mama, I thought that butlers weren't supposed to eavesdrop."

He never cracked a smile. Poor Mrs. Coolidge said, "Now, Papa, you stop that. There is no bug there."

And as a trick on the staff, he would press all the buttons on his desk and chuckle as they popped into his office from all directions. "Just wanted to see if everybody's working," he would say. Later they would shake their heads and talk about his peculiar sense of humor. They just didn't know about him. And he liked to keep them guessing.

Once his staff turned the trick on him. The zoo needed an appropriation of money, and Coolidge was going to attend the meeting at the Smithsonian with the Budget Director to take up this matter along with other affairs. This gave the long-suffering staff time to conspire to train a big parrot-type bird.

At the proper time, the monstrous yellow talking bird was prodded, and started shrieking, "What about the appropriation? What about the appropriation?", and the President almost fell out of his chair with laughter. His funny bone was always more easily tickled by the antics of animals than by those of humans.

Every once in a while, there would be a piercing whistle, and the help would know that the President was whistling for the dogs. The dogs were Paul Pry, an Airedale, who got his name because of his snooping, and Prudence Prim and Rob Roy, a pair of white collies. Mrs. Coolidge had only to whistle very softly under her breath, and the dogs would come bounding to her, but the President had to whistle until he was blue in the face to get their attention. The dogs seemed to know that the President was a very soft fellow under the tough, leathery exterior. He couldn't discipline them a bit.

There were also a pair of cats, Blackie and Tiger, who had the free run of the White House. The President was very much attached to them, and he was always afraid they would run off the reservation, so he had little collars with the words "White House" made for them. Now and then they did disappear and were brought back because of the collars. The President would always feed the cats himself. He kept saucers for them in a corner of the dining room, and Blackie would help the President finish his tea.

The public had its own idea of what boys growing up in the White House needed, and sent a couple of lion cubs. They also sent a racoon, a baby bear, and even a wallaby from Australia. The lions and bear had their moment of glory in the White House, and then were sent to a permanent home in the Washington National Zoo.

The racoon became the President's special pet, and he had a little outdoor house built for it, where it stayed nights. He would go out to see Rebecca, his racoon, and play with it just like a kid. She followed him around the house too, and Mama could never get used to the sight of a racoon in a house.

Visitors at the White House would be startled too, when they saw a racoon coming at them. They would think that a wild animal had gotten into the White House, and would call for help. But Rebecca was different. Though she would let only the President get near her and pet her, she really wouldn't snap at anyone. She even lived at peace with the two cats, one of whom had its own idiosyncrasy.

Blackie loved to use the elevator, and would sit waiting for someone to open the door for him. He would lie on the seat in the elevator until someone stopped it at the right floor. Sometimes he didn't care where the elevator was going, and would recline while he rode up and down for hours. Once, when he strayed away, a radio broadcast sent out an alert for him; he was found and returned because the address was on his little collar. Then he got a *lot* of extra rides. Everyone was so glad to see him again.

Much as Coolidge loved animals, there was one animal that made him deathly afraid, and that was a snake. Every time he went out on a fishing trip, the Secret Service men would have to comb every square foot of the pathway the President would take, so he wouldn't see a snake.

Once they killed a snake and they had a lot of fun passing it around among themselves, but they kept it out of sight around Coolidge.

Mrs. Coolidge loved birds, but hated to see them caged. She had a wire screening put over a large window in the West Hall, and had the birds turned loose so they could

fly around. There was one huge myna bird, which would
alight on everyone's shoulder and pinch their ears. Mama
had a terrible time with the myna, because he would ride
around on top of her head when she was tidying the room,
and if she pushed him off, he would resent it. Once, when
she did this, he flew back and pecked her on the forehead
and drew blood. After that she shunned him whenever she
could.

The first thing that surprised Mama about the Coolidges
was that the President was boss— all the way— and the
menus had to be cleared with him every morning. This had
always been a ceremony conducted by the housekeeper and
the First Lady. Mama reported that poor prim-and-proper
Elizabeth Jaffray— who was still going to market in a horse
and carriage, because she thought automobiles were a
vulgar fad— was going out of her mind from the shock of
it. Coolidge had a nickname for her too— "The Queen"—
but only dared use it when discussing Mrs. "J" with Mrs.
Coolidge.

One of the President's pet economies was to have two
dozen chickens installed in a little coop in the yard. He
would inspect them now and then, and gave word that
only *his* chickens were to be served at the table. But there
was something strange about the taste of the meat— a
minty flavor. The President ordered an investigation. His
trusty aides came back with the report that the chicken
coop was located on an old mint bed of Teddy Roosevelt's.
Needless to say, the coop was moved.

Mama and Mrs. Coolidge did a lot of sewing together.
Mrs. Coolidge loved to sew on the sun porch of the third
floor. She had special glass put in which she said had the
effect of ultraviolet ray treatment. Very few of the staff
knew about this glass, and they would say, "I wonder why
this porch is so warm?", but Mama would not tell them.

Mrs. Coolidge sewed some of her own clothes, and my

mother helped. She trimmed some of her hats. She loved to sew with the music or ball games going on, and she kept the radio on all the time— unless a woman's voice started talking or singing. She couldn't bear to hear women's high-pitched voices on the radio.

She would turn to Mama and say, "Turn that woman off. I can't stand that. Can you, Maggie?"

Mama, of course, would pretend that she too couldn't stand the woman's voice.

Mrs. Coolidge began crotcheting a spread for the Lincoln bed. She worked on it for four years until it was done, and it was beautiful. It was still in use on the extra-sized bed when I went to work there, and it was one of the first things I wanted to see.

The Coolidges kept all the household workers whom the Hardings had employed, but when Brown, one of the doormen whom Mrs. Taft had hired, died, a young doorman named Johnson was taken on in his place. Johnson was a superb dancer, and soon he was teaching John and Calvin, Jr., how to do the Charleston and other dances. Johnson was very proud to be teaching the children of a President, but he was soon taken down a peg by the other help, who volunteered the opinion that the President was just saving money by not having to hire a dancing teacher.

As if to make up for her husband's economies, the First Lady tried to be as generous as she dared, and she was always giving Mama and the other help little gifts.

The White House help had been forewarned about the President's private tight money policy. The waiters at the Willard Hotel, where the President had stayed when he was Vice-President, reported that no one would wait on him except when pushed, because the tips were so small and so far between.

Even so, the White House staff was surprised that the President wanted every penny back when he gave them a coin to buy some little thing for him, like a newspaper. If they thought it was a tip, they would soon find out differently, because the President would go around saying, "Somebody owes me seven cents." And he meant it. They would cough it up, and he would take it.

Mama came home with a million funny stories having to do with the President's sense of economy. He was always coming into the kitchen and personally instructing the help on how to cut the meat. He sought out Mrs. Jaffray and gave her lessons in cutting corners, and once, when he heard the kitchen help griping about his interference, he fixed them with a beady eye and asked them, "Do you have enough to eat?"

"Yes, Mr. President," they agreed, snapping to attention.

"Fine," he said, and walked out.

Mrs. Jaffray finally gave up and left.

But Mama forgave him his economies, because he was so generous with his wife. Very few people around the White House knew that the President loved to go shopping for her, and would slip into the downtown stores and buy the most luxurious gowns he could find, or he'd notice them in a store window and phone to have them sent. Nothing was too good for "Mama," as he called the gracious Mrs. Coolidge, who would always say, "Oh, Papa, how beautiful! Wherever did you find this?" And she would wear the gown as soon as possible.

If he saw her in a dress a second time, he would say, "Haven't I seen that before?", and she would not wear it to a party again, but would get something new. She was his queen, and he wanted to give her everything and do everything for her. Mama was sure that was why he wanted to spare her the details of running the White House, even though he did it with extraordinary economy.

So much did he worship his wife, said Mama, that he

didn't even want to let anyone who had ever neglected her before he was President come to the White House receptions. Certain social leaders found themselves out. He would be heard by the servants saying that so-and-so could not come to his party. Poor Mrs. Coolidge was very embarrassed by this.

She really had a great love for people, and wanted to be nice to everyone, whether they had invited her or not. She was also embarrassed when the President would swing people past him at a tremendous rate at a reception, making them feel unwanted, and brag to her later about how many hands he had shaken in an hour.

What could Mrs. Coolidge do? She was annoyed, but she understood him too, and, being always gentle, would not hurt his feelings.

It was sweet, said Mama, the way the President had made a substitute mother of his wife. Sometimes he acted as if he were a little boy, and bragged to his wife about how he had just learned to do this and that— hit a target, for example— and he would seek her approval, just as he would have done with his mother.

Mama said the President had been raised by his father, after his mother had died, before he reached his teens, and Mrs. Coolidge had once explained that the reason he was gruff with people was because he had not had much contact with them in his youth. He had lived on a farm, and had not had the softening influence of a mother.

His father had been much too busy working to pay attention to his son— farming, running a country store and a blacksmith shop, serving in his state's House of Representatives and then the Senate, and even acting as the local notary public. In fact, when the word came that Harding had died, Coolidge, who was visiting his father at Plymouth, Vermont, became the first President to be sworn into office by his own father.

The President was a chip off the old block, Mama said. As she heard it, his father had steadfastly refused to waste money on a telephone, and the message that his son was President had to be brought by auto in the dead of night. The President had worked his way up the political ladder, starting at the local level too, just like his dad.

When the papers reported that the new President's wife looked young enough to be a bride, she pooh-poohed it to Mama, and said she had practically been an old maid when she married. She told Mama she had met Calvin Coolidge at a church social when she was teaching the deaf and dumb at Northampton, Massachusetts. She had been twenty-six and the President a young attorney of thirty-three.

It was interesting to Mama that Mrs. Coolidge remained serenely quiet, refusing to comment even to her friends, when all kinds of terrible things were being said about the Hardings— that Mrs. Harding had killed her husband; that her husband had killed himself, and that she had committed suicide too; that Harding had had a little colored blood mixed in his veins; that the money that Harding had won in poker bets had really been fixed for him to win by his "Ohio gang," who wanted to keep him happy and out of their hair while they grafted their way through his administration.

Where other women would have been vindictive or catty, she was a perfect lady.

Unlike any First Lady Mama had known, she took absolutely no part in her husband's business. The President would tell her some amusing anecdote, but he did not ask her advice— and she was careful to offer suggestions in a tentative way so that, eventually, he might think the idea had been his.

She was never at a loss for words. He always was. There

never were two people less alike, and yet they seemed perfectly mated, said Mama.

The mystery of the White House was where the President put all that food he ate. He kept nuts around in every room, and nibbled all day long. He kept preserves and crackers in his bedroom, and every morning after his walk, he fixed himself a cheese sandwich. *Then* he had breakfast.

"... LIKE A BROKEN RECORD"

"You see, Lillian, it's just a normal family," said Mama. "The spell of bad luck is broken at last. I'm so glad we have a White House with so much love in it, and harmony, and no more problems."

And then came tragedy. It was in July of 1924, just about a year after the Coolidges had come to the White House. The boys were home from school, and Calvin, Jr., was playing tennis, as he liked to do most any day. But on this day, he had a blister on his foot. He came in limping a little. He developed a high fever, and the next day everyone was worried.

He kept getting worse, so he was taken to the hospital. Everything possible was done to check the poison going through his body— this was before the day of tetanus shots— but he died within a few days.

Mama was shattered again. "It's like I've been through all this before," she said. "It's like a broken record."

It was the President who showed his grief quite violently, and it was Mrs. Coolidge who restrained her sorrow, except when she was alone.

A bud vase was placed beside Calvin Jr.'s picture, and

Mrs. Coolidge put a rose in it every day. If she were not at home, Mama would see to it that a fresh white rose was there. Sometimes, Mrs. Coolidge would close herself in the Green Suite on the second floor, and play the piano she had brought to the White House. Mama knew she was playing her son's favorite pieces and feeling close to him, and did not disturb her.

All the rest of the days in the White House would be shadowed by the tragic loss, even though the President tried harder than ever to make his little dry jokes and to tease the people around him.

A little boy came to give the President his personal condolences, and the President gave word that any little boy who wanted to see him was to be shown in. Backstairs, the maids cried a little over that, and the standing invitation was not mentioned to Mrs. Coolidge.

The President was even more generous with the First Lady than he had been before the tragedy. He would bring her boxes of candy and other presents to coax a smile to her lips.

He brought her shawls. Dresses were short in the days of Mrs. Coolidge, and Spanish shawls were thrown over them. He got her dozens of them. One shawl was so tremendous that she could not wear it, so she draped it over the banister on the second floor, and it hung over the stairway. The President used to look at it with a ghost of a smile.

Mrs. Coolidge spent more time in her bedroom among her doll collection. She kept the dolls on the Lincoln bed. At night, when Mama would turn back the covers, she would have to take all the dolls off the bed and place them elsewhere for the night. Mama always felt that the collection symbolized Mrs. Coolidge's wish for a little girl.

Among the dolls was one that meant very much to the First Lady, who would pick it up and look at it often. It had a tiny envelope tied to its wrist. An accompanying sympathetic letter explained that inside the envelope was a name for Mrs. Coolidge's first granddaughter. Mama knew this doll was meant to help Mrs. Coolidge overcome her grief by turning her eyes to the future. The name inside the envelope was "Cynthia."

The Coolidges' life, after the death of their son, was quieter than ever. John was away at school most of the time. Mrs. Coolidge would knit, and the President would sit reading, or playing with the many pets around them.

Now and then, the President would call for "Little Jack, Master of the Hounds," which was his nickname for a messenger who had worked in the White House since Teddy Roosevelt's administration, and discuss the welfare of some one of the animals. It was part of Little Jack's work to look after the dogs.

One White House dog was immortalized in a painting. That was Rob Roy, who posed with Mrs. Coolidge for the portrait by Howard Chandler Christy. To get him to pose, Mrs. Coolidge would feed him candy, so he enjoyed the portrait sessions as well as she did.

I would like to straighten out a misconception about the dress Mrs. Coolidge is wearing in this painting. It is not the same dress as the one on her manikin in the Smithsonian. People think the dress in the picture was lengthened by an artist much later on. This is not true. The dress in the painting is a bright red, with rhinestones forming a spray on the right side. There is a long train flowing from the shoulders.

Mrs. Coolidge gave Mama this dress for me, and I wore it many times. I still have the dress, and I hope to give it to the Smithsonian Institution as a memento, or, as I more fondly hope, to present it to a museum containing articles showing the daily lives of the Presidents— if I can get it organized.

But to get back to the Coolidge household, Mrs. Coolidge so obviously loved dogs, that the public sent her more dogs— Calamity Jane, Timmy, and Blackberry. The last two were a red and a black chow. Rob Roy remained boss of all the dogs. He showed them what to do, and taught them how to keep the maids around the White House in a state of terror.

The dogs would run through the halls after him like a burst of bullets, and all the maids would run for cover. Mama didn't know what to do— whether to tell on Rob Roy or not— since she had the ear of Mrs. Coolidge more than the other maids. But she was afraid the First Lady would not understand, because Rob Roy was a perfect angel with the First Family.

Every day, when the President took his nap, Rob Roy would stretch out on the window seat near him, like a perfect gentleman, and stare thoughtfully out the window, or he would take a little nap himself. He would not make a sound until the President had wakened and left for the office; then he would bark to let everyone know the coast was clear. His signal was for the other dogs to come running, but it was also the signal for Mama and the other maids to watch out.

Rob Roy was self-appointed to accompany the President to his office every morning. Rob Roy was well aware of the importance of this mission, and he would walk in front of the President, looking neither to the right nor to the left.

At dinner, lunch, or breakfast, the President would call out, "Supper!"— he called all meals supper— after the butler had announced the meal. All the dogs would dash to get on the elevator with the President and go to the dining room. They would all lie around on the rug during the meal, a very pretty sight as Rob Roy, Prudence, and Calamity Jane were all snow-white.

When Prudence and Blackberry were too young to be

trusted in the dining room, they were tied to the radiator with their leashes, and they would cry. Mama tried to talk to them and keep them quiet while she tidied up the sitting room before the First Family returned.

Finally, Mama did mention to Mrs. Coolidge that she felt sorry for the little dogs, and then Mrs. Coolidge decided to leave the radio on for them while she was gone, even though her husband disapproved of the waste of electricity.

Mama was now the first maid to Mrs. Coolidge, because Catherine, the previous first maid, had become ill and died. Mrs. Coolidge chose Mama in her place. It was a high mark for Mama.

Every First Family seems to have one couple upon whom it relies for true friendship. For the Coolidges, it was Mr. and Mrs. Frank W. Stearns of Boston, Massachusetts, owners of a large department store. They seemed to be at the White House half the time. The butlers were amused because when the Stearns were there, the President would say grace at breakfast. If the Stearns were not there, grace would be omitted.

Speaking of breakfast, the President inaugurated a new custom— that of conducting business at the breakfast table. The word was that this too was part of an economy move on his part. A new bill had been passed under Harding that designated the Government, rather than the President, as the tab-lifter for official meals. So the President would make a hearty breakfast official by inviting Government officials to attend.

He caused a lot of talk when he also chose the breakfast hour to have the barber come in and trim his hair while he ate. Mama said that if Presidents were supposed to be colorful, Mr. Coolidge certainly made a good president. He knew exactly how to be colorful!

The favorite guest of the house, as far as the staff was

concerned, was Mr. Wrigley, the chewing gum king. The White House had chewing gum until it could chew no more, and every Christmas, Mr. Wrigley sent the President a check for $100, to be divided among all the help. You can imagine that he got pretty good service.

Another good friend of the Coolidges' was George B. Harvey, who was the Ambassador to Great Britain from 1921 to 1923. He had been a friend of the Hardings, and continued to be invited by the Coolidges.

The first royalty whom Mama ever waited on in the White House was Queen Marie of Rumania, who came to a State dinner given in her honor on October 21, 1926. She was not an overnight guest in the White House, but Mr. Ike Hoover, the chief usher, had Mama check her fur coat when she came in, and take care of her needs. Mama said she was one of the prettiest ladies she had ever seen.

Mama was very patriotic, and one of the duties she was proudest of was repairing the edges of the flag that flew above the White House. Actually, two flags were used at the mansion— a small one on rainy days, and a big one on bright days. The wool would become frazzled around the edges from blowing in the wind, and Mama would mend it. She would often go up on the roof to see the attendant take down the flag in the evening. She used to tell me, "When I stand there and look at the flag blowing this way and that way, I have the wonderful, safe feeling that Americans are protected no matter which way the wind blows."

Even when Mrs. Coolidge was in mourning for her son, she reached out to help other people in trouble. One person she helped was my brother. Mama had told her how Emmett's lungs had been affected when he was gassed in the war. He was in and out of Mount Alto Hospital for veterans any number of times.

Taking a personal interest, she had the doctor assigned

to the White House, Dr. James Coupal, look Emmett over.
As a result, he was sent to a hospital in Arizona until his
health improved enough for him to come back to Washington to work in the Government service. But again, there
was danger that his lungs would suffer in the muggy
Washington weather, and he had to return to the dry clim-
ate of the West to live and work.

When Mrs. Coolidge was in mourning, she did not wear
black. She wore grey every day, and white every evening.
Mama knew that she was out of mourning when she finally
wore bright colors. The President helped her a lot by
selecting some lovely colored dresses to get her started. She
opened the boxes with a tear in her eye and a sad smile on
her face.

On the social side, the chore Mama had at the formal
receptions at the White House thrilled her the most. It was
her job to stand at the foot of the stairs, and, just as the
First Lady stepped off the last tread, Mama would
straighten out her long train before she marched to the
Blue Room to greet the guests with the President. Mama
would enjoy the sight of the famous guests as much as anyone, and would note a gown here and there to tell me about
that night.

One night, Mama came home practically in a state of
shock. She had stood at the bottom of the stairs, as usual,
when Mrs. Coolidge came down, in the same dress that is
now in the Smithsonian, to greet her guests. Mama stooped
down to fix the train, but there was no train there! She
reached and reached around the dress, but there was
nothing there. She looked up and saw that, without knowing it, Mrs. Coolidge was holding it aloft. Mrs. Coolidge
looked down, saw Mama's horrified expression and quickly
let the whole thing fall to the floor. Mama swirled the train
in place, and not a step was lost.

The Coolidges did not always live at the White House

during the Presidency. In that way, they resembled the Trumans, who had to move because the White House floors were about to cave in. In the case of the Coolidges, it was the roof that was in imminent danger of collapse.

Every time there was a big snowfall, the men would have to rush up and shovel it off, because they feared it couldn't hold the weight. A few years before, Washington, D.C., had had a bad lesson in the danger of snow on a weak roof when many persons were killed as the roof of the Knickerbocker Theatre fell in. The White House had cancelled all entertainment for several weeks.

So it was decided to put a new roof on the White House, and the whole family moved to the Patterson mansion on Dupont Circle, which was leased for the purpose.

At a White House dinner on April 23, 1927, President Machado of Cuba was the last important person to be entertained by the Coolidges at the Executive Mansion. When Charles Lindbergh came to Washington on June 10, 1927, after his solo flight to Paris, he was entertained in the Patterson house.

Mama was thrilled to see the great hero, and so was I. I was in the crowd in the park in front of the house, waiting for his arrival.

His mother had come the day before he arrived, and she watched timidly from a window the great ovation for her son. She had gotten off the train at Baltimore instead of Washington, and had the whole staff in a tizzy till they located her and sent a car to Baltimore.

The President took second place to the great hero that day. But Coolidge didn't mind at all. He had stayed quietly in the background once before, when his guest was the most sought-after bachelor in the world— the Prince of Wales. Every prominent family with an eligible daughter had a dance for him, and he had kept all the females swooning.

But when he came to the White House to have lunch with the President and the First Lady, the butler later reported that "Silent Cal" had said exactly three words during the meal. Mrs. Coolidge had carried the whole conversational burden, but she was used to it.

The President and Mrs. Coolidge left for the State Game Lodge, Rapid City, South Dakota, the summer after the Lindbergh visit. Before she left, Mrs. Coolidge walked from the Patterson House, down Connecticut Avenue, and all the way to the White House to inspect the repairs and make final suggestions.

She did not know that two months later, on August 3, 1927, to be exact, the President would announce that he did not "choose to run" for President in 1928. He had not consulted her before making the statement, and Mama was sure that if he had talked to her about it, he would not have put it that way. Mama was sure that the President would not refuse the Presidency— he had only meant that he would not go out looking for it.

It was typical of the President to make such a proud and even haughty statement, because underneath he was very sensitive. Everyone had been talking about whether or not the President would run for office a second time. He had only run for the office once, because he had filled in President Harding's unexpired term. The President was afraid, Mama said (and so did other servants of the White House) that people would think he was greedily trying to get two and a half terms at the White House. So what he was saying, in effect, the White House staff figured, was that he was not pushing himself, and that he did not choose to run, but at the same time he would leave open the door to what *would* happen if the Republicans and the nation *chose him*.

One sign, the White House staff said, showed that Mr. Coolidge did want to be President again— he was acting just like a candidate after his pronouncement, and permitted himself to be made an Indian chief. At other times, he paraded around in fancy cowboy costumes. All the staff agreed that Mr. Coolidge wasn't the type to wear such clothes just for the fun of it.

Mama could tell Mrs. Coolidge was a little sad at his announcement. She was always the one who explained what he meant and smoothed things over so that people would not misunderstand her husband, or be hurt or angry. But this time she did not butt in or interpret it for them. Mama took this to mean that Mrs. Coolidge felt that her husband would be "drafted."

After Coolidge's statement there was nothing else talked about in, or out of, the papers. "What does the President mean?" was on everyone's lips.

Mr. Coolidge showed how stubborn he was when he refused to explain it. It was like him always to want people to be smart enough to figure out things for themselves. But this time, his stubbornness only hurt himself.

The next summer, on June 12, when the convention opened in Kansas City, the President listened to the radio at the White House— he had delayed his trip to his summer home— and he was so upset, that he refused to eat his lunch. He remained in his room until the next day. Late on the night of the thirteenth, the President and Mrs. Coolidge suddenly left for Superior, Wisconsin, for a vacation, and they were on the train when Herbert Hoover was nominated as the next President of the United States.

At the White House, the staff felt that Coolidge would have had no trouble getting elected, because all the visitors who came were talking about how he had kept the nation prosperous. There even was a little saying that Mama brought home— "Wilson made the world safe for democracy, but Coolidge made the Nation safe for Wall Street."

When President Coolidge got back to the White House in September, Mama reported that he acted as though there had never been a convention, and nobody ever heard him mention Mr. Hoover's name. The President did not even pay any attention to the preparations made for the inauguration. He had always been consumed by curiosity, and he would go take a look for himself at any repair work going on, but he would never take a look at the reviewing stand being built outside the White House on Pennsylvania Avenue.

The public never knew how hurt the President was that he had not been "drafted," but Mama knew, and a lot of the White House people sensed it. Everyone thought that the President was very thick-skinned, because he was so rough and tough in his treatment of others, but underneath he was a very sensitive man. To show how touchy he was, when Will Rogers made fun of the President by imitating him on the radio, Mama heard the President tell Mrs. Coolidge, "He will never be invited to the White House again." And he had been hurt by cartoons depicting him exercising on his mechanical horse.

Mrs. Coolidge sadly began packing her things at the White House, and she gave Mama many gifts. Mama's favorite was a lamp that Mrs. Coolidge had brought back from Havana, Cuba. It was made of two starfish and colored beads, so that the finished lamp looked like a Chinese house with little lanterns hanging all around it. She also gave Mama several feather fans, which I still keep with a dainty Oriental fan that had been given to her by Mrs. Taft.

When the sad day came, and the Coolidges left the White House, Mrs. Coolidge asked all the staff to line up before the President's door to say good-by. Mama felt that poor Mrs. Coolidge had chosen this spot, because he would not say good-by unless cornered, and here Mr. Coolidge could not escape. When the President came out, Mrs. Coolidge said, "Papa, here is Wilkins and the staff to say good-by."

The President made a funny little noise in his throat, and that was all. He said not a word.

Mama and Wilkins, the head houseman, and all the rest waited desperately for him to say something, but he didn't, and they were sad. In a few minutes, it was all over, and they had a new boss and a new family to learn about, and there was no more time for nostalgia.

I will never forget one thing Mama said about the President's having cheated himself out of a chance to hold his office another four years. She said he'd made the mistake of following one of his own favorite sayings: "Nobody ever got into trouble or lost a job for talking too little."

"Except himself," Mama added.

All through the years, I wondered whatever had become of the doll with the message about "Cynthia." I wondered if the name Cynthia was ever used.

And then in April of 1959, a great event occurred in the annals of the White House— a meeting of all the living descendants of Presidents. From all over the country, they came to dine with the women of the press at the Statler Hilton Hotel, and then to visit the White House as the guests of Mamie Eisenhower.

Lee Walsh, Gladys Uhl, and Christine Sadler, of the Women's National Press Club, labored mightily to bring them all together. Among those present were Judge George Washington and Mr. Armistead Peter, collateral descendants of the First President, who had had no children of his own. And three great-great-great-granddaughters of Thomas Jefferson were there: Mrs. Constant Southworth, of Washington, D.C., Mrs. Joseph Parkes Crockett, and Mrs. Angus Slater Lamond, of Alexandria, Virginia.

There was the great-great-great-great-granddaughter of John Quincy Adams, Mrs. Harry Hull, the former Louisa Catherine Adams Clement, of Washington, D.C. And the great-great-grandson of James Monroe, Laurence G. Hoes, of Washington, D.C.; and the grandson of John Tyler, Lyon G. Tyler, Jr., of Richmond, Virginia.

The great-grandson of Abraham Lincoln, Robert Lincoln Beckwith, was on hand; and the granddaughter of Ulysses S. Grant, Madame Cantacuzene, of Washington, D.C.; and the grandson of James Garfield, Dr. Stanton Garfield, of Washington, D.C. And a granddaughter of Benjamin Harrison, Mrs. Marthena Harrison Williams, of Washington, D.C., attended.

There were sons and daughters of Presidents also— Richard C. Cleveland, of Baltimore, and Mrs. John Harlan Amen, of New York, children of Grover Cleveland; Mrs. Eleanor McAdoo Wilson, of Santa Barbara, California, daughter of Woodrow Wilson, who added her maiden name after her divorce; Charles P. Taft, of Cincinnati, son of William Howard Taft; John Roosevelt, of New York City, son of Franklin D. Roosevelt; John Coolidge, son of Calvin Coolidge, of Farmington, Connecticut, and John Eisenhower, of Gettysburg, Pennsylvania, son of Dwight D. Eisenhower.

There were many other relatives— the husbands, wives, and children of the descendants.

I feasted my eyes upon the sight of those people, who had meant so much to Mama and me. But most of all, there was one name I was waiting to hear. And then I heard it. John Coolidge arrived with his wife and two daughters. The younger was Lydia, and his first-born was Cynthia.

PART THREE

THE WHITE HOUSE THROUGH THE EYE OF MY NEEDLE

HOOVERS

ROOSEVELTS

TRUMANS

EISENHOWERS

IT'S *MY* WHITE HOUSE NOW ...

I had made it. I was hurrying as fast as my crutches would carry me. I was on my way to the White House that very second. I belonged there. At last, I had a White House job.

"Don't tell me anything more about the White House," I had told Mama when the Hoovers arrived, and I was scheduled to go to work for them. "I want to see everything for myself."

On that glorious rainy morning, in 1929, we were going to work together. Mama was lecturing me all the way. Always remember to say, "Yes, Madam," when the First Lady spoke to me . . . always act dignified . . . never speak unless spoken to . . . never look sloppy . . . remember that what I did would reflect on her . . . don't disgrace her . . . don't act silly . . . don't repeat what I heard . . . don't expect special favors from her just because she was my mother.

"Mama," I said, "will you do me a favor, and just let me enjoy this moment?"

I had been nagging at my mother for years to see if she would recommend me. Mama, being a very ethical woman, was afraid it would not look right if she were to

praise her own child, but she finally promised she would
see what she could do when the new First Lady came in.

As first maid of the White House, Mama had shown
Mrs. Hoover the repair work on the White House linens
that I had been doing at home, and had told her how well
I got along on crutches— I was even able to scrub a floor.
And the timing had been perfect, because Agnes, who
waited on Mrs. Hoover and was married to Leon Thompson,
the head of the receiving room, was expecting her
third child.

Mrs. Hoover had said the magic words, "Maggie, why
don't you have your little girl come to work?"

So there I was at the White House. I waited three tense
days without seeing the First Lady, working on anything
anyone gave me. Finally, Mrs. Hoover sent the message,
which went through the White House like wildfire: "Send
Maggie's little girl to the Palm Room at twelve."

Now that the moment had arrived, I was shaky. I had
been at the White House many times, and had grown up
hearing about it; I felt a part of it all my life, and suddenly
I could hardly move. What if I didn't measure up?

I was glad I had my crutches to hold me up. The Palm
Room? Where was that? Good grief, I couldn't remember
any room like that. And then it came back to me. Mrs.
Hoover, Mama said, had taken the West Sitting Room on
the second floor, and filled it with potted palms and vines
till it looked like a Brazilian jungle and called it the "Palm
Room." I was lost. I could see myself wandering through
fifty rooms looking for the Palm Room.

But I needn't have worried. Suddenly Mama appeared
to escort me there so I wouldn't get lost. I don't know
what Mama was thinking, but I was feeling that this was
the time for her to be giving me advice. Suddenly I felt I
needed it. But all she said, as she directed me through the

right entry, was, "Remember now, if Mrs. Hoover starts walking, that means it's time for you to go."

As I walked the miles, and miles, and miles through the room to the seated figure, I tried to remember what Mama had been saying about Mrs. Hoover's dislike for giving directions. She used little signals for everything— a raised hand or finger or similar signs. And vaguely I was aware that I was in some kind of indoor-outdoor paradise. Birds sang, and flowers bloomed. And then I stood before her.

The First Lady rose and graciously shook my hand. "So you are Maggie's little girl," she said. I remembered the "Yes, Madam," and was surprised at how automatic it had become from listening to Mama.

"Yes, you do look just like your mother," Mrs. Hoover said. "You are a miniature of her. Maggie is very particular about everything she does, so I know you must be too."

I don't remember exactly what else she said as she studied me, but it was mostly in praise of Mama. And then, as she started walking toward a plant, I realized that was the signal. It was over. I was to go.

I floated back to the servants' quarters— Mama had again materialized out of nowhere to escort me. As I surveyed my surroundings, I knew I had made it. I had become a member of the White House. Now I could relax and get to work.

But there was just one thing I wanted to do first— I had waited for this moment for many years. I said, "Mama, would you just show me the Lincoln bed?"

"Lincoln bed," she echoed. "The Lincoln bed isn't here any more. I think it's been taken to storage."

I heard wild laughter behind me and turned around. The servants were laughing at me. "Lincoln bed," said one man and howled with glee. "Where is the bed?" said another. "Bed, bed, who's got the bed?" And everyone was roaring again.

Had they lost their minds? What had I said?

"We're not laughing at you," someone explained. "It's the furniture."

I had hit the funny bone of all the White House staff. Nothing was where it had been. Nothing was where it should be. All the furniture was on the march around the White House. Shelves were being knocked down; shelves were being installed. Bedrooms were becoming sitting rooms; sitting rooms were becoming bedrooms.

Three housemen were especially raucous. They, it seems, had found themselves much in demand by the First Lady as moving men from the very day the Hoovers had moved in. In fact, that was what they now called themselves, the "moving men." Frank and Luther Wilkinson, brothers assigned to the second floor, and nephew William, who was assigned to the third floor, had been sent for within hours following the inauguration ceremony to report to the President's study, and they had been ordered to tear out the built-in bookcases that instant.

Theirs not to wonder why, so they had begun at once. But when they had gotten only part of them down, they had been told to leave the rest, because the President had decided not to use *that* room for a study after all, but another room, which would be changed from a bedroom.

The Wilkinsons thought that would be the end of it, but it was only the beginning. And they became a familiar sight as they trudged up and down the halls— all three carrying furniture. When they had it settled in one place, the First Lady wanted to try it in another place. And when they weren't carrying it, they were hunting for it. And when they weren't hunting for it, they were studying old records that told them where it was supposed to be, assuming that some other administration had not moved it.

As the days rolled by, I was to hear them say a hundred

times, "Well, we turned all the furniture around again today."

To complicate matters, the nephew was afraid of ghosts, and his uncle Frank didn't help a bit when he would ask Mama, "Maggie, did you pass me in the hall?"

Mama would say, "No."

Frank would say, "Well, *something* passed me."

Poor William refused to go into the bedrooms alone because of the stories of Lincoln's and Grant's and William Henry Harrison's ghosts, and Mama had to go with him and stay there while he carried stuff in or ran the sweeper.

Mrs. Lou Henry Hoover was the most elegant woman I had been around. She was tall, very tall from my four-foot-ten viewpoint, and truly stately. She looked like a queen, and she quickly became motherly about me, making sure that I was getting my share of the good things of the White House.

Foods that I had never eaten before were served to the help— crêpes suzettes— not in flames, however— and on top of it, when she ate lunch alone, she was sending her own desserts over to me. She also made sure that a dish of ice cream came to me at every entertainment. "Take this to Maggie's little girl" was a familiar expression.

Too familiar for comfort. The butler would appear with a *soup dish* full of ice cream for me, and stand around waiting for me to eat it so he could take the dish back. I was staggering under the weight of her generosity, but, of course, I was thrilled at the attention, and my heart responded to this magnificent, kind woman.

Mama assured me that this was not standard procedure at the White House and not to expect every First Lady to make a special project of me. I certainly hoped not, because I was interested in staying at my weight of 98 pounds. But naturally, while I ate with the First Lady's butler standing over me, waiting to take back her dish, I was too timid to tell

him I'd already eaten one dessert and hadn't room for another. I was soon up to 104 pounds.

In spite of my tiny size, I noted that a lot of the help
were afraid of me. Small wonder. I was the daughter of
Maggie Rogers, the top maid, who had the ear of the First
Lady, and no one wanted to get into trouble with her. The
men were calling me "Miss Lillian" very respectfully at
the table and looking over apprehensively at Mama if the
conversation got too rough.

Mama, on the other hand, was treating me tougher than
she ever had in my life. For a time, she was practically a
stranger to me as she leaned over backward to make sure
no one would say her daughter was her favorite interest.
If there was any messy, unpleasant, time-consuming job
that no one wanted, that quickly became my job. When I'd
begin to feel sorry for myself, I used to think that if Mrs.
Hoover could see me doing heavy work, when she had
hired me to sew and do light maid's work, she'd get after
somebody. But I only *thought* this.

Still I made good use of the respect I was enjoying from
the other help. I bullied them into showing me all the
things I had only heard about, and wanted to see with my
own eyes.

High on my list was the "gold silverware," as I called it,
until I got used to saying "goldware" as if it were routine.
Where, oh where, was the real gold with which guests at
the White House used to dine at formal dinners?

Mama had told me how Mrs. Harding had sent out all
the silverware to be triple-plated with gold, so that it would
match the Dolley Madison pieces used as the centerpiece
for entertaining. Dolley Madison had bought a gold-bor-
dered mirror, with four gold candlesticks and three big
gold epergnes to hold a large display of fruits (it was still
being used when I left toward the end of the Eisenhower
administration). I noticed that the grapes would be wired

to lie stiff and proud in the epergne, and wondered how the guests would feel if they were to reach for one and strike a wire.

Mama had credited the influence of Mrs. Evalyn Walsh McLean for the gold plating of the silver service. Mrs. Harding, Mama explained, had been completely dazzled by the elegant way in which Mrs. McLean lived, and she used to tell Mama wistfully, as Mama fixed her hair, that Mrs. McLean's showplace, "Friendship," was even more elegant than the White House.

I asked Mama once if she didn't wish she were working for some more elegant place like "Friendship," whose owner had been the daughter of the "gold-mining king" and could afford to fill it with gold.

Mama said, "Heavens no, child. Be it ever so elegant, there is no place like the White House. The White House isn't *just* elegant. It has something else too. Why, I'm living history."

She certainly was. She was living it, eating it, sleeping it, bringing it home to me, and becoming a part of it herself.

Because she had instilled in me the same interest and curiosity about history and the figures of history, I didn't rest easily until I had seen the gold-plated flatware, and the guide had pointed out to me all the history-making furniture around the White House.

I examined the furniture of the past— French Empire, Louis XVI, Heppelwhite, Sheraton and Adam. I was very much amused to hear that the American people had once been practically up in arms about the First Ladies' furniture, which had come from abroad (Mrs. Monroe's Empire pieces had come from Paris, typically enough). In fact, some time after the Monroes, Congress even passed a law that furniture for the White House had to be American-made whenever possible. But the foreign buying went on, because the Presidents' wives said it *wasn't* possible to get exactly what they wanted in this country.

I ventured to bet, as I was being shown about, that Andy Jackson hadn't entertained any fancy ideas like that, and was told that even "Old Hickory," who economized on White House cuspidors— two dollars apiece— had changed after he'd gotten into the White House and been criticized for bringing in still more fancy foreign furniture. All Presidents acquire certain refinements after they've been in office a while, but he had the longest way to go.

The Jackson stories have been passed along by word of mouth from one generation of servants to the next. March 4, 1829, when he took office, is still considered the most rough-and-tumble inaugural reception that ever took place at the White House. "Old Hickory" was so democratic that he invited everybody to his inaugural, and everybody came. And the women showed they were for him by wearing necklaces consisting of strings of hickory nuts. Not only did they come, but they stood on the delicate White House chairs to get a better look at their hero. The men couldn't find spittoons in the crowded room, so they just took aim at the rug. And a bunch of rowdies got drunk and had a fist fight in the East Room.

I looked at the august dignity of the East Room, and could hardly believe my ears. "What did people do when the fighting broke out?" I asked.

"Well," said my guide, "some of them didn't want to get involved, and they couldn't get through to the doors to leave, so they just climbed out the windows and went home, and others tried to protect the President. They wanted to get him out of there."

"So what did they do?" I prodded. "What happened?"

"Well, that's what they did. They got him out of there through the south side door, and he was so bruised and battered that they didn't dare let him go back into the

White House till they'd gotten rid of the crowds. They took him to a hotel, and that's where he spent his first night 'in the White House.' "

"You mean a President actually didn't spend his first night in the White House?" I asked, shocked.

"That's the way I heard it," I was told, "but don't forget about George Washington. The White House is the only house around Washington that doesn't brag 'Washington slept here.' You know, it wasn't completed till the second President, so John Adams was the first President to occupy it. But he didn't spend his first night there either. It wasn't ready till the third year of his term of office."

I listened, amazed, to these postscripts to history. New and fabulous worlds were opening up to me as I learned about the lives of the tenants of the White House.

Mrs. Hoover had given the order that the dining table should have different-colored runners and napkins each day, so I was put to work on that project. Even before I had come to the White House, Mama had brought some of the work home for me to do. Now, since there was so much sewing still to be done, other maids helped me when they had nothing else to do.

As I sat sewing, my mind was not so much on the cloth, and the job of making the stitches as small as I could, but on the ladies who had paraded through the doors— the very doors that I had walked through— and I was as thrilled as it was humanly possible to be.

I tried to get the old-timers to tell me their stories of the past, whenever they were in the mood.

I learned, as I sat sewing, that a number of First Ladies had held sewing bees in the White House, and that the last First Lady to invite ladies in to sew was Mrs. Edith Roosevelt, wife of the "Rough Rider." The gentlemen of the Cabinet shivered about those sewing and knitting sessions she had with their wives, because the ladies would really speak their minds about what was going on around Washington, and there was a saying that reputations were "unravelled by their knitting needles."

But the First Lady didn't escape a bit of gossip either. On the day that Alice Roosevelt was getting married to Nicholas Longworth, Speaker of the House, and the White House was a beehive of happy activity, Mrs. Roosevelt sat alone and aloof, knitting instead of taking part in the preparations. The question was this: did the marriage of Alice remind Mrs. Roosevelt of the fact that the President had been married before to another woman, Alice Hathaway Roosevelt, for whom Alice was named, and did this moment of remembrance make her sad?

Mrs. Taft, who followed Mrs. Roosevelt as First Lady, had heard what went on at these sewing-knitting sessions when she attended them as wife of the Secretary of War, and she discontinued the "Ladies' Cabinet Meetings," as they were called.

I would try to imagine what the city had looked like when the White House was first built, and Mrs. Abigail Adams first saw it. The White House had been in the process of building for eight years, and it still wasn't finished when she was hanging her clothes in the East Room. The story was that Mrs. Adams had hated moving from the refinement of Philadelphia to the unfinished house in the wilderness by the Potomac, and she had asked her husband what in the world the men had been doing for eight years if they hadn't finished the job yet?

Her winter there was one long war against the dampness— the only heat was from the fireplace, and the plaster wasn't dry. The shacks the workmen lived in were set up on the grounds around the White House. The grand staircase was still to be installed— as well as a lot of other things— and the building materials were all stacked outside in the mud.

Speaking of mud, even the road in front, Pennsylvania Avenue, was mud, and its purpose was to join the White House to the Capitol, one-and-a-half miles away. Mrs. Adams couldn't see why they had put these two buildings so far apart, and when I saw some old pictures of the city, I had to agree.

I had never heard before how the plan for the White House had materialized. Thomas Jefferson, I learned, had offered a $500 prize for the best plan for a "President's House." The winner was an Irishman who hailed from Kilkenny, and had been eking out a living as an architect in Charleston, South Carolina. His name was James Hoban. What the judges liked best about his three-floor Georgian plan was that it allowed for the addition of wings on each side later on. I wish he could have known how well his plan worked out, for wings were added on both sides, and they vastly improve the picture.

The White House has seen many new inventions installed to keep the First Families in tune with the times. President Benjamin Harrison brought in electric bulbs, but left the old gas lights "just in case." Actually, he never did trust electricity and refused to touch the switches, or have them touched, because they might shock and kill somebody, so the White House still continued to use gas light.

But what the White House did get, along with those first light bulbs, was a wonderfully friendly man, who had been introduced to me as the chief usher. His name was Irvin Hoover, but everyone called him "Ike" Hoover. He had come to the White House to install the first electricity for the Harrisons, and had been invited to stay on as an usher. I had heard Mama talk many times of his fabulous memory for names, and how he never forgot a name when introducing people to the President.

The big news about Ike Hoover when I arrived was that

Mrs. Hoover had forbidden anyone to call him "Mr. Hoover" any more, because that was the President's name, and everyone was to call him "Mr. Usher," when speaking to or about him.

I thought Ike Hoover would be disturbed by this, but he laughed and said he was used to having his name changed about at the White House. When he was installing electricity, and gave his name as I. H. Hoover, he had been mistakenly called "Ike" Hoover, though his name was Irvin, and he let it go, because he didn't want to be correcting Presidents.

Not all the ladies had been as thrilled to live in the White House as Mrs. Hoover so obviously was, I learned. Mrs. Zachary Taylor had shut herself up in a bedroom on the second floor, and would not even attend State dinners. Her daughter, Betty Taylor Bliss, acted as hostess. When she came reluctantly to the "President's House," she announced that the whole business of making her husband President was a plot to deprive her of his company.

Just as reluctant to live in the White House was Jane Appleton Pierce, who also refused to have anything to do with society. But at least she had a reason. She had lost a child, right before her eyes, in a train wreck two months before her husband took office, and she felt it would never have happened if her husband hadn't been elected, because then she wouldn't have been traveling.

An aunt acted as hostess for Mrs. Pierce, but it was pretty sad entertainment. Everyone said that she had lost her husband the re-election, because the public wanted a real hostess, and the bachelor candidate, James Buchanan, had promised them as hostess his beautiful and socially-prominent niece, Harriet Lane, who had gone to London and been received by Queen Victoria. The voters responded, and Harriet Lane gave a performance as Acting First Lady that is still talked of backstairs as the last word in regal entertainment— so much so that the Japanese Ambassador addressed the President as "Your Majesty."

I was surprised to learn that the bits of gossip my mother had been bringing home to me were mild compared to the gossip about the First Ladies of the past. It was said, for example, that Mrs. Zachary Taylor smoked a pipe, and that that was why she didn't attend parties; and that Dolley Madison sniffed snuff and flirted shamelessly in order to be the middle-aged belle of the ball.

When Mary Todd Lincoln was First Lady, it was rumored around Washington that she was mad, and on top of that, that she was actually a spy and went out in her carriage to deliver messages to the Confederates. Thus, she was even denied credit for one of the nice things she did do. The White House staff could have explained that she was seen in her carriage, because she was working at hospitals for the wounded soldiers.

The talk about Mrs. Lincoln's extravagance was true enough, and many a story was told backstairs of how insatiable she was in her demand for pretty things; but the rumor that she was out of her mind was groundless, according to the household staff. They knew her simply as a moody and sometimes bad-tempered woman, but surely not to the point of "madness."

My head was really swimming with stories of the White House past, and I gloried in the fact that I too had become a part of it. Every time Mrs. Hoover would order another change, the help would remember some story connected with the room or the furniture.

As the Wilkinsons Three toiled, we domestics were amused by the manner in which one wheel had come full circle— President Chester Arthur had thrown out twenty-four wagon loads of fancy fripperies from the White House, and Mrs. Hoover was bringing them back. It wasn't true, of course; it only looked that way because of all the activity. Even many of the paintings grew restless and marched around. The portraits of George and Martha Washington left their home in the Red Room and settled down at last in the East Room, where they look very much at home today.

The Hoovers couldn't decide where to sleep, or where to work. When the dust of moving had cleared, the "moving men" discovered that Mrs. Hoover had appropriated the bedroom that was traditionally the President's bedroom, and called it her dressing room. Only it wasn't used for that at all. It was her *workroom.* She used the bed for her "desk" and had it completely covered with papers. She sat beside this bed, working all day long, and when she went out, we had to cover the bed with a sheet and tuck it in so the papers would never be disturbed. Mrs. Hoover had turned three bedrooms on the third floor into offices for three secretaries she had hired to help her with all her projects and her correspondence, but preferred a bedside office herself.

And then, at last, I saw the Lincoln bed! Mrs. Hoover had brought it back, I was thrilled to hear, and it was now in the First Lady's suite, in the larger of the two rooms, where the President and she slept. The smaller of the two rooms was the one the poor President had to use for dressing.

The Oval Study, traditionally used by Presidents, became a furniture storage room for the First Lady, and the President found himself doing his nightly studies way down the hall in the same room in which Lincoln signed the Emancipation Proclamation. It was a pity he couldn't do the same— emancipate himself— because he worked till all hours of the night, and soon earned the title of the "hardest working President" from the staff. His hours were even worse than Wilson's, they said, and added that Mr. Hoover had better watch out for his health.

Hoover worked at the Lincoln desk, called the "Resolute" desk because it was made from the timbers of the ship
Resolute. As an added touch, the President had brought
from his home a painting of "The First Reading of the
Emancipation." And it was a red-letter day for Mrs. Hoover
when she brought back to the White House a little mirror
that had been stolen by a British soldier when the White
House was partially burned in 1814.

It was wonderful, historically speaking, for the President
to work in the Lincoln room, *but* it meant that the White
House was short two guest bedrooms, because the smaller
room next to the Lincoln Room was also without a bed,
and had been turned into a drawing room for the President to use with his male guests.

Suddenly, Mrs. Hoover discovered she had four sitting
rooms on the bedroom floor— the second floor— and she
started reshuffling again. The moving men told me that not
one place on the second floor ended up as it had begun on
March 4, 1929, "except the grand staircase and the elevator,
and we're waiting to see where they're going."

Not only were furnishings moved, but they were redyed
and redesigned. The Oval Room, formerly known as The
President's Study, eventually became a "Chinese" room,
painted black and gold, for which the grey rug and blue
furniture had to be sent out and dyed black. It was used
for small teas, and as a family sitting room.

It went on and on, with more and more wicker furniture
and grass rugs and specially-built bird cages and trailing
plants arriving for the "Palm Room," formerly the West
Sitting Room; and then things were torn up again to install
a motion picture projection unit.

One of Mrs. Hoover's projects, over which she labored
for several years, was her pride and special, special love—
the restoration of the Monroe Room, a sitting room on the
other side of the Oval Room. It contained copies she had

had made of priceless furniture, just as it had been when used by the elegant James Monroe and his wife, according to the descriptions in old records.

The Monroe Sitting Room restoration is the only Lou Hoover change in effect today. But even in that there was one break in the continuity of the room's décor, and a strange twist to the story. It has to do with the day that Mrs. Eleanor Roosevelt came to inspect the house which she would "inherit" within a month or so.

Proudly Mrs. Hoover showed Mrs. Roosevelt through all the rooms she had redone, emphasizing most of all the Monroe Room. Mrs. Roosevelt then asked to see the kitchens. They went to the servants' area, but when they approached the kitchens, Mrs. Hoover suddenly stopped, drew herself up, and said, "I'm sorry, but the housekeeper will have to show you the kitchens. *I* never go into the kitchens."

When Mrs. Roosevelt moved in, the first thing she did was to order all the Monroe furniture taken out to storage.

A CLOUD OVER THE
WHITE HOUSE

There was panic in the streets. Mama said that never in her experience had she felt such anger and desperation in the city, and such uncertainty in the White House.

A lot of people were unfairly blaming all their troubles on the President, and he received many threatening letters. President Hoover did not take a single vacation, for as the newspapers reported, he was far too busy. He would only go to the seclusion of his Rapidan Camp near Washington for a week end, and only a few old trusted friends would be in the Hoover entourage.

In the White House, he seemed tense and utterly pre-occupied with the nation's ills. Such were the security precautions, that the order was given that none of the servants were to be in sight when the President came out into the halls. So whenever the help heard three bells— the signal that he was emerging from his quarters— they would jump in every direction in order not to be seen. They jumped into rooms, and they jumped into a particular hall closet.

Mama was around the First Lady much more than I was, so she did much more jumping, but even I had to resort to the hall closet once in a while. That broom closet, near the President's elevator, was eliminated during the Truman period of White House reconstruction, but in the Hoover administration, it was a very popular place, and butlers would hold their trays high over their heads to make room for others as they tumbled in.

Mama said that the Secret Service needn't have gone *that* far, since we were on the President's side. But when he went out, that was a different matter. Sometimes hecklers would boo him, and then he would return to the White House looking grimmer than ever.

Actually, there was a very good reason for the tightening up of security. Soon after the Hoovers had moved in, a man managed to come in right off the street, and he got to the President as he sat in the dining room with the First Lady and a handful of guests.

It was a ludicrous moment for the President, as he watched this stranger approaching him— and even the butlers seemed frozen in their tracks.

The President said, "I don't have an appointment with you," and the man replied menacingly, "You'd *better* have an appointment with me."

Then Mrs. Hoover rose to the occasion. In the twinkling of an eye, she ordered the butlers to shove the man out, and called for the Secret Service men. But the incident marked the beginning of a new era of tension.

Looking back, Mama always said that the business of popping into closets in order not to be seen was very funny, but the whole atmosphere of security was no joke when you had to live in it. All kinds of people wanted to get to the President, to tell him their troubles, or to threaten him, though he was no more responsible for the economic crisis than the Man in the Moon. The letters from the public were not calculated to give anyone in the White House peace of mind either.

Things got worse and worse, starting with the stock market crash and a rash of suicides from windows (the help referred to them somewhat callously as "dry dives"). Everyone on the staff agreed that President Hoover was really trying to solve the problems of the unemployed and the poorly employed. No man could have been asked to work longer hours than he did. He would come out of his study at night in a state of exhaustion. He appointed study committees right and left to decide what to do about the economy, but his problems were endless.

The President hardly took enough time to eat, so anxious was he to get back to work. All the servants and kitchen staff made bets on how long it would take him to eat. He averaged around nine to ten minutes, and he could eat a full-course dinner in eight minutes flat. They would come back saying, "Nine minutes, fifteen seconds," or whatever the time had been. Eight minutes seemed to be his record. For State dinners, though, he would slow down for the benefit of the guests.

Mama said that poor Mrs. Hoover didn't know what to do about it, but there was really nothing she could do, and she would explain to the startled guests that the President had an appointment or had a lot of work to do, and she would do her best to put them at ease. There were always friends at dinner. The staff said they could count on two hands the times the President and his wife ate alone, and even when they did, they dressed for dinner, and used the formal State Dining Room rather than the little family dining room.

They did a lot of entertaining. Everyone backstairs said that this was part of the President's policy of "business as usual," and that he wanted to make everything seem as normal as possible, as if he had a lot of confidence that everything would turn out all right.

There were a record fourteen receptions in one social season. It seemed rather incongruous, with all the strife and soup lines, to be talking about the number one social problem of the day— whether or not Alice Roosevelt Longworth, as wife of the Speaker of the House, should sit higher at the White House table than Dolly Gann, who was not married to a high official, but was the sister of, and hostess for, the Vice-President, Charles Curtis. The President side-stepped the whole controversy by adding one more official dinner to honor the Vice-President, so that Dolly Gann could have top honors at that party.

By having a separate dinner for the Speaker of the House and another one for the Vice-President, the Hoovers kept the feuding ladies from ever meeting at the White House. Neither lady was satisfied about this arrangement, according to gossip which I overheard, and each lady was quoted as desiring a showdown, so that it would be on the record of the social history of the town that she had been the second-ranking lady after Mrs. Hoover.

I used to see all of those controversial personages and hear the comments made by other guests about them, because I had the job of presiding over the water pitcher whenever the Hoovers had guests. I would have my glasses and water set up on a little table on the ground floor, and guests, coming and going, would stop nervously for a drink.

But there was one guest who was never nervous, and that was Alice Roosevelt Longworth, who had the self-assurance of having lived at the White House. Some guests, who were on the Alice Roosevelt side of the feud, said that even on the grounds of being the daughter of a former President, she outranked Dolly Gann.

On the other side of the fence were those who thought that Alice Roosevelt Longworth had ruled Washington society too long, and that she was afraid a rival might grab a little glory. I never had to feel sorry for Mrs. Longworth, who could take care of herself. Everything she said was widely-quoted, and sometimes the quote had a lot of sting in it, as when she commented that "Cal" Coolidge looked as if he had been "weaned on a sour pickle."

She was quoted all right, but she was also feared.

As for Mrs. Gann, she was good-looking, with a touch of grey in her blonde hair. Her half-brother, the Vice-President, did not resemble her in the slightest. He had pitch-black hair, touched with grey, and he was said to be half Indian.

At the Inaugural Ball, there was a procession of American Indians in full feathers. The White House help had a little fun with that one, because it brought back memories of Wilson's second wife, who had Indian blood.

"Just you wait," someone said. "The Indians will still take over Washington."

Actually, the way the White House staff saw it, Dolly Gann should have been very grateful to Alice Longworth, because without the feud, Mrs. Gann's name would have been forgotten by historians. As it is, people are still asking me about her.

After every party, Mrs. Hoover would hold a conference just like a football coach, with her three secretaries and the new housekeeper, Mrs. Ava Long, and a few others, discussing what had happened and how the next affair might be improved. She worked almost as hard at her White House "job" as her husband did. Money was no object when the Hoovers entertained, and they used much imported and out-of-season food, paying for it out of their own pockets.

Mrs. Hoover's gowns were perfectly fitted, and I was happy that I had a part in keeping them that way. Mrs. Hoover would send for "Maggie's little girl"— I don't think she ever found out my name— and I would go hurrying down the hall with my pincushion and scissors as fast as my crutches would carry me. I learned that Mrs. Hoover was so particular about her clothes that she would direct the fitting to the most minute detail, and would put most of the pins in herself to show exactly how she wanted a gown fitted.

She even had me fit her riding habit to perfection. She had an excellent figure. At some of our sessions, she would try on dress after dress, and I would have enough work to keep me busy for weeks at a time, without touching the linens that needed mending and that were piling up waiting for me.

The biggest hit I made with her began with a dress that had been made for her by Madame Ricciardilli, a French dressmaker. It had dots on the sleeves. She sent the dress to me by way of Mama, with the vague instruction to "tell the 'little girl' to cover those dots." I had no idea what to do to them, and I ended up redesigning the dress to give it a collar-and-cuff set.

Suddenly my collar-and-cuff sets were in demand. The First Lady wanted them made for almost every dress that took her fancy. Once I had to come to work on a Sunday morning to get a collar-and-cuff set made for a dress she wanted to wear to church, but I didn't mind because I was thrilled to be *needed* at the White House at last.

As the personal maid, Mama had to keep a record of the costumes that the First Lady wore every day, so that she would not be seen wearing the same clothing by the same people. It is a real rat race for a personal maid to keep track of those who have attended an affair, so that the First Lady will not be embarrassed by hearing a comment that some lady has seen her in *that* dress before.

Mama was such a whiz at remembering people, that Mrs. Hoover got into the habit of simply telling her that she was

going to such-and-such a wedding and to "pick out something nice to wear, Maggie." Mrs. Hoover's favorite colors
were brown and beige, which Mama tried to keep her from
overdoing, because she looked better in any color *but!*

When the King of Siam came in 1931, Mrs. Hoover had
a yellow taffeta made. Though King Prajahipok and his
Queen, and their in-laws, Prince and Princess Svasti, only
saw the gown once, it became forever after "the Siamese
dress."

Mrs. Hoover used imagination in her hair styles, and
changed them to suit the dress she was wearing. With her
"Martha Washington" dress, which looked as though it
belonged at Mt. Vernon, she wore her hair low on the
neck, with a black velvet bow in the Colonial style.

Other gowns required a more sophisticated hairdo. At
first, only Mama took care of Mrs. Hoover's hair, but
when the First Lady decided to try some of the high-style,
New York hairdos, she sent Agnes, another personal maid,
to New York to take a concentrated course in hairdressing.
She still preferred Mama to do her hair for the more official
occasions, and would let Agnes experiment for the more
family-like entertainment.

Somehow the White House became a place of seclusion.
The Hoovers stayed close to the Executive Mansion, even
on week ends, and yet there was a lot of "entertainment
as usual" at the White House. Mrs. Hoover had the President's valet, Boris, put on his white tie outfit, and stand by
the stairway on the ground floor to greet old friends. She
felt that this would "make them feel at home" since they
were used to seeing Boris when Hoover entertained as
Secretary of Commerce. The valet was a Syrian, tall and
handsome, with salt-and-pepper hair, who looked more like
a diplomat than a valet.

In her striving for perfection and uniformity, Mrs.
Hoover decreed that all the butlers should be the same

size in the dining room. So you can imagine everyone's surprise when Mrs. Hoover proceeded to hire the tallest man some of us had ever seen— six-foot-four Alonzo Fields— thus breaking her own rule. But Fields was so good, that he quickly became chief butler, a giant among Lilliputians.

Though Mrs. Hoover was a kind and considerate woman, she was so busy concentrating on making each party the finest, that she didn't see the worried faces of the staff, who were losing their savings while the banks went under, and had to take care of their unemployed relatives on the small salaries of the White House.

Mama was making $80, and I was making $48 a month.

Elegance was the word when Mr. Louis B. Mayer, of motion picture fame, arrived as a guest from Hollywood. The White House certainly was a different place to live in from what it was in the Coolidges' time. Instead of economy, the byword was "the best of everything." Sometimes it seemed that *only* out-of-season food was served, and much of it was imported.

Unlike the Coolidges, the Hoovers practically never saw each other at a meal alone together. The President would have stag breakfasts and lunches to talk politics— frequently out under the magnolia tree in the garden, where special dining furniture was set up— and there were always fourteen to eighteen at dinner.

The only time Mrs. Hoover would see her husband in the morning was after breakfast, when she walked to the office with him. Before breakfast, he would have his own strange form of recreation— a workout with his medicine ball. This was his only relaxation.

Whenever an employee was sick, a basket of food and flowers was sent with Mrs. Hoover's card attached. Once Mama was sick with a cold, and suddenly there appeared Mrs. Hoover's station wagon, and cooked food was carried in, complete with get-well flowers to look at while eating.

Mrs. Hoover did a lot of welfare work for dozens of people, but she never wanted it to be known. She was very strong, and everyone around her would be exhausted, but she would always have the strength to do anything else that was requested of her.

She also did a kind thing that meant more to me than anything else could have. Whenever she gave away hats and shoes to her maids, she would let me have my choice of them too, even though it was obvious that I couldn't wear them. My feet were size three, and the hats were miles too big. But it was the gesture that counted, and it gave me the feeling of belonging.

I think she knew what she was doing. It was in keeping with her action every holiday, when I would be off, but Mama would be on duty. Mrs. Hoover would say to Mama, "Have 'the little girl' come in for Thanksgiving dinner," or whatever the occasion would be.

I didn't dare refuse, and I would cancel an invitation from my girl friends in order to eat with the help at the White House. There seemed no way out, for I now had two "mothers."

I think that Mama never got as close to Mrs. Hoover as she had been to some of the other First Ladies. This was partially because both ladies were independent and maternal women who enjoyed having others lean on *them*. Other First Ladies had leaned on Mama, and she had loved feeling maternal.

Don't think for a minute that we didn't have any dogs to share the White House with the Hoovers. I don't believe the White House has ever been dogless. There was Pat, a large police dog, and Weegie, a small black dog, who were quite at home in the Executive Mansion. They were strictly Mrs. Hoover's dogs, and paid little attention to Mr. Hoover, or he to them.

When Mrs. Hoover would walk to work with Mr.

Hoover, the dogs proceeded at a distance, but on the way back, they would walk with her, and she would accompany them on a walk through the grounds. Under this administration, and unlike the Coolidge one, the dogs lived outside the White House in their own houses; Mrs. Hoover would go out to see them, and help the young man who cared for them.

She loved having her grandchildren— Peggy Ann, Peter, and Joan— at the White House, even though the reason they were there was a sad one. Herbert Hoover, Jr., had developed TB and was in Asheville, North Carolina, recovering from it.

On the first Christmas at the White House, Mrs. Hoover had a Christmas party for fifty, using a horseshoe table, with a smaller table in the center for the children. Mama and Boris, the President's valet, had to stand over the children's table during the entire meal.

Mama came home saying, "I almost had to referee a couple of fights before I took Peter from the dining room." Peter was aged three, and he had reached the "demon" stage.

Mama brought home some of the table decorations— little bells for the ladies, and brass candlesticks for the men. I still have them. The Christmas tree was decorated with real cookies, and I also received a box of those.

After the dinner, the President, whose dignity we admired, led a march all through the parlors. His partner was his little four-year-old granddaughter, and all the ladies who followed had to ring the bells that were at their places, and the men carried the candles in the darkened room. The march continued up to the second floor, where a surprise was waiting— a motion picture.

The servants couldn't get over the fact that the President, who had once been a great outdoor man, roughing it in the wilds, and a mining engineer, who was used to mixing with all classes of people, was completely aloof with the White House staff. He never spoke to them, and never paid the slightest bit of attention to anything they were doing. However, he was *respected* by everyone. They knew how busy he was. At Christmas, when the servants would have a big party in the East Room, the President would simply walk in, say, "Merry Christmas," and leave, and Mrs. Hoover would give us a little talk.

Whereas we referred to the dignified Mr. Hoover as "His Majesty," Mrs. Hoover was to us the "Girl Scout." She was very much engrossed in the Girl Scouts, and made an outstanding contribution to this organization, which helps its prestige to this very day. Knowing how maternal she was, the Girl Scouts must have represented all the little daughters that Mrs. Hoover never had.

Two paintings were made of Mrs. Hoover while she was at the White House. One depicted her in her Girl Scout uniform. Mama used to get it out of the cedar room whenever she was scheduled to pose in it.

We were all sure that this would be the portrait that would be chosen to be hung in the White House. But when she was asked to send the White House a painting, after she had left the mansion, she sent a small head-and-shoulder pose, which does not do her justice. I still feel that wherever it is, the portrait of Mrs. Hoover in the Girl Scout uniform should be hung in the White House as a tribute to the Girl Scouts of America.

The First Lady loved to hold picnics outdoors, and one person for whom she threw a picnic was a boy hero from Towner, Colorado, who had kept fifteen other children alive in a blizzard-stalled school bus. He had taken off all of his clothes except his underwear to give to the other children, and had saved them by keeping them moving— singing and dancing— until they were rescued after a day and a half. The bus driver was not with them because he had gone for help. The little boy, Bryan, had received the invitation from the President to come visit while he was still in a hospital recovering from frostbite and exposure.

Bryan was the best thing that had happened to the White House in a long time, and backstairs, he was greatly applauded because he had treated the President in a thoroughly casual way. Too casual! He failed to rise when the President entered; instead, he held out his hand. He had come with a beat-up old cardboard suitcase, but he left the White House with two additional suitcases to carry the new clothes that the First Lady had given him.

Backstairs, some of the help said that while the President, who was a great friend of youth, was happy to have Bryan at the White House, they wanted to see him invite people who had some real ideas on how to lick the depression.

The President would never make a move without a heavy Secret Service guard. Gone were the happy-go-lucky days Mama remembered, when Harding or Coolidge would try to sneak away from the Secret Service men.

The classic example of evasion was that of Theodore Roosevelt, who would elude his protectors to go to the White House stables, which were located below the Washington Monument. He would get a horse and ride off into the southwest section of the city, where he wouldn't be easily recognized. A gang of little boys would be waiting for him at 13th and C Streets, S.W., and he would give them rides on his horse.

One of these riders, Fred Brill, is still living in Washington, and works at the pharmacy in the Woodner Hotel. Little Fred would have to climb up on his mail box in order to mount behind the President.

To protect the Hoovers, the Secret Service even stayed on the second floor at night while the First Family slept, continuing the practice that Mrs. Harding had initiated—

something that hasn't been done at the White House since.

In September of 1931, when the bank panic spread until it closed over three hundred banks, Mama's money was cut off like everyone else's, and in the backstairs area, the help was looking just as grim as the President.

The next spring, when a thousand men, including subversives and a lot of chiselers, converged upon Washington, calling themselves the "Bonus Army," the President was busy with his advisors. Soon the ranks increased to seventeen thousand, and their leaders issued the statement that they intended to stay until Congress authorized cashing in full the soldiers' bonus certificates. We realized that the whole show was Communist-inspired.

The President was reluctant to go on his campaign tour for reelection, but he went, despite the very real danger that threatened him on every hand. One man had been caught attempting to remove the spikes from the track on which the President's train would pass on his way from St. Paul to Beloit. In November of 1932, Mrs. Hoover, with great confidence, went to California to vote. She returned to Washington crushed.

Mrs. Hoover took her husband's defeat so hard, that she didn't make any effort to begin moving any of their possessions out of the White House until the very last possible moment. When there was little time remaining, an extra force of men had to be called in, in the emergency, from another building, to help us pack for the Hoovers.

Agnes and Mama had set up the third floor for packing Mrs. Hoover's personal belongings. Trunks, suitcases, and boxes were brought out of closets, and two Philippine boys came from the President's summer camp to assist with all the clothes, shoes, pocketbooks, and jewelry.

Mrs. Hoover had, perhaps, the largest wardrobe of any First Lady in the White House up to that time. Each pair of shoes was wrapped and labeled, as were the pocketbooks.

By Thursday of the second week, they had gotten to the evening gowns. I was called in to help. From 9:00 in the morning until 9:00 Friday night, I did nothing but fold evening gowns. We only had until Saturday morning to get ready for the next First Lady— Mrs. Eleanor Roosevelt.

Mama was the one whom Mrs. Hoover trusted to carry out the task of removing all of her personal papers from the filing cabinets and packing them. These were in what Mrs. Hoover called her dressing room. It was Saturday morning, and the White House was a madhouse. Mrs. Coolidge had taken two months to do what the Hoovers had left undone until the last two weeks.

Mr. Sheppard and his crew from the White House carpenter shop took out furniture with about ten extra men, and made bedrooms out of the rooms that Mrs. Hoover had turned into sitting rooms and offices for her three secretaries. Mama blacked out from leaning over the filing cases so much, and had to be carried to the third floor and placed on the housekeeper's bed— the only one that was in any order. As soon as she had recovered sufficiently, she went back to the second floor, and finished her job.

"I just don't have time to be sick, Lillian," she said. "I'll wait till I get home."

Mrs. Hoover stood near the elevator and bade good-by to Mama. It was the first time Mama had ever seen her with tears in her eyes. She said, "Maggie, my husband will live to do great things for his country." Mama was very sorry, years later, when the prediction came true, and the ex-President was called in to help reorganize the government, that Mrs. Hoover had not lived to enjoy that moment. Mama always felt that Mr. Hoover grew a lot in understanding once he had left the White House.

He did show that he had a heart and had noticed Mama in the White House, though he had hardly spoken to her,

when he sent her a dish from his wife's collection after
Mrs. Hoover's death in 1944.

My own farewell with Mrs. Hoover was not so dramatic.
She surprised me by calling me to the Palm Room, where
I had first seen her, and inviting me to take my choice of
two victrolas. One was a portable, and the other was almost
four feet high, made of fine mahogany. I chose the latter
one, and had it remade into a beautiful cabinet to hold
all of my White House souvenirs. Ellis, the head butler,
told me he was glad I had chosen that one, because now he
was the one to get the other victrola, and he had wanted the
small portable for the beach.

The word came that at 10:00 A.M., a new man, named
Irvin McDuffie, valet to President Roosevelt, would be
bringing in the luggage. I was still packing odds and ends,
and the entire hall on the third floor was still cluttered
with trunks and boxes to get the "deck" clear. We called
the third floor "the deck," because it was like the deck of a
ship, even to the nautical-like doors. So many people were
rushing by, carrying beds and giving orders, that I didn't
dare look up; I was afraid that someone would think of
something else for me to do, and give me more orders.

To top it off, a lot of our help were leaving with the
Hoovers, and they were milling around saying good-by—
Annie and Nora, the two Irish maids; Catherine Buckner,
the head cook; the head butler and a houseman, as well as
the housekeeper. Even Miss Hall, the personal secretary,
was rushing to the train, because she was going to California with Mrs. Hoover. Agnes was going along to unpack,
and would be back in a month.

Mama and I were the only maids left to assist Mrs.
Roosevelt and the seven servants she was bringing. At
twelve o'clock, I was helping Mrs. Long put hangers in the
closet. Ike Hoover— who suddenly didn't have to be addressed as "Mr. Usher" any more— came up to inspect the

third floor. We paused for a moment, and heard him remark, "I don't know how in the world it was done, but
everything *is* done."

Mrs. Long and I looked at each other. Her face was
sweaty and smudged, and so was mine. We smiled. We
knew.

While we were making our big "putsch" on the last day,
March 4, 1933, the First Family was having its own
troubles. The President received some threats right up to
the moment of his departure, and arrangements were made
with the railroad for extra guards to accompany the
Hoovers to New York.

Mrs. Hoover was very concerned about the two canaries,
which she was going to carry with her by hand on the
train. As I raced against time, in order to get the mansion
ready for the new First Lady, Frank Wilkinson came running with two bird cages, one in each hand.

"Hurry, hurry," he said. "Mrs. Hoover is leaving, and
she wants two covers made for these right away."

Bird cage covers!

I looked up at Frank from where I was working on my
hands and knees, and suddenly I realized that for the first
time I could refuse to do something.

"Put a couple of towels around them," I said. "I don't
have time."

He gasped. But he went and got the towels.

". . . THERE CAN BE ONLY
ONE MRS. R"

You would have to have been a part of the White House under the Hoovers to appreciate the difference under the Roosevelts. In the pantry, you had to whisper so that the Hoovers wouldn't hear you as they ate; and Mrs. Hoover's hand signals told you when to move and when not to move, when to speak and when not to speak.

Under the Roosevelts, doors stood open, and happy voices rang out, and there was no more popping into closets, and no more hiding when the President or the First Lady took the elevator. You were invited to "come in and ride along." We walked freely down the halls, and kept running into members of the big, sprawling Roosevelt family.

Mama used to say that success was relative, and that a man didn't know how many relatives he had until he became President. Well, that certainly applied to the Roosevelts— everyone who had any kinship with him, or with his wife, Eleanor, made his or her Washington headquarters at the White House. It was family in and family out all the time.

We heard funny, crazy little things that made us laugh. I remember one version of a birthday song that I heard some grandchild— was it Sistie?— singing:

> "Happy birthday to you
> You belong in the zoo . . ."

In a way, we felt we were a part of the family as we overheard family affairs being discussed freely and openly. It might have been called eavesdropping, except that it would have been impossible *not* to overhear the Roosevelts. As Mrs. Roosevelt told a bunch of movie stars, whom she was showing around the White House, "You will find us a noisy family."

They were also a family that engaged in "happy talk." The President's "happy talk" was contagious. Backstairs and frontstairs, and all through the nation, emotions suddenly ran rampant. "Happy Days Are Here Again" blared from the radios, and even old-timers at the White House, who had seen a lot of broken campaign promises in their day, believed it! The banks closed, and the banks reopened, and everyone had a feeling we were on our way.

FDR was the perfect picture of what a President should *look* like, but he was no world-beater, as the nation would soon discover. Some people seemed to think so, and were ready to clobber anyone who didn't agree. The President was human, and no one knew that better than the servants at the White House, who had to maintain a certain serenity in the midst of chaos.

Yes, we knew that the father image, the hero, the "perfect man" was besieged by his own set of problems. Now and then, he was torn between the two women in his life, his mother and his wife. Sometimes, he would revolt against his wheel chair, and the fates that had put him there; then he would complain and become irritable. At such times, there was only one thing to do— give him a rubdown to soothe his weary, wasted muscles and relax his mind.

No, he was no god, and he had his special phobia. Strangely enough, it wasn't a fear of being assassinated while in office, even though an attempt had been made upon his life two months before his inauguration, when another man, Mayor Anton Cermak, had been killed instead. That wasn't what bothered him. And though he kept a gun under his pillow, it wasn't guns that bothered him, or bombs from the sky or in the mail, or any of the usual things, like aeroplane accidents or drowning.

No, his special fear was fire. It always had been. He was obsessed with the fear of being trapped by fire and unable to escape.

For a man with that fear, he lived in the worst possible house, because every time the Interior Department men came to inspect this choice bit of Government property, they would shake their heads and call it a firetrap.

The Secret Service installed special chutes to get him out of his window and down to the ground in record time, and they held regular drills for handling the President in such an emergency.

I also knew of several underground escape routes that had been built under the White House, but I would never reveal these for all the world. When the new bomb shelters were built at the time of the renovation, the escape hatches were improved too. I think the public will feel better to know that their President cannot be trapped in the White House.

In the backstairs sections we used to talk about the President's fear of fire, and speculate on its origin. Some said it went back to childhood and firecrackers, and some said it came from having an over-protective mother— we heard that once she had even climbed a ladder outside his window to read to him when he had scarlet fever and she couldn't go into his room.

Everyone was struck by another interesting event— he had fought a brush fire at Campobello just before he came down with polio. Was there any connection, we wondered? And at Harvard, a dormitory fire disturbed him so greatly, that he wrote an article in *The Harvard Crimson* calling for better fire prevention and protection.

The White House help knew that the Roosevelts would be a very different kind of First Family from the moment they set foot in their new home. It was a day full of surprises. The President escorted his mother, instead of his wife, to a buffet inaugural luncheon. His wife, the First Lady, *started helping the butlers serve the guests.*

There were guests for luncheon, and there were guests for a tea. The guests stayed for both instead of one or the other. The First Lady didn't try to bring any discipline into the proceedings. The butlers couldn't believe their eyes or their ears— the President was not served first, but had to take his turn like everyone else. What was going on?

Then there was the matter of the Inaugural Ball. The Hoovers had been different. They had not attended it at all, but had let the Vice-President steal the show. FDR didn't attend either. *But his wife did.* She simply left her husband, who was working away at the White House, and went off to the Ball with all the young members of her family.

But that was only the beginning.

Mrs. Hoover would not set foot in the kitchens, but Mrs. Roosevelt brought the kitchen into the dining room. As soon as she was settled, she would immediately call for a chafing dish, and calmly cook Sunday supper at the table herself— usually scrambled eggs and sausages.

The Wilkinson "moving men" were popeyed when Mrs. "R" pitched right in and helped them move furniture, and unpack and carry books to the bookcases. They claimed that she could carry more books at one time than any one of them could.

Mrs. Roosevelt was definitely the fastest-walking First Lady the White House had ever seen. The staff couldn't keep up with her. She would answer your question if you could catch her. She would go through the usher's office talking so fast that no one knew what she was saying over her shoulder.

Mrs. "R" will probably learn here for the first time the effect she had on one employee. Harold Thompson was in training to be an usher, but he couldn't understand Mrs. "R" when she was talking and walking, so he gave up and joined the engineering department, where he became head engineer of the White House.

But getting back to the kitchens. Mrs. "R" paid practically no attention to decorating the rest of the White House, but what she did do was to redesign the White House kitchens, making them more comfortable to work in, and equipping them with electric stoves and dishwashers. All the changes that Mrs. Roosevelt made were for the comfort of other people— for example, she assigned a nice dining room for the help, and a room to lie down in if you were ill.

There was only one other room in which she took a special interest— again, as if in defiance of Mrs. Hoover— and that was the West Sitting Room, which Mrs. "H" had made into a Palm Room. Mrs. "R" made the same space into a showcase for Val-Kill furniture.

This was the factory that Mrs. Roosevelt had helped finance so that farmers and other workmen who lived in the area around Hyde Park would have work. Proudly Mrs. "R" would bring in reporters, such as Bess Furman of the New York *Times,* to show them the good furniture that the factory made.

It is interesting, and typical of Mrs. Roosevelt, that today she lives in the Val-Kill factory, which has been converted into a home, rather than in the family mansion. The Hyde Park home is a museum, open to the public, which flocks in by the thousands each year to see how FDR lived.

Mrs. "R" did everything she could think of for the comfort and happiness of all those who shared her White House home. The President loved ship models and pictures of ships, and she made sure that his study walls were lined with his ship collection, with all pictures numbered so that they would be in exactly the order he wanted.

Col. Louis Howe, who was the most intimate friend of the family, and who had moved into the White House to live, wanted to sleep in the Lincoln bed, and so Mrs. Roosevelt had it moved into his room. The youngest son, John, who was also the tallest in the family— six-feet-four — needed a giant bed, so she had one made for him, rather than hurt Colonel Howe's feelings by having the giant Lincoln bed taken away from him.

For herself, she wanted nothing. She once directed that a bed be put in the sewing room, and I wondered whom it was for. Then I found out. It was for *herself*. She was going to sleep in there and let the overflow of guests and relatives take her room and sitting room. She was going to use the wardrobe outside her maid's door, down the hall, and would have to walk there to check herself in the mirror, which was on the outside of the wardrobe.

I was really touched when I heard of this act of kindness, and I joined the help who were painting and fixing up my sewing room, to make it halfway decent for the First Lady when she would move into it the next day. I looked over the situation, and seeing that her shoes would be kept on the shelves of a little open bookcase, I quickly made a little curtain for it, which, in turn, touched her heart.

She was so grateful for any little thing we would do for

her, that all of us tried to think of something we could do to please her, protect her, or shield her from any trouble or embarrassment. Of course, this was hard to do, because her manner of living provided a perfect opening to all the humorists and cartoonists, who delighted in burlesquing "Eleanor on the go."

Some of the criticism wasn't too funny either, and everyone thought Mrs. "R" was thick-skinned. But she wasn't, and she wanted to know what people were saying. For this reason, she had one of her secretaries stationed in the crowd whenever she gave a speech or made an appearance, and the girl would take down the "critical" things people were saying.

Nor did people realize that most of the time, she was traveling at the suggestion of the President. He needed someone to give him a first-hand report, and he could trust her to tell him the unvarnished truth.

Mrs. "R" never let anything interfere with her work. She would go directly to her desk as soon as she had finished breakfast. In fact, the only time Mama was scolded by her was in the very beginning, before Mama knew her work habits, and didn't have Mrs. "R"'s desk ready for her. Mrs. Roosevelt told Mama very severely, "Don't ever let it happen again, Maggie. Always have my desk dusted first."

On days when Mrs. "R" went horseback riding at six, breakfasted at seven, and worked immediately, without a pause, Mama would say that she put in as much work by noontime as other people did by the end of the day. And she was still fresh as a daisy.

She used to come back from a trip and dictate a report to the President, just like an employee. Sometimes, when he was surprised at something in her report, he'd call her, just as if she were a paid worker, and ask for an explanation. She took herself very seriously, and so did the President. He made no allowances for the fact that she was his wife. We used to say that she was one of the lowest-paid Presidential advisors— "not even room and board"— because she was seldom home.

Everyone thought the First Lady was getting rich on her "My Day" column. We longed to tell them that almost every cent of her earnings went to charities. We heard guests say, "She doesn't need the money, and look at her writing a daily column."

It was certainly true that she didn't need the money. She had inherited money. We overheard many stories about Eleanor Roosevelt's early years, when she had been raised by a couple of aunts, because her mother had died when she was eight. She seldom saw her father, but she'd been smothered by so much good care, that a personal maid was always in attendance, traveling with her wherever she went.

No, she didn't need the money, and few people realized how often she would use her own instead of going to her husband. It was just easier.

In fact, few people realized that a certain Dutch thrift was the particular idiosyncrasy of the President. Those who worshipped the President thought that Mrs. Roosevelt was lucky because she was married to the "perfect" husband. That wasn't exactly so. The First Lady had to cope with a husband who considered his mother before he considered her, and who was strangely economy-minded when it came to running the White House.

Every once in a while, he would go on an economy binge, and check up on how the White House was being run. We thought we were living back in Coolidge's day when we found out that he too was afraid that too much food was being wasted. He used to carve the turkeys and other fowl himself, and prided himself on his ability to get every scrap of meat off the bone. Mrs. "R" would have someone else carve the second turkey on the excuse that the meat would get cold if everyone waited for the President to serve. Actually, it took so long because he insisted on not wasting a single morsel.

Then there was the famous case— among ourselves, that is— of the missing lobster. It was in the refrigerator, and the President was going to have it for a snack. But when it came time for the snack, the lobster was missing. The staff was practically frisked, but the lobster was still missing. Years later, after the President had died, and we were packing to get Mrs. Roosevelt moved out of the White House, the missing lobster was found— or what was left of it— behind some mattresses in the attic. The case remains unsolved.

One of the President's pet economies was his clothing. He simply would not let anything go, and his pajamas and underwear would get threadbare. Mrs. Roosevelt gave the order that we were to use our own judgment, and throw out things so that he couldn't use them any more.

When, in his third term, the President gained too much weight and was put on a diet, this penchant of his for home economy was responsible for those first reports that he wasn't looking too well. No wonder he wasn't— his neck size had shrunk, but he refused to throw out "good" shirts and order others. I longed to point this out to him when I saw newspaper pictures in which his neck looked so scrawny and shrunken in the large collars, but I was only the maid, and so I merely expressed my opinion to his valet.

Another of the President's economies was aimed where it hurt the help the most— right in the pocketbook. The White House servants have always been paid on a very low scale, and many have been forced to work outside the White House in their spare time to make ends meet. But the President decided to cut our meager salaries. He didn't have to do it, but his excuse was that salaries elsewhere in Government were being cut, and, therefore, ours should also be. So, *whang*— off went twenty-five per cent of our salaries!

When FDR went off on his economy kicks, he would send notes to Mrs. Roosevelt, telling her about the bills and why he couldn't afford them. In one such note, which made the rounds backstairs, he told her what amount he could afford to pay each month, and informed her that she would have to run the White House on that budget. But we never knew whether she did or not.

The President was forever firing notes about the food too. Once he complained that he'd had chicken six times in a week, and within a month, he was writing another note to "E. R.," complaining that he was not *getting* any chicken, but sweetbreads instead, with the result that he was becoming very "unsweet." With typical Roosevelt humor, he ended by saying that as a result, he had bitten two foreign dignitaries.

Miss LeHand, FDR's private secretary, was the one best able to handle the President on any and all matters, including money. Mrs. Roosevelt would give the information to "Missy," as she was called, if she were afraid the President would balk at paying something. Once she sent a note to Missy that told of money needed for a particularly big bill, and added, "I know FDR will have a fit!"

FDR found the note on Missy's desk and wrote on it, "Pay it. Have had the fit. FDR."

People ask me about the relationship of the President with the woman who had been his secretary ever since he had run unsuccessfully for Vice-President as running mate to Cox against Warren Harding in 1920. Now that it is all over, and Missy and the President are both gone, I can say that Missy was more than a secretary— she was the warm-hearted listener, the boon companion and, yes, a sort of mother substitute for the President.

She was the one who worried about drafts and got ex-

cited if he appeared to be catching cold— FDR was prone
to colds that kept hanging on and on. She was the one who
shared his private jokes; the one who first learned of his
ideas, and the one who applauded them without reservation.

She was always there. Until her health broke, she kept
his hours, eating dinner with him in his office, when the
First Lady was not around, or when he was working on a
speech, which was often during the era of the fireside chats.
She even went swimming with him to keep him company,
though it was common knowledge that she hated the water.

As we saw it backstairs at the White House, Missy gave
him the companionship, the rapt attention, the ego-build-
ing boost that men sometimes find in their wives. Mrs.
"R" was not the kind of woman who would give blind
praise or blanket approval. For that kind of warm support
and recognition, no matter what he did, the President
turned to Missy. There was definitely no question of anything improper. It was a spiritual attachment, although
Missy built her whole life around him and never married.

When her health broke, Mama was called from retirement back to the White House, to sit in Missy's room and
spend long, lonely nights with her, because she could not
sleep, and needed someone to talk to. Mama supervised
her dinner, and talked with her any time she woke up during the restless night. Even in her sickbed, the force of
habit was so great, that Missy's sole concern was the welfare
of the President. All the while, three nurses were required
round the clock to take care of her.

Before her breakdown, Missy's dedication received family recognition. She *did* live in the White House. She *did*
get to attend many formal White House functions, and she
even acted as hostess when Mrs. "R" was absent, and
poured at teas.

Mrs. "R" had turned over a suite of rooms to Missy on

the third floor. She had her own sitting room, bedroom, and bath. She also had breakfast in bed, because her hours would run late into the evening. Backstairs, we used to wonder if Mrs. "R" wasn't a little jealous of Miss LeHand, but she never seemed to be, and they were the best of friends. When Miss LeHand served as hostess in Mrs. Roosevelt's absence, the First Lady seemed grateful to have a "substitute First Lady." At official parties, Miss Le-Hand was frequently a guest.

Mama grew sadder as she saw the stout heart of Miss LeHand grow weaker. She finally had to go to a hospital, and after that to Warm Springs, Georgia. She came back to the White House, but she never regained her health. She went back to Boston to her family, and a year later, she died. Mama felt that she might have been better off at the White House, where she would have been near her true adopted family, the President and Mrs. "R."

Mama said that Missy knew that she was dying. When Missy died, Mama cried just as if she were one of her own family. "I should have been there to take care of her," she would say.

But by then, Mama's health was very bad too— high blood pressure and hardening of the arteries. It had first been diagnosed in the Coolidge administration, and a doctor had ordered her to eat "brown bread." It used to be a White House joke that only one loaf of brown bread would be ordered, to be shared by two people—President Coolidge and "that Maggie gal."

After she had retired, I used to tell Mama, "You'd better start taking care of yourself and quit worrying about the White House."

It was a pathetic twist of fate that Mama had become the one who waited for me to come home and tell her the White House stories just as I, when a little girl, had sat at home, waiting for her to come and tell me the latest adventures of Charlie Taft and the Wilson girls.

I would tell her how the fabulous Mrs. "R" was doing with another "adopted" member of the family, Diana Hopkins, who was known as "Washington's youngest hostess." When Hopkins' wife died, Diana, at the age of seven, took her place at the table. She had come to the White House so wistful and sad, that Mrs. "R" and the staff spent a lot of time making her feel at home. And I explained to Mama that Diana had become so much at home, that she rebelled against telling us where she was going; she would try to sneak out to visit a girl friend at one of the embassies, and, just in case she were asked to spend the night, she would take along her pajamas and a change of clothes in a laundry basket.

I brought home a much more scandalous story one night, when Molotov was visiting the White House.

Poor Fields, the butler, had had a terrible shock to his nervous system. Molotov had sent him to fetch his valet, and so he knocked on the door. The valet turned out to be a woman! And not only a woman— but a naked woman, who wasn't at all ashamed to yell, "Come in," when she hadn't a stitch on.

However, it wasn't so funny when the houseman discovered a neat little gun in Molotov's suitcase. What the Secret Service did about it, I don't know.

Mama was quite amused by one hilarious misunderstanding. When Mrs. Roosevelt called for a "bulb," Sarver ran around the room with a flit gun, looking for a "bug."

Then there were all the dogs, and we would marvel over the intelligence of Fala, who had been a gift from FDR's cousin, Margaret Suckley, and I would tell Mama about our difficulties in getting around in the White House though the snowstorm of dogs. Even Buzzie and Sistie had their Jack and Jill— the latter had the loudest toenails of any dog ever to live in the White House.

One of the more monstrous dogs, which had been locked in a bathroom because it had been barking, made an absolute shambles of the place. And Mrs. "R" had been very understanding about it all.

And I told Mama that Johnny Boettiger was in the habit of feeding Jello to his dog, Ensign, a retriever, under the table, because he didn't like the stuff and the dog did. Johnny had told me plaintively that his nurse, Mrs. Williams, "thinks more of Ensign than she does of me."

I can remember a day when I too almost thought more of Ensign than I did of Johnny. He had taken my long measuring pole, which I used for making draperies and curtains, and had broken it while playing with it on the grand staircase. But how could I stay mad? He had taken matters into his own hands, and tried to rectify them by going to the carpenters and asking them to make another one. When I called the carpentry shop to tell them that my pole had disappeared, and to ask them to make me another, the carpenter laughed and said, "Lillian, it's already been taken care of."

Johnny also tried to take care of his own need "to get out." He got into a car with a Secret Service chauffeur, and announced that his grandmother was sending him on an errand. Well, with Mrs. Roosevelt anything was possible, so off they went. But when Johnny's directions got vaguer and vaguer, the Secret Service man knew he'd been had. He turned him right around and brought him back.

We talked a lot about the President and the First Lady, trying to figure out how they had happened to marry, since he had been so handsome, so much the "big man on campus," and she had been so shy as a girl.

We had our own theory as to why FDR had married Eleanor— whose name had been Roosevelt too before her marriage. She was the exact opposite of his mother. We figured he had spotted his sixth cousin as the woman least likely to try to dominate him, as his mother, Sara Delano Roosevelt, did; she qualified as being most likely to allow him room to breathe, and least likely to smother him with attention.

Much as he loved his mother, the President did admit she was a bit bossy, and once, before we got into the war, she was worried about an aunt who was in Europe. It was the talk of the White House that she had wanted her son to send a warship over to pick up the aunt.

It was also true that she not only acted very much at home in the White House, but she also objected to the other guests she was falling over, and felt that there was too much of a hotel atmosphere. We always did whatever she commanded, of course, as long as it didn't run counter to any orders we'd received from the President or the First Lady.

We admired Mrs. "R" for being able to cope with a mother-in-law who didn't mind acting more like a First Lady than the First Lady did herself. But most of all, perhaps, we admired her for the way she lent a helping hand to everyone within her reach. I would bring home new stories of Mrs. "R" 's amazing generosity; we would discuss it and just shake our heads, unable to believe it.

Once, I was standing near the door when she came in from a walk in the park with her secretary, Malvina Thompson, who was called "Tommy" by everyone. They had picked up and brought back a destitute man in the park and were as concerned about him as a couple of Girl Scouts. I could see the guards stiffen and groan, because "Eleanor had done it again." The order was given that he be taken back to Mrs. Nesbitt, the housekeeper, to be fed and helped.

Secret Service men and White House guards were always

busy trying to keep track of complete strangers who had not been cleared for admittance to the White House. They might have been assassins, posing as bums, in order to get in. One such man, I remember, was invited to join the Roosevelts at dinner, and the valets and housemen had a terrible time getting his clothes in some kind of condition for the occasion. They finally got him scrubbed and dressed— his clothes were quickly spot-cleaned, in the nick of time— and off he went to the dining room.

On another occasion, the Secret Service men were almost pleased, because it seemed that one of these impromptu guests had made off with some silver. They thought it would discourage Mrs. "R." But it didn't.

One of the favorite stories around the White House concerns a time in New York when her husband was Governor, and Mrs. Roosevelt gave her card to a down-and-outer. She told him that if she could be of any help, he should call on her. Acting on her promise, the man came to call, and a policeman stopped him. The poor man showed him the card. The policeman snatched it away, and sharply sent the man on his way, ordering him not to show his face again. Just then, Mrs. Roosevelt drove up, and the policeman told her about chasing away a young man who wanted to see her, and added "somewhere he got hold of this."

Mrs. Roosevelt gave the policeman a scolding, told him never to turn anyone away, and demanded to know which way the young man had gone. Then she hurried down the street to find him.

I used to keep Mama informed concerning the latest goings on in the Roosevelt family, and I would tell her all about the new thing Mrs. "R" was knitting and "botching up" for some relative. We used to chuckle over Mrs. Roosevelt's habit of knitting and dropping stitches whenever she became distracted by something. Then when I would block the piece and get it ready for presentation, I would try to make it look as good as possible. Mama and I would laugh and say that we wished we had a penny for every stitch Mrs. "R" dropped. But we also wished we had had a sample of her work as a souvenir.

Mrs. "R" was in her element among her riotous family of sons, grandchildren, and daughters-in-law, and she seemed to love her daughters-in-law as much as her sons. Perhaps this was to make up for the fact that she had never been able to make the grade completely with her own mother-in-law.

As a matter of fact, Mama and I marvelled and applauded Mrs. "R," because she continued to be good friends with her daughters-in-law after they had been divorced from her sons, though her sons may have wanted their mother to be a little more on their side. Her attitude seemed to be that though they were no longer *in-laws,* they still weren't *outlaws.*

The daughters-in-law adored her. The only thing that bothered them when they were in the White House was their loss of identity so that they became "Mrs. James," "Mrs. Elliott," "Mrs. John," and "Mrs. Franklin." They hadn't married a Roosevelt to become a "Mrs. Franklin" or a "Mrs. James."

Some of them would become doubly irritated when the staff would slip, and the name would come out *"Miss* James" or *"Miss* Elliott" or *"Miss* John." They had not married a Roosevelt to become a "Miss James" either. One of the nursemaids who had come with one of the daughters-in-law finally complained to me about it. She insisted upon calling her mistress "Mrs. Roosevelt."

"That's her name, isn't it?" she said to me belligerently.

"Not at the White House it isn't," I told her just as tartly. "In this house, there is only *one* Mrs. Roosevelt."

WITH MRS. "R" IN PEACE
AND WAR

FDR had his hundred days of "honeymoon with the Congress," in which everything he demanded was rubber-stamped. But his honeymoon there on Capitol Hill couldn't last, and our honeymoon at the White House couldn't last either.

Sure enough, the rumors were starting to seep through and circulate backstairs that there wasn't enough dignity around the White House, and that it was becoming a "Little Hollywood."

"Hollywood people are not dignified enough for the White House," said someone. "All those movie stars around the White House, and one of them even in the family."

The old-timers backstairs laughed and laughed about that. It reminded them of Coolidge's time, when a bunch of bathing beauties came to the White House, and were photographed there in their bathing suits. They told us with relish how those femmes of the roaring twenties had sat posing in the White House with high heels, stockings rolled below the knees, jewelry, *and* scanty bathing suits.

Nothing so undignified had taken place since. It had been a riot— but in tune with the times.

It was also in tune with the times when Elliott Roosevelt married a movie star. All the maids were wild about Faye Emerson, who was lavish with her tips and her praise. She smiled at us, one and all, and never tried to play the movie queen around the White House.

Whenever Mrs. "R" saw a play, she would bring the whole cast in for supper. One season, she had a series of luncheons, when an artist would sing in the East Room afterward, at 4:00 P.M. These Four O'clock Musicales were quite a success.

A screen was placed outside the East Room door, beside the window, and I was assigned to help the performer change costumes— some of them fairly scanty. I thought we were shielded from everyone until one day, when a singer was making a quick change to do the number "Darktown Strutters Ball," I glanced out the window, as I helped ease the tight dress over her head, and saw the policeman on duty at the front door looking in at us, and smiling with relish. In a second, the entertainer was back in the room, singing and dancing, and only the policeman and I ever knew that he had enjoyed a strip-tease view of the White House entertainment.

It was true that every actor or actress available was invited. We sometimes wondered whether Mrs. "R" would have liked to have been an actress— did she have a secret, hidden desire to perform?

The stars were more than happy to come to the March of Dimes celebrations, which were held for the victims of polio on the President's birthdays. They would have lunch at the White House with the President, Mrs. "R," and as many of the young Roosevelts as could come. All the White House secretaries would come too, and there would be between forty and forty-five at the table.

Marsha Hunt, Mitzi Green, Jean Harlow, and Robert Taylor were the first to come. Mrs. "R" took them on a tour of the mansion. When they got to the third floor, she opened the linen closets, and showed them how things were kept at the White House. Mama was still in charge, and everything was in the right place. I was taking a peek at Robert Taylor when Mr. Pettijohn, who acted as manager for the visiting stars, spotted me and called out, "Have you ever met Robert Taylor?"

I said, "No."

Then he yelled out, "Come here, Robert."

I began to shake in the knees, but there was nothing to do but take a few steps out into the hall to meet him. However, in a moment I was not alone. Other maids materialized out of thin air. Robert Taylor was so friendly, that I found myself telling him, "There is a great resemblance between you and Franklin, Jr." Robert Taylor acted quite flattered.

When Tyrone Power and Annabella came to the White House, I was sick in bed with a cold, and the snow was heavy on the ground. I wanted to go to work anyway, but my mother insisted I stay home. That day, I wasn't half as sick from the cold as I was from not having seen Tyrone Power.

I didn't miss any more. George Raft, Gene Kelly, William Bendix, Dorothy Lamour, Myrna Loy, Diana Durbin (she almost fell down the steps), Judy Canova, and Carol Bruce are just a few of the many who came. Red Skelton saw a suitcase sitting in the hall and said, "Eleanor is off again." There was a big laugh from everyone. People were always telling jokes about her.

Few knew that we had our own star at the White House, and backstairs at that; she was Lizzie McDuffie, a maid who was married to FDR's valet. The President used to love to hear her recite, and once she got a leave of absence to try out for the role given to Hattie McDaniel in *Gone With the Wind*. It seemed so likely that Lizzie would be chosen for the part, that Winchell broke the news in his column.

She also went campaigning for the President, and she was one of the very few persons invited by Harry Hopkins to attend his wedding to Louise Macy in the White House. He told her not to dare come in her uniform, but she was so busy that she put on a silk coat over her work outfit, and a fancy hat on her head, and marched into the room with the rest of the guests.

One of our biggest troubles around the White House was getting rid of guests. Mrs. "R" 's softheartedness sometimes led to tense moments, when we wondered if she could manage to get rid of one guest before another arrived to take his or her room. At first, we would hold our breath, and sigh with relief as one guest left an hour or so before another arrived to take his place. But then it got worse, and guests would actually be waiting in the hall while previous guests were still packing. I remember Mrs. "R" serving coffee to some while they waited.

The classic case, however, was when Alexander Woollcott came to dinner, and stayed and stayed and stayed. His room was needed for Prince Bernhard of the Netherlands. The tension was mounting, because the day of the Prince's arrival dawned, and Woollcott was still in his room. Finally, that morning, Mrs. Roosevelt herself went to Woollcott's room and knocked and knocked. He took a long time coming to the door, but when he did, Mrs. Roosevelt told him that she did hope he would come again soon, and that she wanted to say good-by because the Prince was arriving soon. Woollcott did leave and *did* come back again soon for another long stay.

We had a lot of fun behind the scenes when another visitor wouldn't stop talking. Gertrude Stein came to visit Mrs. Roosevelt, but instead of listening and answering questions, she just rambled on like one of her poems. We found out later that her "Rose is a rose, is a rose, is a rose" type of conversation was caused by her difficulty in hearing. She hadn't heard a word Mrs. Roosevelt had said.

One of the guests who impressed us most at the White House was Amelia Earhart (Mrs. Putnam), who visited several times as an overnight guest. Mama waited on her. On her last visit, before she disappeared mysteriously on her flight over the Pacific, the aviatrix combed her hair and clipped off an unruly curl, tossing it on the dresser. When she had left the room, Mama put it in a small envelope and saved it (I still have that curl). When the news came that Miss Earhart could not be found by any of the search planes, Mama reported that Mrs. "R" was very upset.

Mrs. Roosevelt had a wonderful gift of kindness in little things. She knew, for example, that we who worked at the White House would want to see the King and Queen of England— George VI and Elizabeth— when they visited in 1939. She sent word that we were all to assemble on the South Lawn, so that we could see and be seen, as they left to tour the city with the President and Mrs. Roosevelt.

I rushed out to the South Lawn at 2:30, and it was so hot that I thought surely I would faint, but my mind said this was not the place nor the time to do it. And somehow I stood and watched as the President and the King started off in one car, and Mrs. Roosevelt and the Queen followed in the next car, moving very slowly; they bowed to all of us. It was sort of a thrill, I must admit. I confess that, like very many Americans, I protest that royalty means nothing to me, but I get a feeling inside when I see them.

The First Family is the nearest thing we have to royalty in this country. They are supposed to embody all the dignity and prestige of our land. I think that one thing that people objected to in Mrs. Roosevelt was her insistence upon acting too independently for the wife of a President.

There was one time when she was a real queen to us, and that was at her first meeting with Queen Elizabeth. Mrs. Roosevelt and Queen Elizabeth had both been presented with thin woolen material by the International Wool Growers of Australia, South America, New Zealand, and the United States. Both ladies were to wear new dresses made of the material at their first formal meeting, which was to signify international "togetherness." It would help the wool industry— especially the British— and it would show that the two First Ladies shared mutual interests in the products of their countries.

Mrs. Roosevelt wore her woolen dress, because she had committed herself to do so, and good sport that she was, she would wear it or die. The sun was blistering. The Queen did *not* wear her woolen dress.

Everyone asks me what it is like at the White House when royalty is there. I must say that sometimes royalty is more gracious than their entourage.

We had a terrible time with the servants of the King and Queen. On the third floor of the White House, which had been turned over to them, nothing satisfied them. A long table had been placed in the third-floor hall for the meals of the Royal servants. They were constantly eating and drinking. While doing so, they complained about the food. Poor Mrs. Nesbitt was almost out of her mind. The Royal servants demanded menus— they wanted a choice of foods, as in a hotel. They told us that in the Palace, they had their own set of servants to serve *them,* because *they* ministered to the needs of the Royal Family.

The Queen's maid was a nervous character, who was always rushing by. I could hardly get a good look at her face, because she was always in motion. I can see her now, fairly flying through the hall, with a second maid carrying the Queen's ball gown, running behind her. The dress had just been pressed, and the poor second maid was frantically trying to keep it from touching anything, especially the floor. She was yelling, "Come, come, you mustn't keep the Queen waiting! Come, what is holding you?"

I'll take our American way. I must add, however, that when the Queen's daughter, Elizabeth II, came to visit, in both the Truman and Eisenhower administrations, things were different. But I mustn't get ahead of the story.

When the King and Queen were invited to go to Hyde Park, the fun really began. Mrs. Roosevelt's mother-in-law was uncooperative, because her daughter-in-law was bringing colored servants to take care of Her Majesty. Encouraged by her supercilious attitude, her own English butler, to avoid being present, started his vacation just before the White House party arrived.

Poor Mrs. "R" had to pitch in and really organize things with her own butlers, and, as happens at such times when someone is standing by with a disapproving air, everything went wrong. In the same evening, first the serving table collapsed in the middle of the dinner and the dishes clattered to the floor.

Then later, when all the guests had gone to the library, a butler, carrying a tray of decanters, glasses, and bowls of ice, missed a step and landed right on the library floor. Mrs. James Roosevelt was really embarrassed, but we were also pretty sure she would use this as further proof that her daughter-in-law should have done as she had advised and had white help.

Everybody asks me about the picnic that the Roosevelts gave for Their Majesties— "Did they really serve hot dogs to the Queen?" they ask. "What a shame!"

Americans act shocked about serving hot dogs to royalty. Certainly it's true, we did serve hot dogs to the King and Queen, but we also served ham and a million other things at the picnic. And the servants felt that it was nice of the First Family to introduce the uninitiated English to one of America's favorite foods. Smoked turkey was served, which the King and Queen had never tasted before; also baked beans, salads, and, to top it off, strawberry shortcake.

At the special request of Mrs. Roosevelt, Mama had stayed long enough to see the White House through the visit of the King and Queen— she was the head maid and responsible for having everything shipshape for them— but right after their visit, she retired.

Mama deserved a rest. She had worked very hard through all the years, and had even helped take care of Colonel Howe when he was so ill. Toward the end, he would allow no one but his secretary and Mama in his room, and between them, they even had to make his bed.

Once, a tremendous wardrobe that stood in his room broke loose from its moorings in the wall, when Mama was putting something away in it, and she had to hold it up by main force, to keep it from crushing her until help could come. This didn't improve her health either.

When she left, Mrs. Roosevelt gave her a gold watch, inscribed "To Maggie Rogers, in recognition of thirty years' faithful service in the White House, from the President and Mrs. Roosevelt— 1939."

The whole staff had a dinner for Mama— turkey, with all the trimmings, and beautiful flowers. John Mays, who had worked with Mama thirty years, and always called her "Margaret," shed the most tears. I knew I would miss her as my boss as much as the others would, but she had taught me so much and guided me for so many years, that I wasn't afraid to be on my own in the White House.

Mrs. Nesbitt asked me what my mother would like as a gift, and I suggested a desk set, because a publisher wanted her to write her memoirs. Not only did she get a desk set, but a beautiful silver tray and pitcher as well.

Mrs. Roosevelt knew that the publisher wanted Mama to write a book, because he had been a guest at the White

House when he first met Mama, and he had talked to the First Lady about it. When Mama left, Mrs. Roosevelt said, "Maggie, you must write that book."

Mama was thrilled that the First Lady had said this, and that was the thought she brought home with her— that she would write the book. But she never did. She wrote down her notes, and she talked to me about all the things she was going to do, but her health gave out, and she didn't accomplish them. When she died, just after the Eisenhowers arrived in 1953, one of her deathbed requests was that I write the book as soon as I had left the White House, and not let it drift by as she had done.

I'll never forget how Mrs. Roosevelt gave me the job of taking care of the checking stand used by the tourists, who streamed through the White House for four hours a day. On January 2, 1934, she called me in, and asked me to take over this chore. From 10:00 A.M. to 2:00 P.M. every day, I had to check all cameras, brief cases, and suspicious-looking packages. It was a strange new world of danger and excitement for me, working with the White House police and Secret Service agents.

And I got acquainted with the public. Of all the people I dealt with, I think I had the most trouble with a midget, who simply refused to hand over his camera, and was most belligerent about it.

All kinds of things happened, some funny and some not so funny. There was the little lady who kept coming and trimming off the lace from the curtains, and finally, in my other capacity as seamstress, I put plain curtains in that particular window. Another woman kept asking for a souvenir, saying that the White House was hers as much as anyone else's. At last, a policeman gave her a little sliver of wood and said, with a laugh, "All right, here's your share."

In 1939, we did a landslide tourist business at the White House. As early as April, sightseers began pouring into the

Executive Mansion at a rate nearly double that of the previous year. Over a million visitors passed through the portals in April, May, June, and July. In June alone there were 335,724 callers.

I looked at people, and people looked at me. I answered questions, and checked cameras, wet umbrellas, and packages. Some people brought cameras, and didn't know how to put the films in. I had to do it. Some would pull out a road map and ask, "Can you show me how to get to Baltimore?" Others had city maps and asked for help.

I remember a professional football team sightseeing the day after one of the elections. One of the young men asked me, "Do you ever see the President?" My answer was, "Yes, of course I see him, and I shook his hand when he returned yesterday morning from Hyde Park." Then he asked, "May I touch your hand?" For a second I didn't know what to say, but finally I said, "Yes."

To my surprise, the whole team stroked my hand. I didn't enjoy it. I felt rather silly, being everyone's good-luck charm, and I was glad none of our backstairs gang was around to see it. I would never have heard the end of it!

I have never done more sewing in my life than I did under the Roosevelts. Everyone kept me busy, and after my hours were over in the White House, I would go to Miss LeHand's suite and sew for her. She was very style-conscious, but had no time to go shopping.

I loved sewing for Mrs. "R," because she was so easy to please, and because she looked so well in some of the things I made for her. People were always surprised at how much prettier the First Lady looked in person than in her pictures. Her complexion was lovely.

One morning, I heard a butler say, "Mrs. R certainly did look good last night." I asked him what she had worn. He said, "A pretty white dress and some kind of coat that the President bought for her." I had a hard time convincing him that I had made that particular gown. Again, it was a copy of a pink chiffon tea gown that she had liked very much. She always wore it when she was home for dinner with the family, with a black-and-gold Chinese coat that the President had brought her from a trip abroad.

I made a million gifts, to be given away by Mrs. "R" and others around the White House— shoebags, handkerchief cases, lingerie covers, to name a few. Once, when I was all packed and practically on my way for a much-needed vacation in Atlantic City, the White House called and asked me to do some emergency sewing. I had to cancel my trip. The emergency turned out to be linen towels, which the First Lady wanted embroidered. I knew that Mrs. Roosevelt herself would have been surprised to learn that the housekeeper had asked me to stay because of the towels. Mrs. "R" would lean over backward not to upset anyone's schedule.

Christmas time was the best time to be at the White House. I have never seen a person more excited by the holiday season than Mrs. Roosevelt.

Even Mrs. Henrietta Nesbitt, the housekeeper, who didn't have to lift a finger in the kitchens, would catch the fever and become a whirlwind of energy, calling for supplies and baking up a storm. She would have me stitch up bags in a hurry, so that she could put puddings in them, and hang them up for days. Fruitcakes and plum puddings were her specialty. She would make so many of them, that Mrs. "R" would give a lot of them away as gifts.

Every Christmas season, I would get a little sick because of one of my jobs, which was to fill certain little boxes with cookies, and cut them to fit. Three of us maids would cut the ends off the cookies and eat right along, because they were so delicious. We would be woozy for a few days thereafter.

As far as Mrs. Roosevelt was concerned, one of my big-

gest jobs was to make large red stockings for all the grandchildren and some adults, to be hung on Christmas Eve.
Christmas was the real fun time for the First Lady, the time
of year when she seemed to be most thrilled and happy.

Christmas started in October for Eleanor Roosevelt.
There was a room on the third floor that we called the toy
room, in which she would stack all of her presents. She
shopped with loving care for everyone. There were over
a hundred policemen, and one year it would be neckties for
them, and the next year it might be pocketknives or handkerchiefs. Then she would shop for the chauffeurs, the
soldiers who attended the riding horses at Fort Myer,
the carpenters, plumbers, electricians, painters, florists,
groundsmen, cooks, butlers, maids, housemen, valets, doormen, and the rest.

To top it off, she would buy gifts for the children under
twelve of all the White House backstairs family. There
would be a tremendous party in the East Room at 3:30
every Christmas Eve. And it was a party that would really
include the whole country.

Long before the party had begun, Mrs. Roosevelt would
be busy going about the city, passing out baskets in the
poor homes of Washington, and at the Salvation Army
headquarters. She would come panting in at the last minute, but fresh and eager for the main treat.

At 5:00 P.M., the President would light the Community
Tree and broadcast a Christmas message. Next he would
read Dickens' *Christmas Carol* to the family. After it was
all over, Mrs. "R" would go to midnight service at St.
Thomas' Church with Miss Thompson ("Tommy") accompanying her.

I can only remember two occasions when the First Lady
missed her Christmas party— one was the Christmas when
Franklin, Jr., was sick in the hospital in Boston, and she
flew to be with him. On another Christmas, she flew to

Seattle to be near Anna, who was sick. But even then, she made sure that everything had a festive Christmas air before she left the White House.

One Christmas season, soon after the Roosevelts came to the White House, was marred by the death of Mary Foster, Mrs. Roosevelt's personal maid. Mrs. Roosevelt cried openly as she finished wrapping the gifts that Mary had left undone. Mama helped her.

But getting back to happier Christmas seasons, a Christmas dance was Mrs. Roosevelt's favorite affair of the year. She liked to invite engaged and young married couples at this romantic season. I remember seeing Ethel du Pont at the first of these parties in a most beautiful white dress. Myer Davis' orchestra would play, and afterward a supper would be served.

The staff was greatly amused by Mrs. Roosevelt's custom of ordering raw onions to be served. "She gets all these romantic young couples and then tries to kill the romance!" they laughed. The rest of the meal was always typical of Mrs. "R"— scrambled eggs, which I think was her favorite food, and link sausages.

Mrs. "R" was always just as busy waiting on the guests as the butlers. After everyone else had been served, she would take her plate and sit on the backstairs steps between the usher's office and the family dining room. And that's where she would eat.

Brother Hall, Mrs. "R" 's only brother, would whoop it up like a youngster, and he would grab the First Lady and dance the Virginia reel with her. Everybody would applaud like mad. I think that Mrs. "R" was never so happy as when she would dance that fast, happy dance with her brother. There was a great bond between them.

Proper Washington's reaction to Mrs. "R" was to avoid the White House. There was a rumor that one woman had spotted her own maid in the receiving line ahead of her.

Mrs. Alice Roosevelt Longworth, the Roosevelts' own cousin, made herself scarce around the White House, and we felt that the differences were perhaps more than political.

Mrs. James Roosevelt gave her own interpretation as to why the "Teddy" and the "FDR" sides of the family didn't get along— "Our side of the family is better-looking, and they're just jealous," she told somebody at the White House. In the servants' quarters, we often quoted her on that one.

One group with whom Mrs. "R" particularly enjoyed letting down her hair— the newspaper women— responded by teasing her goodnaturedly. When the Gridiron Club— composed of the gentlemen of the press and top Government officials— had their annual stag dinner, Mrs. Roosevelt countered with a party for the newspaper women and the wives of all the gentlemen at the Gridiron Club. The Ladies parodied the gentlemen's skits. Once two newsgals, dressed as one horse, made fun of Mrs. Roosevelt's penchant for horseback-riding at six in the morning. Another time, one woman, imitating the First Lady, rose and sang, to the tune of "Home on the Range":

"Oh, give me my home, where the New Dealers roam,
 And the Congressmen vote as they may.
 Where never is heard an encouraging word,
 And the press keeps on printing My Day."

As the war clouds gathered, and unemployment continued, there was a certain tenseness in the White House, which even the liveliness of the Roosevelts could not cloak. Everybody knew about the President's stamp collection, but few people knew that every time the President was troubled, he would wheel himself to his study desk and work with his stamps, studying and sorting them and mounting them in the books. Somehow it soothed him and cleared his mind for decisions, and we servants would get the word that the President was "busy stamping out a problem."

He gained comfort too from having his little figures of dogs and pigs placed just so on his desk and bedroom mantel. Only two people knew exactly where FDR wanted each one of them— Sarver and Cesar, houseman and valet. And I was the person entrusted with packing the whole fragile kit and kaboodle of them each time his study was painted. I tried to simplify the procedure by packing two boxes— dogs in one, and pigs in the other. I had inherited the job to help out, and discovered that nearly all the dogs were standing on three legs because of nervous-fingered maids. So I spread a pad on the fireplace hearth to avoid further breakage.

Once, one of the fellows challenged my packing, and claimed that I had gotten them mixed up. I told him that "Pigs is pigs and dogs is dogs," and added that I had lived long enough in the world to know the difference.

When FDR died, I sadly packed the little animals for the last time. At the suggestion of Lizzie McDuffie, Mrs. Roosevelt told us to help ourselves from the collection, because the rest would go to Hyde Park, and we would never have another chance. I picked out my favorite two little dogs and two little pigs, which I still have. There wasn't one left. But you can recognize the home of any former FDR employee by the tiny sign of the pig or dog on the mantel.

FDR was probably the man with more hobbies than any President we have had. He collected a million things, including, for some obscure reason, the china dogs and pigs. He'd get very annoyed because everyone would send him the Democratic symbol— the donkey— when what he really wanted was dogs and pigs.

Besides collecting, FDR had a hobby of identifying birds, and before the war, we would have many a laugh over his Hyde Park routine of making everyone get up with him before dawn to go out "bird-listening." Everyone had to sit quietly and listen, and when a bird would sing its joy at the approach of the sun, they had to try to guess what kind of bird it was. If a person said "robin" for every bird call, he was labeled a "bird brain," and those who knew their birds rated high with the President. There was many a heated argument over birds, and much consultation over books.

I think he used humor to help himself relax, and he was a great teaser. To illustrate the President's love of practical jokes, I remember that the day before he was to address the Teamsters' Union, the word came down that President Roosevelt had awakened with laryngitis. A procession of doctors came through the house, but nothing seemed to do him any good. His daughter, Anna, who was looking after him, was very upset, especially as the time for the speech drew near.

Backstairs, we knew that some of the remedies had eventually worked, and that his voice had returned. But, for some reason, his daughter looked as worried as ever. We couldn't understand it. Then, just before he left to make his speech, she asked him again, practically wringing her hands, "How are you doing, Father?"

The President whispered, "I can't say a word."

Anna Boettiger looked so distressed, that the President soon let out a big laugh, and assured her that he was all right.

"I was going to let you worry some more, but I just didn't have the heart to," he said.

That was typical of the President. He loved to kid everyone, and made up the names "Harry the Hop," and "Ickes the Ick," and many others. He reminded me in that way of "Cal" Coolidge, who had been a genius at inventing funny but unflattering names for his staff.

World tension was mounting. I remember the diplomatic reception held on December 12, 1937, the day after the U.S. gunboat *Panay* was sunk in Chinese waters by Japanese planes. I watched, with a little group of staff members, the whole procession of the diplomatic corps, with the dean of the corps first in line. Everyone acted as if nothing had happened. The Japanese, however, stayed only a few minutes, and the Chinese only a few minutes longer. We had all been curious to know how people act under these circumstances, and we saw that the diplomats truly deserve the name— they are *very* diplomatic!

When America entered the war, the White House doors were locked. We became a "closed corporation." No more tourists were allowed. We all worried about protecting the President in case of an attack. Since there was only one elevator in the White House, it was reserved for the President's use only. And we all were briefed as to how we would get him to safety in the bomb shelter, which had been hurriedly constructed.

Everyone was equipped with a gas mask, and trained to use it. We kept our gas masks hanging nearby, to be grabbed when an alert was sounded. The first time we had a drill, and I put on my mask and started walking through the tunnel, I thought I'd faint. Everyone who was fighting had my sympathy. Whenever the alarm sounded, we had to take to the steps and dash to the bomb shelter.

A large switchboard was set up near the shelter and manned by soldiers. Whenever we heard the alert, we never knew whether or not it was a real air raid, but we prayed just as hard as if it were.

It didn't make me feel any better to have to attend classes in the recognition of gases, and their effects upon a human being. During the demonstrations given by the army officers, all the gases would smell alike to me, and I used to hope that no one's life would depend on my knowledge in the event of an attack.

Just to the right of the Diplomatic Waiting Room, on the ground floor, the President set up his war briefing room. A group of soldiers brought him all kinds of maps and other data pertaining to the war. And the President would be wheeled in there every morning on his way to the office. By looking at the maps, he could see the location of the ships at sea, represented by tiny pegs.

Next to the President's office, that was the most carefully-guarded room in the White House. Only one houseman was allowed in the map room to clean each morning. And when he carried out the trash basket, soldiers would accompany him and stand watching until every scrap of paper had been burned.

One day, the regular cleaning man was off duty, and a trusted substitute was assigned to clean the map room. This resulted in a small catastrophe. The inexperienced man had knocked the pegs to thunderation with his vigorous dusting. The President sent out the word, "Don't let that fellow stay off duty again. The fellow who was in here yesterday sank the entire fleet."

But the worst thing that happened was when a very important paper, having to do with the timing of the Normandy invasion, didn't burn completely, and was found on the roof of the White House, where the antiaircraft guns were manned. It had blown up the chimney. Thank goodness, it got no further than the roof, but it scared the backstairs boys responsible, and, after that, papers had to be burned in a mesh basket.

One of the things that had to be changed during wartime was the handling of my laundry baskets. Locks had to be put on the tops of them to keep anyone from slipping in a bomb, which could have blown up the White House when a basket came back from the laundryman. A special driver, Richard Tracy, who is still at the White House, where he is affectionately known as "Dick Tracy," would stand guard at the cleaner's as the basket was being packed with the clean laundry. I was the one who had to unlock each basket, since I was in charge of the linen room, and if anything had been detonated, I would have been the first one to go.

Mrs. "R" took an office in the Dupont Circle Building, and busied herself doing Civil Defense work.

At the White House, part of her "defense effort" was to cut down on the servants' food. She called a meeting of all the help who ate at the White House, and explained the new rules. She sat on the edge of the desk in the hall of the second floor, and explained that we would have "one egg instead of two, one slice of bacon, toast and coffee for breakfast. And the large midday meal will consist of whatever is available on the market."

To save Mrs. Nesbitt a lot of trouble with the ration stamps, we were instructed to bring our own sugar. But, wouldn't you know, there was never any sugar. Someone was always dipping into someone else's sugar, and we had our own spy system backstairs.

We didn't have any fights, because Mrs. Roosevelt was apt to fire people who couldn't get along, but we did indulge in a few choice words whenever someone was caught with his hand in the sugar bowl.

Anyway, I wasn't in much of a fighting mood in those days. A spur-of-the-moment marriage hadn't worked out. After my husband entered the armed forces in 1943, we lost touch, and in 1946 we were divorced.

During the grim war years, Churchill was the most important White House guest, but even he gave rise to some innocent merriment backstairs. We were amused when he, who wore such "way out" clothes, of his own design, poked fun at Harry Hopkins because he dressed "like a bum."

But the funniest Churchill story for me was when Roosevelt ordered up the pigs' knuckles with a particular sauce that he had been bragging about to Churchill, and the Prime Minister, trying to be gracious, shut his eyes and ate them. Churchill said he had never heard of eating pigs' knuckles, and he became sicker by the minute as he pretended enthusiasm. But then the President went too far and suggested that in a day or two, they would have pigs' knuckles cooked still another way, and the Prime Minister "chickened out" and "surrendered," the President laughed, and promised he wouldn't have pigs' knuckles again after all.

During the President's last spring, we didn't have many house guests, and things were very quiet around the White House. Everyone was saying that the President felt very tired, that he was going to Warm Springs for a rest, and that he would bounce back to his old self. Knowing that this trip had always given him renewed vigor, I had no idea that he would die soon.

We were glad to see him go, so that we could do a little house-cleaning in the President's suite. In fact, something seemed to be driving us to get everything shiny. We even cleaned in the attic, where the clothes are pressed. All kinds of little things were being done for him on the day he died. Shoes were being shined, small articles washed.

About 3:00 P.M., two maids, Wilma and Bluette, and I were in the sewing room, taking what we considered a well-earned rest before going home, and feeling very good, because everything was so clean and in such good order. All of a sudden, we stopped laughing and talking and congratulating ourselves and just listened. Wilma said, "Why is the house so quiet?" We didn't have an answer, and we just sat listening to the strange quiet. Then suddenly Mrs. Roosevelt rang the bell for her maid. It was a rare thing for Mrs. Roosevelt to ring the bell, but she did. She told Mabel to put a few things in a bag, because she was going to Warm Springs right away.

Shortly after 4:00 P.M., when I left for home, we still didn't know anything was wrong. When I walked into my apartment, my phone was ringing. The White House pantry girl, Willie Collins, was calling to tell me that the President was dead. I just put the phone down in a stunned condition and walked into my mother's bedroom, where she was taking a rest. I stood by her bed, and she asked me, "What happened?"

When I told her, she didn't say very much. She could have been thinking about the day that President Harding died. She often talked of that day. I called the usher's office in the White House, and Mr. Crim told me it would not be necessary to return that evening.

In the midst of tragedy, there is always some funny thing that happens. Mrs. Boettiger told me that when she had carefully and with great control, told Johnny that his grandfather had died, his first comment was, "Goody, now I guess we can move." Then realizing what death meant, he burst into tears. He did not like White House restrictions, and had been told by his mother that they had to live at the White House to help his grandfather. He had been waiting anxiously to get away.

The next day, everyone arrived at the White House. Mr. Elliott and his wife, Faye Emerson, arrived early, and later that morning, I heard voices. Looking out of the sewing room window, I saw them walking very slowly on the roof, holding hands. There is a wide walk way around the entire roof. Whenever any activity took place, we would run to the roof to see what was going on. It's strange, but the only thing my numb mind could think about, as I saw them up there, was the time I had run up to the roof so many years earlier, to see FDR arrive to take his place at the White House for the first time, and I had run into the butler wearing Mrs. Hoover's hat.

I've always been able to accept death when it comes, and I never cry. Some of the maids began to cry as the horses drawing the caisson neared the gate that Saturday morning, April 14, 1945, but I stood there dry-eyed. Then a loud scream came from a woman in the crowd, watching with me from the northwest bedroom with its Lincoln bed, and somehow this triggered my own tears. I will always remember her shriek, and the sound of the horses' hooves as they came up the driveway to the door. I sometimes wake up at night still hearing it.

People always ask me why the President's casket was never opened, and why it remained closed while in state in the East Room, so that no one ever actually saw the President's body. They imagine all kinds of sinister reasons —foul play or some kind of secret about his health that had supposedly been kept from the public.

I'm sorry to disappoint those people, but there was nothing dramatic or sinister about the closed coffin. That is simply a family tradition. While the Roosevelts were there, other caskets lay in state in the East Room, and they were not open either— the casket of Mrs. Roosevelt's brother, Hall Roosevelt, for example.

We all lined up to say good-by to Mrs. Roosevelt, and every person but one cried. The servants cried, and the members of the Roosevelt family cried, and daughter Anna's husband, Major John Boettiger, was so affected, that he preferred to sit in the usher's office. "I cannot bear to say good-by," he said.

Only one person remained dry-eyed. She shook hands and thanked us and seemed calm with a control that had been learned through a dozen White House years. Strangely enough, the woman who had cried copious tears at the death of her maid, was the only one who did not cry.

Mrs. Roosevelt was beyond tears.

THE "THREE MUSKETEERS"

Backstairs, the help said, "Poor Truman, he has a hard act to follow." But they needn't have worried about Harry Truman. He was soon establishing himself as a colorful character in his own way.

True, he didn't resemble everyone's ideal version of a Chief Executive. But the man from Independence was very peppery as soon as he opened his mouth, speaking his mind in plain, undiplomatic terms, and letting "the chips fall where they may."

He wasn't afraid to do a little cussing either. It had been amusing that FDR had been so conscious of his proper upbringing that he restricted his cussing, but he used to encourage Colonel Howe to cuss like a sailor by laughing uproariously whenever Howe let go with some choice profanity. It would tickle FDR, for example, when Howe would be invited to come to dinner "provided he would dress," and Howe would send back the message that it wasn't worth the blankety—blank—blank—blank trouble, and the President could keep his blankety—blank—blank—blank dinner.

At first the help would soft-pedal Howe's language, but

Roosevelt would insist that they give him the exact quote of what Howe had said, and he would chortle like a naughty schoolboy.

Well, nobody had to do Harry Truman's cussing for him. He could do his own.

And there was no one who appreciated it less than his wife. If ever there was a prim and proper woman, that was Bess Truman. Again, how they had ever gotten together was a big mystery to the backstairs help, but we finally decided that the bad little boy in Harry Truman was what really had intrigued Bess Wallace, and had made her decide to marry the man. She tried from then on to soften the edges, and she kept right on trying throughout the period of his Presidency.

And just to show you how far she'd progressed by the end of the second term— almost eight years— let me report what happened when the newly-elected Eisenhower sent a man to look over the White House and start changing things. After the man had left, Truman exploded, "I had to tell that blankety-blank of a blank that I was still President around here." There was that cussing again to bother poor Bess.

Well, that was her problem. Backstairs, we felt a letdown as we realized that the old easy days were over. We had grown a little spoiled. We had become accustomed, when the coast was clear, to taking, not a coffee break, but a movie break, in midday, and we had used that movie projection machine more than President Roosevelt had. In fact, we had felt a little sorry for FDR, because he didn't appreciate a good movie. When *Gone With the Wind* played, he started watching it, but then went to bed instead. "That's too much torture for me," he said. But he didn't object at all to having the crashing and shrieking and the roaring of the cannons right outside his door. He was a "hearty" sleeper.

He was used to noise. Why, when his two youngest sons were roughhousing, it sounded like the battle scenes from *Gone With the Wind.* John once had his ankle in a bandage for two weeks as a result of one of those roughhouse sessions.

Suddenly, with the Trumans came deafening silence. When we first saw the valiant little trio of Trumans, we kept looking around for the Presidential family— where was the family of giants we were used to? In the Roosevelt family, everyone had been tall. And even FDR himself had had a tall look in his chair.

So we hunted desperately for something about the Trumans to catch our hearts and our fancies, while we fought the urge to look back and back at our bigger-than-life Roosevelts. But everything reminded us of our former residents. We had a "thing" for a while of trying to solve the mystery of the new President's non-existent middle name. What did the "S" without a period stand for in Harry S Truman? It stood, we found out, for the names of both grandfathers— Shippe for one, and Solomon for the other.

Well! When the name Solomon came up, that made some folks wonder if Truman had any Jewish blood. He didn't, and that reminded us of the rumor, which wouldn't be stilled, about Roosevelt's name and the question as to whether *he* had had Jewish blood.

For the first time, I heard the story about where the name Roosevelt had come from. Someone had been around when the question of his ancestry had been put to Roosevelt, and he had said that while he didn't have Jewish blood, he wouldn't have minded having a little of it. Then he explained that the original member of the family who came to America in 1650 had added "van Rosevelt" to his name to indicate the town he had come from in Holland. His name had been Claes Martensen, but he became known as Claes van Rosevelt, meaning "from the world of roses."

It was very interesting to hear about the names of Presidents, and until they tired of it, the staff went around calling President Truman "Sol" Truman— but only behind his back, of course. They were amused because "Sol" Truman had not made a go of his clothing store. "He was a traitor to his class," they would josh, paraphrasing what had been said about Roosevelt.

When Harry Truman finished off the war with the dropping of two atomic bombs on Japanese cities, the men backstairs gasped and said, "Wow, he's topped any act Roosevelt ever dreamed up. He's front and center stage now for sure."

They were right— hardly a day passed that President Truman was not on the front page. He quickly got the nickname "Give-'Em-Hell Harry."

It was definitely the salty language that first captured our imaginations backstairs. Everybody was saying that Truman was just an accident of politics, and he would answer reporters and critics with pithy comments.

Everyone was suddenly very interested in his background. People wanted to know whether he had been a tool of the Pendergast machine, and he would fire back in an equally vituperative way. Did Congress think it could shove him around, now that he wasn't up there in the Senate any more? Well, he would blankety-blank see about that.

Whenever she heard of such outbursts, and especially when they came out in the papers, Mrs. "T" used one phrase that became a byword around the White House: "You didn't have to say that."

Pretty soon the staff was saying to one another— no matter what the occasion— "You didn't have to say that." We would say it in a hurt voice, and then laugh and enjoy our private joke.

We wondered where he had gotten the habit of cussing

and expressing himself like a tough sergeant on maneuvers. And then we found out that he *had* learned it in the military, of course, and we also learned that it had taken him longer than any other veteran of our wars to capture the Presidency. Grant and Teddy Roosevelt had done much better, after the Civil and Spanish American Wars, but it had taken Truman twenty-seven years from World War I, when he was a Major, to reach the White House. We thought of that when the next military President, Eisenhower, stepped into office, with a hop, skip, and a jump, following World War II.

But everything that Harry Truman did had a delayed reaction, we agreed backstairs. Even his military career was supposed to have begun in his teens, when he was a whiz at math and was scheduled to go to West Point. The simple fact that he couldn't get in because he wore glasses was his first bitter disappointment, and his first great challenge and toughener.

It is amusing, on looking back, to realize that the next President, with whom Truman carried on a salty feud, had been scheduled to go to Annapolis and hadn't made it. Instead, he had settled on West Point as his second choice.

Harry Truman had turned to the National Guard to fulfill his yen for the military, and he had worked like a Trojan as a charter member of Battery B. This paid off when he went into World War I as a Lieutenant, and came out a Major, after having seen plenty of action.

He'd been an equally slow starter in everything he did in life. He didn't enter politics until he had failed in his haberdashery— which he'd opened with an army buddy— and he had had an amazing array of jobs, from timekeeper for the Santa Fe Railroad and mailroom clerk at the Kansas City *Star* to County Judge in Jackson County, Missouri. And in middle age, he was still paying off the debts of that haberdashery. That's why he had searched for a better job in politics, and ended up as Senator. And, in 1948, the slow-starter became, at sixty-four, the oldest man to run for the Presidency since Buchanan in 1856.

And, we noted that he'd been equally slow at starting his married life. Thirty-five! But he'd had his usually happy ending too, and the marriage was spectacularly successful, blessed with a daughter who was the apple of his eye. Mother and daughter both rode herd on the President, clucking over him, and appointing themselves his advisors on speech and habits. And we, watching the busy little trio from behind the scenes, nicknamed them the "Three Musketeers."

Though the ladies might scold him in private, whenever he would break into the papers with another "Give-'Em-Hell Harry" story, they presented a united front to the world, and backed him to the hilt. It was "All For One and One For All."

They were even a perfect team at the piano— one played, one sang, and one applauded. The President could hardly sit down at a piano without making news. But we thought that the best postscript to the piano-loving President was when he put "patriotism above pianos." It was really his own, and only, decorating touch to the White House. When he found out that the gorgeous Honduras mahogany piano in the East Room was a gift from Steinway, Truman decreed that the White House must have an American-made piano too, and bought a beautiful black Baldwin for the other end of the room. It made no difference to the President that the Steinway had been manufactured by the American firm of Steinway & Sons, and not by the German firm, which makes the "Hamburg" Steinway.

When last I saw it, during the Eisenhower administration, the Truman piano was being put to good use by the entertainers who come to the White House to participate in the musicales. It stands in the library on the ground floor, where the entertainers limber up and get ready to go "on stage" in the East Room and perform before the President. I think Mr. Truman will be happy to know that his piano is helping many a nervous performer to calm down. I know, because I've stood by many a time with the smelling salts.

It wasn't long before we learned that although our new First Lady was shy, and hid from newspaper reporters, she was not exactly mousy. When the housekeeper, Mrs. Nesbitt, didn't change to conform to the new First Lady's ways, and insisted on saying that "This wasn't the way Mrs. Roosevelt did it," she was soon out of a job. The rest of us domestics had learned long ago never to tell one First Lady about another's ways— a cardinal White House rule.

And for the first time, to my knowledge, a First Lady took the bookkeeping part of the White House in hand, and ran it herself. She took a look at the food bill and cut out breakfast for the daily sleep-out employees. Every day, she sat down at a desk and tried to run the White House as though it were a business, which indeed it is. We tiptoed around and marvelled.

She answered her own mail too, in longhand, commenting that she just couldn't dictate; it was too rich for her system. But eventually, of course, she did have to learn that trick, because the mail was overwhelming.

We gasped again when she solved the problem of requests for "something from the White House." She simply sent out for a box of buttons, let them mellow a while in the White House, and had them sent to all who wrote for a souvenir. This lady we were starting to like.

We soon found out the kind of woman Bess Truman is. She would make more of a fuss when her old bridge club came from Independence, Missouri, than when she was entertaining the social queens of Washington— Gwen

Cafritz and Perle Mesta— because those bridge buddies were the ones she was going home to in a few years, and she never lost sight of realities.

And she was the kind of woman who, once she became acquainted with the help, got to know them as no First Lady had done since the first Mrs. Wilson. She was the kind of woman who would keep track of each member of my family, and was genuinely concerned about my mother's condition, which prompted her to compare notes about *her* mother's condition. She would stop and talk to me now and then— really *talk*— and not in a superficial way.

I would say that the Trumans were the most informal of any of the First Families I have known or heard Mama talk about. They did nothing for show; they simply behaved naturally.

The Roosevelts had been kindly and good to the staff, and had even kidded with us, but there had always been a sort of barrier, as if you had to look up. The Trumans' attitude said that you were just as important as anyone else, and you were treated with the respect of an equal. And for that, the whole gang of us looked up to them even more.

We used to talk about the difference in attitude between the Roosevelts and the Trumans, and we recalled how once Lizzie McDuffie had asked Mrs. "R" if the help could watch a certain entertainment— it wasn't a State occasion but just some little affair, which all the White House secretaries and such could attend. Mrs. Roosevelt said, "Yes, they can come if they stay in the back." So we knew that even she had reservations, and we didn't bother about going. We had come to know the difference between a high-sounding speech and actual performance.

To demonstrate the kind of woman Bess Truman is, after the Trumans had left the White House, Vietta went back to Independence with Mrs. "T," and built her own little house near the family so she could still work for Mrs. "T." Mrs. Truman herself would hop into her car and chauffeur Vietta home after work. That's a real lady.

Mrs. "T" was the kind of woman who put her family and servants first. She really thought about the menus, and served the best and most carefully-cooked food of any of the First Ladies. And she believed in home-cooked food even for the guests who came to teas; there were no more thrown-together snacks, as there had been under the Roosevelts, nor cake-mixes, such as the Eisenhowers favored. No, she really believed in equality for everyone. What she liked and found good she wanted everyone to enjoy too. She did not hoard it for herself.

And Mrs. "T" was the kind of woman who gave many things away anonymously. She had a standing order that all gift labels be removed so that the sender could not be identified. And she was always packing something for the needy.

She was the kind of lady who was so sensitive to criticism, that when the papers made fun of her, or her daughter, or her husband, she had a sick headache. The papers made fun of her "poodle cut." Then her husband announced, when asked how he thought she looked, "just like a woman her age should look."

Mrs. Truman was tickled pink when Alben Barkley, the Vice-President, courted and married the beautiful young secretary from Missouri, Jane Hadley, who became the star of the Washington show, because then the newspapers would pay less attention to her. Any vain First Lady would have been biting her nails at the most publicized romance of the century, next to that of the Duke and Duchess of Windsor.

And she was the kind of First Lady who hated fussiness, loved cleanliness and neatness and an all-things-put-away look, but who didn't want her servants to keep working all the time and would order, yes *order,* them to rest.

At first, I didn't think that she returned my feeling of friendship. She acted very cool toward me, and eventually I learned that when she had arrived at the White House, someone had given her the impression that I was giving her only the mended towels and holding back the good ones. That was not true! The policy of the house is to mend and use an article as long as it does not look badly. The towels are very expensive, and just cannot be thrown away because of a tiny hole.

A First Lady soon learns what it costs to run the White House, and she begins to go along with the ones who know. It was not until we were in Blair House and Mrs. Truman had learned the truth about many things, that she changed her attitude toward me. From then on, she was very nice to me, and has been ever since she has left the White House. I have a number of lovely letters she has written me, and when she visits Washington, she will give me a ring on the phone, or I will call her.

Looking back, I know that the appearance of the bathrooms happened to be her very sensitive spot, and we always had to pay special attention to keep new bars of soap on hand.

How differently the household was run! Mrs. Truman had breakfast with her husband; the Roosevelts rarely saw each other before dinner time, if then. Meals were on time. The Roosevelts would wait for a quorum to start eating, and let the rest of the members straggle in whenever they chose.

The "Three Musketeers" led as quiet and orderly a life as they could— Father tending to his politics, Mother tending to her housekeeping, and Daughter tending to her school books. But it seemed that no matter how the Trumans tried, life couldn't run smoothly. Even the backstairs bunch were affected.

Once, when President Truman was eating alone, Fields, the butler, turned the soup over on him. Then Charles Ficklin toppled over a quart of milk on the red carpet just at the time the doorman was bringing the President and Mrs. Truman to breakfast. And once, when Mrs. Truman was away, it was up to the President to order his breakfast. He called the pantry and said, "Breakfast for Mrs. Wallace and me."

The voice on the other end said, "Who is *me?*"

The answer was, "I happen to be the President of the United States. Who are you?"

The poor fellow sweated that one out all day, waiting to be fired for "insubordination," and we sweated for him. But we soon learned that the President was a good sport.

Then Margaret announced to a startled world that she would have a singing career, and we servants echoed the question that others were asking, "With *her* nose?" We had fierce arguments about Margaret's nose, and I vacillated back and forth, but finally decided that she should have her nose bobbed, because she is a beautiful girl except for the nose.

Every once in a while, we would see an item in the paper suggesting that Margaret might have had her nose made smaller by plastic surgery. Margaret said she had thought about it. But she ended up by saying she had one good angle. Well, when sewing for her, I saw her good angle. I agree, but a girl on a stage should have all good angles. It was amazing how lovely she looked except for that one feature.

How I longed to advise Margaret to go ahead and have plastic surgery performed on it. It would have changed her life, and increased her chances for a successful singing career. And if she ever goes back on the stage, it still would. She just doesn't look like an entertainer with that nose.

The papers seemed to rebel against the idea of a President's daughter having a career, just as they had when Wilson's daughter Margaret tried for a concert career. Was she taking advantage of her father's position? Could she really sing?

I'm no Paul Hume, and, to me, Margaret sounded fine. But what it did to our backstairs life was not too fortunate— we had to be as careful of the young star as though she were a fragile rose. No sounds could disturb her practicing. No one who even felt as if he were catching cold could touch her or come near her. No one dared raise dust anywhere near her sensitive nose. And even so, she would become ill before every entertainment.

The papers made the most of it. Backstairs, we wondered too if it were just nerves, but we found out it wasn't when the White House physician went to Margaret— in Detroit, I believe it was— to bring her home to the White House. She was really sick.

It wasn't just her troubles with a career that upset her; she also had difficulties with her boy friends. The White House was a terrible hazard for her, because she never knew if a boy friend were dating her to further his career, knowing the publicity it would automatically bring, or if he were really fond of her. And once in a while, she would like someone, and he would marry some other girl and she would mope around for a while. We felt sorry for her and whispered, "There goes another one, poor little Princess."

Her father didn't help her romantic life any. When he thought she was staying out too late, he would simply send a Secret Service man to get her. She would leave the party sweetly, like a good Musketeer, but she'd come home raging.

No, the White House wasn't the best thing that ever happened to Margaret. And, somehow, even the White House building seemed to have it in for the Trumans. Though the voters had wanted Truman in the White House as their Number Two choice next to FDR, it seemed as if the building were creaking and groaning and making the family unwelcome. Termites were discovered in the President's office, and the baseboard had to be replaced. As Truman would say, whenever the butler walked across the room to hand him something, "The dining room seems to be shaking." And the chandelier would actually sway.

Then, as a last straw, a false fire alarm nearly drove *everyone* out. Looking back, I find it hilariously funny. Irving Harley, a houseman, came running to me for the key, shouting, "The Cedar Room is on fire!" My linen room was right across the hall from it.

I said, "It can't be. I'm looking right at it."

With the sound of fire engines clanging, and the police rushing around, Harley and I looked in the Cedar Room. There was no fire.

By this time, the sound of the sirens was deafening, and firemen and policemen were swarming all over the third floor.

George Thompson, who had been running the vacuum, came over and said, "What can I do for you gentlemen?"

The policeman said, "You've done it already, when you touched the ceiling with that gadget."

George said, "I'm sorry," and continued sweeping as though nothing had happened. Watching George try to maintain his dignity set me to laughing until the tears ran down my cheeks. After that, he was careful not to bang into the fire alarm attachment.

The only thing the Trumans didn't have, which had always been a news-maker for other Presidents, was a pet. And even here, by a quirk of fate, the greatest pet story in the annals of the White House was thrown on their door-step, so to speak, in the form of a fat cat called "Mike the Magicat."

Mike appeared at the White House, and was well fed by the backstairs crowd, who were still lonely for Fala. He was then sent home to the address on his collar— eleven blocks away— in a chauffeur-driven White House limousine.

Mike knew a good thing and returned, and again was taken home in a chauffeur-driven limousine. Mike was getting rotten-spoiled, and by the time the reporters covering the White House had discovered Mike, he was a feline with two homes, and a real bay window full of cream, and, quite possibly, the fattest cat on two continents.

Mike made the papers in a big way, but the cutest story was in the Scripps-Howard paper, the Washington *News*. Society writer, Evelyn Peyton Gordon, headed her column, "Mikey Is Running For President In His Own Way." The publicity ruined everything, as far as Mike was concerned. Now, when he ran away from home, his mistress, Jeane Dixon, socialite wife of the Washington realtor, James L. Dixon, and famous Washington seeress, would simply receive a phone call to "come and get him." There was no more cream. So he just stayed home.

As if by magic, his mistress got into the news when she predicted that her crystal ball showed Harry Truman was going to win the election. The White House staff was much amused by her prediction, because we were convinced that Harry Truman was not going to win any election. Cabinet officers, it was rumored, were sending their furniture home preparatory to leaving Washington, and nobody, but no-body, was contributing to the cost of the campaign. Who wants to throw money down a drain?

It was a pity too, we all were saying, because we had grown fond of our cocky President. We wouldn't have minded another four years of listening to the "Tales of Truman" and said so. But we "knew" it was hopeless.

And we were backed up by practically every pollster in the business. In fact, one pollster announced that he was not going to bother with any more polls, because old Harry hadn't a chance against the handsome young Tom Dewey.

Backstairs we talked long and heatedly about Truman's decisions and more decisions; all of them were getting him in trouble with the public. No wonder he couldn't win. The slogan was going around, "To err is Truman," and we servants agreed.

He had fired his Secretary of Commerce, Henry Wallace— and you just didn't do that sort of thing. But "Pepper Pot Truman" did. Wallace had made a speech counter to his foreign policy, and that was that. And Wallace had retaliated by running against him on the Progressive ticket.

Truman had dropped the atomic bomb, and people were not going to vote for a man who would do that. But Truman said that he'd done it to save the lives of American soldiers. And as far as he was concerned, that was that.

Didn't he have trouble sleeping, Truman had been asked, when he justified his act with the statement that in wartime you use every weapon you have. No, said the peppery President, he didn't have trouble sleeping. He just put himself to sleep every night reading about the troubles of some other President of the past.

He had delivered a civil rights message, calling for a Federal law to end discrimination, and that had killed his chances of getting "a single Southern vote." But Harry Truman had felt that an American is an American, no matter what his color or the number of fillings in his teeth. And that was that. And the South had retaliated by running Governor Strom Thurmond of South Carolina against him on a States' Rights ticket.

He had also dreamed up the Truman Doctrine to "contain" Russia, and that was receiving its share of brickbats. And he had approved the Marshall Plan, which would "give all our money away to foreign countries."

So he wasn't too popular. Especially with Congress, which had turned Republican. What more of a slap in the face could you give a President, they said backstairs, than to elect an opposition party to Congress for him to try to work with? This was the voters' way of telling him that they didn't want him. And some people seriously suggested that the Vice-President-turned-President resign, so that, under the Constitution, the Republican Speaker of the House, Joe Martin, could take over as President and bring some harmony to the country.

And back came those cries of "Pendergast machine." Boss Tom Pendergast had given Truman his start in Missouri politics. Pendergast had been slapped into prison for not reporting some of his ill-gotten gains on his income tax return. Could HST escape the stigma? Hadn't Truman been involved somewhere? Politicians hunted unsuccessfully for any blemish on his record. Reporters took the question to Truman himself.

Yep, he'd stolen a little money too, he said, chuckling. When he'd handled all that money for highway construction, he had misappropriated some to get a statue of President Andrew Jackson erected in Jackson County, his namesake.

And then the final straw: Harry Truman had built a balcony on the South Portico of the White House, and it had cost the taxpayers $10,000. A President should be working and not have time for rocking on a back porch, said lots of people, who, unlike the loyal but helpless backstairs White House crowd, *did* have a vote.

So that was the situation at the time of the election,

and nobody gave him a chance to win except two people, one of them being Jeane Dixon, whose hobby was her crystal ball. She was always much in demand for political social functions, and had predicted FDR's death and a lot of other things.

The other person who predicted Truman's victory was Leslie Biffle, Secretary of the Senate, who had gone around the country pretending to be a salesman, and had reported back to Truman that, according to *his* poll, Truman would be elected.

Truman attacked the campaign as he did everything else. He brought in his two faithful pals, Bess and Margaret, and off to the campaign went the "Three Musketeers."

The country called it the whistlestop campaign. We of the White House called it the stage show of the "Three Musketeers." Mrs. Truman had said she would go if he would promise that she didn't have to speak a word. Margaret Truman had given up her singing career for the duration of his campaign.

It wasn't too big an act, and it wasn't too theatrical. The stage was the back of the train. Harry would "give 'em hell," and talk about the "Do-Nothing" Congress, and then he'd introduce his fellow troupers, Margaret and Bess. All they had to do was wave and smile and say hello. But backstairs, we knew that though Margaret was eating it up, Mrs. Truman was quaking in her shoes every time the crowd looked at her. Her timidity was real, and only her great love for her husband could induce her to go through the torments of passing before the public eye.

Something about the act must have pleased the public, because on election night, the commentators were describing a Truman lead, which, they said, would be wiped out soon. Commentator H. V. Kaltenborn had been so reluctant to admit Truman's chance of winning, that at 4:00 A.M., when Truman was leading by two million, he was still saying that didn't mean the election, but only that the contest would be thrown into the House of Representatives for a decision.

That tidbit gave Harry S Truman the material for a smash third act, "Victory Morning." The President had more fun with that third act than anyone except the other two Musketeers when he went on the air and indulged in an imitation of Kaltenborn in questionable taste.

Privately, one of the Musketeers wasn't sure he should have done that on the air— "you didn't have to say that." But, publicly, it was *all for one and one for all,* and so it remained through all of their days in the White House.

The President went his way as usual. He decreed a "police action" in Korea, because the North Korean Communists had not taken heed when he had told them they could go so far and no farther. There was much criticism about the action, which involved us in the affairs of a nation so far away.

Mrs. David Wallace, the First Lady's mother, criticized the President when he relieved MacArthur of his command.

Why did he have to fire that public hero, Douglas Mac-Arthur? Why? And so soon before an election too. Why hadn't he let the General run the Korean War his own way? Those who defended the President backstairs said that was what made him so great. He made up his own mind and "let the chips fall where they may."

Others felt that the President had behaved rashly, and perhaps spitefully. After all, MacArthur had been trying to *win* the war in Korea, and the boys who had died in battle would have demanded nothing less than total victory. And from the tremendous reception the General received upon his return to the United States, it was evident that the American people felt the same way too.

The First Lady never criticized her husband in public, nor did she like to hear her mother criticize the President in private. As far as she was concerned, the President could do no wrong, though he could speak out of turn.

When Mrs. Wallace persisted, and asked from her sick-bed, "Bess, why did Harry fire that nice man?", Mrs. "T" refused to discuss it. Instead, she threw back her shoulders like a true Musketeer and marched out of the room.

. . . BUT BESS IS BEST

Well, the balcony cost $10,000, but that looked like chicken feed when the White House was saved from disaster by a re-building job that cost $5,000,000.

The mess began right after HST's election— wouldn't you know it?

And some of that moving made a very undignified impression. People staggered across Pennsylvania Avenue from the White House to Blair House with a bunch of pots and pans in their arms, or armloads of pillows.

We got the order to start moving about the 9th or 10th of November. The family had left almost immediately for Key West, Florida, for a rest. It was good that they did go, because Blair House had to be almost made over in two weeks.

Mrs. Victoria Geaney had been the housekeeper there for a number of years, and was to continue her job. Mrs. Mary Sharp, the new housekeeper, was to see that everything was moved out of the White House, before she took a year's leave. It took nearly four years to do the renovations.

The very day the moving started, Mrs. Sharp informed me she would be leaving. I said, "When?"

She said, "Now! At twelve o'clock. Looks like you are going to be left alone in here. I'm leaving this job."

I gasped. Then I got back to work.

Maids and housemen were carrying out the personal clothes. All the carpenters, plumbers, painters, and electricians were in the Blair House working. The house was strictly antiquated. A coal stove was still being used in the kitchen; this had to be taken out. A door had to be cut to connect the two kitchens— the one in the Blair Government Guest House, the other in the Lee Guest House. The same thing had to be done on the first floor, to make two dining rooms and two drawing rooms.

Blair House had a small elevator, so small the houseman would have to stand on the side of the laundry basket to close the door. The stair was very narrow and winding. In the Lee House, the stairway was much wider, with large landings on each floor.

A small door was cut on the fourth floor between the two houses, enabling a person to ride up to the last floor, pass through the hall and walk down the steps in the Lee House. Many improvements were made. Coolers had to be placed in some of the rooms for very hot weather.

Meanwhile, back at the ranch, everything was a grand mess— everyone was walking out, like rats leaving a sinking ship. All the beds were left as they were. In fact, everything was left in the rooms.

Mr. Crim spoke to me about the lace scarves under the glass on the furniture. I told him, "If you want me to dismantle this house, you will have to send up some men."

He sent four. I had everything brought to the third floor. A lot of linen had to go to the Blair House, and the rest to storage. Mr. Reynolds and his crew of inventory men brought in boxes on top of boxes for the packing. When he read the instructions written by Mr. Crim, the last line said, "Lillian Parks will remain in the White House until everything is moved out." I thought it was a joke. I had to read it for myself to believe it.

And then I felt tears in my eyes. I was now a part of the written history of the White House. Fifty years from now someone would be reading my name, just as I had thrilled as I read the names in the old records of the White House.

But a greater thrill was yet to come. In the linen room, high on a shelf, I found a box that I had never paid much attention to. I thought it held an old tablecloth. It turned out to be a flag from Lincoln's time— all black squares. On each square were the names of Presidents and prominent men, done in gold. The flag was sent to the Lincoln Museum by two men who had taken the inventory, after consulting Mr. Crim. And there I hope to see it again some day.

I found many other things that hadn't been used for years and must have rested once in the hands of such men as Abraham Lincoln, or Teddy Roosevelt, or James Garfield. They were old-fashioned things of heavy red velvets and blues and golds. There were draperies, baskets of lace curtains, dozens of sofa pillows, chair and sofa covers. Whose hands had touched these sofa pillows, I wondered? Whose head had taken a nap on them?

Never once did I go to Blair House during the moving. I kept in touch by phone, finding out what was needed, and sending it over by houseman or maid. In the midst of it all, came bad news.

Mr. Crim called four of the housemen and myself to his office and told us, "Since Blair House is rather small, the entertaining will be limited. There will be no sightseers to clean up after, and Mrs. Geaney still has a staff in the House. I'll have to transfer you elsewhere until we return to the White House." This was true for the men, but my story was different. Someone had come up with the idea that my work could be taken over by some of the other maids, so I told him that I would like to go to the U.S. Treasury to work when I had finished packing what was left in the White House. But I felt dejected. I felt "fired."

B. Altman sent men from New York to take all draperies, while another group was taking out the furniture for storage. A very interesting old man put the name and value on each rug so fast, that I stopped work just to watch him. The house began to take on a sad look— every room was empty. We packed all the lamp shades in tissue paper, and put them in large boxes. Truckloads went to Fort Washington for storage.

I told Mr. Reynolds and his men, "Pack these things so you can find them when the new house is ready, because I won't be here."

He laughed and said, "Lillian, you are going to be the first person to come into the new house," and it so happened that I actually was the first person to come in, on March 15, 1952. But don't let me get ahead of the story.

The Trumans came from Florida in time for Thanksgiving in Blair House. I had my Thanksgiving dinner at home with my mother, since I was no longer a member of the White House staff in the Blair House.

It was well into December before the mansion was cleared of everything except a room full of rubbish, which had to be taken away by the inventory men, and a big pile of trash in the center of the hall on the third floor, which I sat on while I slipped into my street shoes for the last time.

A few of my tears fell into the rubble, for I was feeling very sorry for myself as I got ready to leave. I was leaving *my* White House. Would I ever come back again? Knowing how things go, I was afraid that once in the Treasury, I would stay in the Treasury.

And, even if I were to return, it would never be the same. It would be the White House, but not the same floor on which I had walked "the longest mile" to the Palm Room, to speak to the first President's wife I had ever spoken to. I wouldn't be in *that* White House.

I have never forgotten how the White House looked stripped of everything. I guess I am the only person who will carry this picture in my mind always.

No one ever came to see if I were working, so I took it for granted I didn't have a boss. But I respected Mr. Reynolds, with whom I was working, enough to ask him, "Is it all right for me to leave?" This was a few days before Christmas.

As I walked away, not looking back any more, I comforted myself with the thought that at least I had some lovely souvenirs from the White House. Mrs. Truman had ordered several tables set up before the real moving had begun, and had placed on them many odds and ends of things that would not be used in the *new* White House. Many of them were gifts that had come in from the general public. I had gotten a lovely embroidered, natural-color table runner, among other things, and Mrs. Truman herself had given me a gift of a silver evening bag, which she wanted me to have.

Mrs. Truman had been there to help distribute the gifts. She had on an old pair of gloves, because many items were old and dusty. But the way we felt about it, the more dust there was, the more history a particular item had seen.

I was saved from the Treasury Department by a phone call saying that I was wanted and needed at Blair House. I tried to be tough and say I was all set for the Treasury Department, but, of course, I was bluffing, and I was delighted to be back among the Presidents.

It thrilled me to know that now I was going to work in

the house where Lincoln used to go to escape the crowd of people waiting to see him at the White House. Here his Postmaster General, Montgomery Blair, lived, and I don't know if it's true or not, but this was the house in which Lincoln was supposed to have sat while composing the notes for his Emancipation Proclamation.

Yes, I felt pretty good as I reported for work at Blair House. The words of Mr. Crim's assistant, Mr. West, rang in my ears. He had phoned and said, "Lillian, will you come down here and straighten out this house?" I knew he was partly kidding, and that they could survive without me, but my heart sang.

As I came in the door, I heard Mrs. Truman's voice calling down the stairs from the small room that she and Miss Odum shared as an office, wanting to know if I had come in yet. Mrs. Mabel Walker, the new housekeeper, who had replaced Mrs. Sharp, said, "Here she is, Mrs. Truman." Mrs. "T" stepped out in the hall to meet me, and said, "Lillian, I am glad to see you. We have to get ready for a full house. I remember now, you are used to large crowds."

Mrs. "T" was all in a dither. The President's family and hers were coming for the inauguration. We soon had everything ready for the house guests. Mrs. Truman and Margaret were very busy with their new wardrobes. I think most of the excitement was centered around the fact there would be a large ball, something that had almost become a thing of the past.

When 10,000 people got all dressed up for one evening, you can see how hungry Washington was for an old-fashioned Inaugural Ball. Mrs. Truman's three brothers and their wives, and the President's brother and sister, all arrived for the big day. There were just two children this time, David and Marian Wallace, the nephew and niece of

Mrs. Truman. This was quite a letdown in the children's department from the last inauguration.

David must have been nearly fourteen years old on this trip. He had been quite a character when he was at the White House before. He liked to go into the small kitchen on the third floor and make a sandwich between meals. He and Miss Margaret were always in a squabble. When he was younger, he was heard offering his services to Mrs. Truman. "Aunt Bess, what can I do to help you?"

"Just get out of my way" was her answer.

But David was enjoying himself on this eventful day— he seemed to be carried away with the big cars in the parade. It was just wonderful to be able to see an inaugural parade. Blair House is so close to the street, that I could see it right out of the window.

Tickets had been issued to the employees for the grandstand, but they all passed them on to their families. Lizzie McDuffie, who was a dear friend from the Roosevelt days, had come from Atlanta, Georgia, so I gave my ticket to her. She soon found herself surrounded by many old friends. The day was beautiful, but cold enough for the ladies to have cold feet when they returned from the reviewing stand to dress for the 6:00 P.M. reception.

President Truman remained in the reviewing stand until every unit had passed. It was just about dark when he came in to join Mrs. Truman and go to the reception at the National Gallery. They were already one hour late. It was 7:30 P.M. when they got back to Blair House for dinner.

A large crowd had formed around Blair House to watch the comings and goings of the family. At the moment, they were watching David, who had perched himself on the windowsill in Mrs. Truman's office on the fourth floor, and was yelling, "Hi, Aunt Bess!"

Bluette said, "Don't you dare yell out of that window."

"Oh, Bluette, you're always taking all the joy out of life," he complained, and dashed out of the room.

I had already seen the black *panne* velvet gown with a side-draped skirt, floor length, that Mrs. Truman would wear to the ball, but I enjoyed seeing it again. Miss Margaret always looked beautiful in pink, and Madame Pola had designed a Margaret-pink gown of yards and yards of tulle for her, which resembled a beautiful cloud.

Friday was another gay day for the Trumans; their old friends gave them several receptions. Then it was "fun's over," and back to the old routine.

At the end of January, Margaret left for New York, taking Miss Reathal Odum, her mother's secretary, with her as a companion. I knew how it hurt to have the "Three Musketeers" cut down to two. Whenever Margaret would return from one of her concerts, they'd act like a bunch of kids at a school reunion, so happy were they to be together— flipping bits of things at each other at the table and laughing and joking.

Miss Margaret had never failed to keep me busy with her wardrobe on each trip she made home. She even had her dad helping out. I saw the President leaving early one morning, and I asked Prettyman, his valet, "Where is the Boss going so early?"

He said, "To Silver Springs. He is taking a box of winter hats to the train for Margaret."

This little station, or stop for a train, was often used by Presidents to avoid a crowd, or even to slip a VIP into town.

At the Blair House, we had time to talk and exchange more bits of information than in the more hectic days of big entertaining at the White House. Personally, I wondered where Truman had picked up his cocky ways, and the answer, I was quickly told, was "From his mother, of course." I hadn't met his ninety-two-year-old mother personally, when she came to visit him, but now I heard how Mrs. Martha Ellen Truman had made her mark among all the help when she announced, on arrival, "If I'd known there was going to be all this fuss, I wouldn't have come." And she had frowned at the news photographers as if she meant it.

Then one day, at the table, she demanded to know if a certain person was a "Yankee." Her son hastened to assure her that there were good Yankees as well as bad Yankees, and she replied tartly, "Well, I haven't found any good ones yet."

That took care of that. She wasn't going to let any old President change her mind at this late date. Harry Truman knew when he had met his match, and he called her the "Old Rebel." But he still followed her dictum that nobody should have to wash anybody else's socks or underwear, and he did his own.

There was a story backstairs that the President had asked his mother if she would like to sleep in Abraham Lincoln's bed, and she had declined; she was probably the only person who had visited the White House who didn't even want to inspect the famous bed. That part of the visit I'd already heard about, but it was just as funny on a second hearing.

Poor Margaret had her troubles with both grandmothers. One didn't want her to marry a Yankee, and the other, Mrs. Madge Wallace, didn't want her to go on the stage. So she disobeyed both of them.

I wasn't at all surprised when I saw the pictures of Margaret's husband, Clifton Daniel, a Yankee by choice, though born in North Carolina. I knew the type she liked. The clue was her fondness for the movie *The Scarlet Pimpernel*, which she ordered to be run twelve times, so that she could moon over Leslie Howard. And another

clue popped up when she met Anthony Eden. She came
floating on air into the sewing room.

"Oh, Lillian," she said, starry-eyed, "I just saw my
dream man."

I knew she would marry a man with an aesthetic look
and a little grey in his temples, and he would be an in-
tellectual. And I wasn't wrong.

The Blair House was wonderful to be in, because it gave
me a chance to live in close quarters with a First Lady,
but there were all kinds of little things that would go
wrong— like the entry rug that kept coming apart, and had
to be sewed and resewed and inspected every time before
guests arrived. Mrs. "T" had visions of some woman
catching her heel in it, or a wounded soldier catching his
crutch.

Then came real bad luck for *me* when we were washing
the nylon curtains that had been made new for the Trumans. They fell all to pieces, because the material wasn't
any good, and we decided to buy several bolts of material
and let "lucky me" make curtains for the two houses— the
Lee and the Blair. Eventually, the whole world looked
like one more length of nylon to me. But I survived.

Then there was the cook who refused to wear a cap, and
didn't survive. And there was the matter of the upside-
down Chilean flag to greet the Chilean President and
Señora Videla.

This was an unforgivable insult to our guests, and could
have embarrassed the Government. When the car pulled
up to the door, with Presidents Truman and Videla, the
mistake was seen at once, and Carl Ferguson, one of the
doormen, came running.

"Let me in the linen room," he panted. "The flag is
up wrong."

I went in with him and kept watch out of the window

to see who might be looking. The reporters and photographers were so busy, that no one looked up, and the flag was changed so quickly, that there was no story.

On one occasion, the City of New York was not as lucky as we were. There, they made headlines by flying the wrong flag when they gave a ticker tape parade for Sékou Touré, President of the young African Republic of Guinea. It reminded me of the day we goofed at the Lee House.

Being in charge, in any capacity, is no bed of roses— especially in the most important household in the country. If the doilies were ironed the least bit crooked, or the pillow cases had too much bluing in them, or the uniforms had too much starch, it was to me that all the complaints were made. We had three different laundries, and I had to be nursemaid to everything going out or coming in.

A little room— which I had to back into— on the fourth floor, across from Mrs. Truman's office, was used as the linen room. I just could not get used to the limited space in Blair House. Sometimes Mrs. Truman would literally "squeeze" in while I was counting the linen, to ask me to do some sewing for her.

But at least there was one compensation. While working in this little room, I could enjoy listening to Mrs. Truman talking to her friends on the phone. How she could laugh— the thing that people thought she never did!

For recreation, she read Westerns, but she didn't care for television.

Mrs. "T" had high blood pressure, and had to be on a salt-free diet. In fact, she had to be careful not to get excited, because it would make her ill. Sometimes she would have to lie down till the pressure became more normal.

I never saw President Truman more excited when Blair

House called him to tell him Bess was sick. He ran out of the Executive Offices— an adjunct to the White House that was not being renovated— and across the street to Blair House before the Secret Service men realized what had happened and hurried after him. Nothing in the world could upset him more than a crisis or setback that concerned his womenfolk.

Blair House saw a lot of action, particularly the attempt on the life of President Truman by the Puerto Rican assassins. When the dust had cleared, the truth came out that the Secret Service had wanted to rope off the front of the house when the family moved in, but Truman had said, "Nobody wants to shoot me. No, I don't think anyone wants to do me harm."

After the attempted assassination, everyone of the help had to show a pass to get in to work. Bullet-proof glass was installed in the windows on the street side, and shades were drawn when the lights were put on. Everyone was nervous for a long time. I had a feeling someone was crawling up the steps. It was such a strong feeling, that I would stop sewing, and go to the door and look, because these steps did lead to the basement door that one of the assassins had tried to enter.

Blair House also saw a lot of illustrious visitors. Prime Minister Nehru of India, laden with gifts and never removing that white cap from his head; Mme. Vijaya Lakshmi Pandit, then the Indian Ambassador to the United States, who was with her brother when he arrived at Blair House. To me, she was a beautiful lady, as she gracefully walked along with the wind blowing her hair and *sari*.

The front door of the Lee House was kept locked all the time for security reasons, but it would have to be opened so that the housemen could bring in the baggage. Without an elevator, Sarver and George had to carry everything up to the third floor. When the Shah of Iran came, I really felt sorry for those boys— he brought gifts in two boxes nearly as large as caskets. As I stood on the top floor and looked down the stairway, I could see their legs buckle under the weight. If they'd been in the White House, everything would have been put on a truck, and rolled to the elevator.

It was very hot during the arrival of President and Madame Auriol of France, and the maid to the First Lady of France took off her shoes as soon as she arrived. "I would have liked to take them off at the airport," she told me, when she brought me a heavy black dress to press for Madame Auriol. I thought she could never wear such a heavy dress in that weather, and learned, next morning, that she hadn't worn it after all.

President Aleman of Mexico was another Blair House guest, and so was Mrs. Eleanor Roosevelt, who came to tea. But the guest we made the most fuss over was Princess Elizabeth, who arrived with her Duke.

I was still in the midst of my curtains. It had taken Mrs. Truman, Mr. West, Mrs. Walker, and myself a full month to get the Lee House ready for the Princess. The sewing room was too small for me, so Mr. West suggested that I work in one of the rooms on the third floor in the Lee House. Not having a long table, I had to use the floor. But I was used to this. I'd had to use the State Dining Room once for the same purpose. I was on the floor so much there, that Mrs. Helm, Mrs. Truman's social secretary, said to me once, "Lillian, it looks funny to see you standing up."

In October, 1951, all the talk at Blair House centered on "when the Princess comes." New curtains were hanging at the windows, and some of the new tables that had been purchased for the White House were brought in for the bedrooms.

Mrs. Truman gave up her bed for the Princess, because it was the right size— three-quarters, with a canopy top. The carpenters put the bed up, including the wrinkles in the ruffles of the top. When I walked into the room and saw this error, I was too tired even to bawl them out for not letting me iron the ruffles first. I had a tall ladder brought into the room. Mrs. Truman saw me with an iron and a long cord. "What in the world are you going to do, Lillian?" she asked.

I said, "Press the top of the bed."

She just shook her head and walked away, as if to say she didn't want to see *that* job. It took a little time, but with a bath towel and a hot iron, Mrs. Walker and I did it.

Our troubles were not over. When we fixed up the sitting room, the air conditioning had to be taken out, and when it had been moved, the carpet beneath it was spoiled from dampness. Since there was wall-to-wall carpeting in the whole house, Mr. West, Mrs. Walker, and I just stood there and looked at each other, and wondered what in the world to do.

Then someone got a brilliant idea. We put a small rug over it, and a table, and set it up like a bar. It worked. We fiddled and fumbled and fixed until we had to take off our shoes and keep going in our stocking feet.

When I began to make the bed with pure linen sheets and a beautiful pale-blue blanket, I could only picture a little blonde girl sleeping in this bed, not a grown-up Princess. My mind went back to the day in 1939 when I had helped dress the bed in the Rose Room for her mother, Queen Elizabeth.

Fixing up the Duke's room was no trouble; it was strictly a man's room. In fact, all the bedrooms in the Lee House were on that order, and that is why we had to add a feminine touch to the Princess' room.

When November 1, 1951, came, what a different day it

was from last November 1, 1950, when tragedy had struck at Blair House. Now a real live Princess was coming to visit.

Mrs. Truman had made many trips riding up in the elevator in Blair House to the fourth floor, then walking down the steps in the Lee House, to inspect our work, and just before leaving for the airport, she came by for one last look. She was so pleased. Flowers were in all the rooms; a small tea table was set with a lace cloth; silver was in the Princess' room, and the new lamps were very pretty. We felt wonderful when she said, "You have done a splendid job." Then she was off to the airport, with the President and Margaret, to meet the Princess.

While she was gone, Wilma, Julia, Rose, and I changed into our best black uniforms. This is a *must* for the help— to change before any kind of an affair. Mrs. Walker told me, "We want you to be on the first floor by the stairway tonight. That tiny room under the stairway will be used as a powder room."

This was the first time I had worked at a dinner in a long time. Most of the dinners had been given at hotels while the Trumans were at Blair House. There would be eighteen for dinner, and at 10:00 P.M. there would be a reception for one hundred, with refreshments served.

When the President and the Princess arrived at Blair House at 5:00 P.M., a large crowd had gathered on the opposite side of the street to see her, and during her two days' visit, people were always there in crowds to catch a glimpse of the Royal couple.

Everything went smoothly. The party rushed right up to their rooms and had tea. The Princess changed from her red fitted coat to a silk dress and grey fur cape, all in thirty minutes. I saw her as she came down the steps, and I could hear the rustle of the silk dress.

When the Princess came in from the Statler Hotel, where

she met the members of the press, radio, and television, she had less than an hour to make herself still more beautiful for dinner. It was rush, rush, rush! Before dinner, during dinner, and after dinner, I had too many experiences to mention here. I sewed hems in dresses that had been stepped on. And then, just a few minutes before eight, Mr. Searles, one of the ushers, went up the stairs to bring the Princess and the Duke to dinner, and as I knew they would pass me, I stood very straight and close to the wall.

My heart was beating very quickly. The Princess looked beautiful, with her head held high. She said to the Duke, "Nana said my dress is too long."

The Duke asked, "What?"

She repeated, "Nana said my dress is too long," to which the Duke gave no reply.

The Princess looked as though she were saying to herself, "Men! They never pay attention!", and I wished that the housewives of America could have seen this too.

Both the Princess and the Duke of Edinburgh gave me a faint smile, and went into the drawing room to meet the dinner guests. After dinner, the Princess went to her room, the Duke walking three paces behind her. I could just imagine an American husband's reaction to those three paces!

In five minutes, the Royal couple returned for coffee. And after coffee, there was a reception. I didn't know how *they* felt, but I was exhausted!

Incidentally, the maid Nana, whom the Princess had quoted, looked like a petite model, but since she had been with the Princess so long, Her Majesty still called her "Nana."

The next morning, John Dean, the Duke's valet, informed us that he was going sight-seeing. Later, the Duke came from the second floor to John's room on the third floor, and yelled, "John! John!" I stepped out of the sewing room, looked over the balustrade, and said, "He went sightseeing." The Duke said, "OK," and sailed down the steps in his shirt sleeves— I imagine he was going to the usher's office. It is very hard to make people understand just how human these people are, regardless of their position in life.

On Friday night, the Princess gave a dinner for the President and Mrs. Truman at the Canadian Embassy. Before noon on Saturday, the couple was ready to leave, and Mrs. Truman brought the Princess to the Glass Room to see her mother, Mrs. Wallace.

When they had gone, and Rose and I were cleaning the room, I saved one thing for a souvenir— the linen towel the Princess had used to wipe her pen. I could have gotten the ink out, but I didn't. I kept it, and I also answered for it to the inventory men.

When we reviewed the visit, the most surprising thing that struck us was what the Princess' maid had told us in the Royal bedroom: "It looks *so* like her room in the Castle." No one had had any idea as to what her room was like. It was just a case of doing our best with what we had. From what the maid told us, I understand the room is quite beautiful, and I hope to make a visit there one of these days.

Then, suddenly, it was time to go back to the White House. The employees were invited to show their families through before the President was due to move back. I asked Mama if she wanted to see it.

She said, "No, I want to remember it as I've always known it."

It was a sad inspection tour, and I felt a deadness as I walked up the stairs and through the rooms. All I could think of was that it looked like a glorious "Home Show." Sadly I told Mrs. "T" about my visit, and she said, "I should spank you for walking up all those steps. You should have waited till we moved and the elevator was working."

But what she really meant was "so you wouldn't have had to be alone when you saw it."

That was Bess, all right— warm and friendly in her talk, concerned in a personal way, and feeling more than she said.

I thought, "I can't help it, but Bess is best."

LIFE WITH MAMIE

When Mrs. Eisenhower came to look over the White House before moving in, Mrs. Truman said to one of the maids, "Julia, by this time next month, you are going to have a fluffy White House."

We wondered what she meant. But we'd find out soon enough. We'd also find out the significance of the hat Mrs. Eisenhower wore on her visit.

Mrs. Eisenhower had looked very dignified when she visited and very conservatively dressed, but on her head was a cute pink hat. That color pink was the clue we weren't smart enough to see. But pink and fluffy were what we became at the White House. And fussy.

I've sewn a lot of things for a lot of exacting First Ladies, but I think the strangest or the fussiest items I've ever had to make at the White House were a cover for an inlaid hand mirror, whose beauty should have been enjoyed, and a cover for a lipstick holder, which was gem-encrusted. Both these items— I'm sure you have guessed it— were for Mrs. Eisenhower.

I also made a cover for the chandelier at Gettysburg. The work got so bad, that for the first time in my career at the White House, I even considered quitting before I was ready to retire. What stopped me was that Mama was bedridden, and needed nursing care round the clock. I was home nights, but since her pension was only $111.00 a month, I had to dip into savings for the nurses, both in the daytime and when I was working late for the White House entertainments, zipping zippers, and standing by in the powder room, with my SOS kit of needles and pins.

Mama had been living more and more in the past. But even so, her mind was sharp. When I would tell her about a President or First Lady, she would remember, and pick a name from the past. When I told her how fussy the new First Lady was, she said, "Mrs. Taft."

Mrs. Roosevelt's life had recalled to her the second Mrs. Wilson. Pepper-tongued President Truman had been "Calvin Coolidge." She would just whip out the name as if that explained everything.

I told her how everyone had expected President Eisenhower to be exceptionally friendly, because there had even been a slogan, "I Like Ike," and yet the President hardly knew we were there, and was definitely not friendly. She snapped, "Herbert Hoover."

She was right when I thought about it. And every Mamie Eisenhower assignment I would tell Mama about at home would always bring forth the same name, "Mrs. Taft."

I remembered the stories Mama had brought home about Mrs. Taft, and how she had striven to turn the White House into a palace. The two ladies were alike in many ways. Mrs. Eisenhower had also known the rigors of tropical life, and she often told me how she had been beset by every form of insect and reptile life, and every hazard of the elements.

She now showed great concern for public opinion, and I remembered that Mama had said that when the public complained because Taft played golf, instead of doing something for the people in order to get himself re-elected, the only thing Mrs. Taft worried about was that people might see her playing cards on the Sabbath.

Mrs. Taft always worried about the impression her husband would make on the public, and even sat in on his meetings to keep him from making a bad impression. Similarly, President Eisenhower didn't dare appear in his golfing outfit when his wife was entertaining at the White House.

Once, when Mrs. "E" had invited a group of ladies to the East Room, at about 3:00 P.M., to hear the Little Singers of Korea, President Eisenhower was in the yard, knocking his golf balls around, when the children arrived. I was surprised when I saw someone's head thrust through the center of the green draperies that are used to close off the corridor when guests are in the house on the ground floor. I had to look a second time. The cap was on sideways.

Then the President came close to where I was standing at the foot of the stairway that leads to the East Room, and said to me, very softly, "Vice-President Nixon phoned me to be sure to hear these children sing." He had on a sweater and golf shoes. He eased up to the top step, and sat down to listen. Soon he said, "I guess I had better get out of here," and tiptoed down. He went to his room, changed to a suit and rushed down to shake hands with the Little Singers, but they got away in the bus before the usher could catch them.

When I told Moaney, "Your boss was on the steps wearing that cap and sweater," he said, "Miss Mamie would have had a fit if she had known he was near the guests in that outfit."

So a group of youngsters missed a handshake they would have remembered all their lives, because a First Lady wanted only "properly dressed" people in the White House, including her husband.

My first shocker in the work department was when Mrs. Eisenhower ordered me to make thirty-two pairs of curtains, because she didn't like the looks of the natural-color raw silk curtains on the second-floor living quarters. She wanted them made of "that white silk that is used for making parachutes" that you can "just swish out." Thirty-two pairs!

When I heard that I was to make enough for the whole second floor, I protested, "I don't see how I can do my regular work and make thirty-two pairs of curtains too," and said that for such big jobs we used outside help. Mrs. Eisenhower said, "My husband is in here to balance the budget, and we are going to do them ourselves."

So I sewed enough parachute material to float to the moon.

It took time, but Mrs. Eisenhower was always in a hurry. As I strained to please her, I remembered the new White House as we had moved in after leaving Blair House, and how the natural-color raw silk curtains were one of the things we particularly liked, because they took away from the "home show" look, and toned things down a little. Now the bright white of the parachute cloth would be more "home show" than ever.

And then, shades of pink! The order came for rose drapery and pink curtains. I was to make rose drapery for Mrs. "E"'s dressing room, and pink fiberglass curtains to replace the white ones in her bathroom and her mother's bathroom.

I remembered that when we were moving into the renovated White House, and there were still workmen around, we had to keep the doors locked, and Mrs. Walker had gone around with a big ring of keys around her waist. We maids kept borrowing the keys, and we would end up accidentally locking each other into rooms. I wished now I could tell

Mrs. Walker to just lock me in, because I was losing my mind for sure.

The newest order of the First Lady had me really punchy. It was to make covers for the bottom of the rose drapery. I had to take old sheets and make a long case, open at one end. Every night, the maid would have to slip the bottom of the drapery into the sheets and tape them halfway up, to hold them onto the drapery. This was to keep them clean while Mrs. "E" slept.

I was not the only one going out of my mind. The kitchen help reported that pink had crept onto the dining room table, and pink food was also the order of the day. Whatever wasn't peppermint-pink was mint-green.

Finally, the papers were making too much of the pink White House, or as we called it backstairs, "The Pink Palace," and so the table decorations became yellow, and yellow and gold were suddenly the only colors in demand.

I heard the head gardener say to the housekeeper, "I had to tell her this morning that if she didn't stop using so much yellow, the newspapers would be on her soon."

So we went back to "Mamie Pink," and a pink carnation was named for her.

It got so bad that on one occasion, *pink* candles were used at a *luncheon*. Some one passed me in a hurry and said, "Can you see candles on a table this time of day?"

The servants never fail to see every little detail and comment on it. After the luncheons, the ladies usually came to the ground floor to see a movie. I could leave the powder room and go to the theatre also. *Gigi* was shown five times, and the President saw it three times.

When Mrs. "E" had the annual luncheon for the "Senate Ladies"— the wives of the Senators— she wanted pink tablecloths, so the housekeeper sent to a hotel for them. When I saw them, I asked her, "What are you going to do, use *pink* cloths and *white* napkins?"

She said, "We can't use the pink ones anyway, because they have the name of the hotel on them." I thought this was the best thing that had ever happened, because it turned out that the small tables with white cloths and "Mamie pink" flowers were just right.

Mrs. "E" would give favors to the ladies. Once they were little hat boxes with tiny hats inside. I remember having seen Mrs. John Kennedy at the Senate ladies' luncheon; she was the youngest person present, and the most simply dressed.

Mrs. Eisenhower broke with tradition in many ways in her entertainment, but, in the jive talk of the young folks today, of all the parties I have ever seen in the White House the Halloween party that Mrs. Eisenhower gave October 30, 1958, for the wives of the White House staff members, was really a "gasser." Even the old-timers backstairs could think of nothing to compare it with.

Some of the guests described it as "the most interesting" party they had ever seen at the White House, and I had a feeling they were simply at a loss for words. I guess it *was* "interesting" to come into the dignified White House and see scary-looking skeletons hanging in the ornate State Dining Room. Witches on broomsticks perched on the white tablecloth. Swinging from the elegant chandelier were black cats, witch heads, black owls, and goblins, mingled with fall foliage. Outside the room, brown corn stalks, huge real and fake pumpkins, and rosy-red, giant-sized apples clustered at the base of the corn stalks, and transformed the red-carpeted corridor into a harvest scene. Orange light bulbs were placed in the chandeliers in the marble corridor.

The worst part of it was that this spectacular was to be left over the week end for the sightseers to view. Most of them thought the children had had a party, the backstairs folks reported.

When another maid told me to please look and tell her if she were justified in shuddering at this sight in the White House, I looked, but I had just come through a one-and-a-half-day shock treatment of my own, and was beyond shuddering at anything. It had to do with the preparations for this same party.

Just two days before the party, Mrs. Walker came rushing into the linen room and said, "Put aside everything. Mrs. E wants you to make pink flowered draperies to match the paper we are putting on the wall in the powder room off the library, and a skirt has to be made for the long dressing table."

The library on the ground floor is one of the choice rooms of the House. The walls, lined with books, are made of the natural wood, nail holes and all, of the old White House before it was renovated. There is a dark red rug on the floor with an eagle in the center, that was formerly in the Red Parlor. The black Baldwin piano, which President Truman ordered, is in this room. Well, when I was told to get out two pink rugs, for the bathroom and entry floors, I thought, "This is the last straw!"

They were salmon-pink, and whenever I opened the door to the powder room, something would hit me right in the face— clash! Mrs. "E" thought the room looked fine, and on her way to the movie, she told me, "Lillian, the room looks very nice."

Frankly, I was too shell-shocked to shudder much for anyone else. Forty-nine guests sat at the E-shaped table, scattered with autumn leaves, ears of dried corn, autumn nuts, squash, and dried gourds, and backstairs, we hoped that none of the guests would make a mistake and eat some of them in the eerie light.

It wasn't just the fussy parties and the striving for perfection that was putting a strain on the folks backstairs. It was the effort to hurry so, and to be perfect even in what we said.

For example, Mrs. Eisenhower decreed that there would be no slang or nicknames. It began with her hearing the help call the houseman Enrique "Ricky." Everyone called him that. His full name was Enrique Aflague. She not only decreed no nicknames, but commented that she didn't like to hear her husband's name bandied about as "Ike."

Taking away nicknames was taking away the spice and fun of backstairs life. The handsome chief usher, James West, was called "Perry Como" because of a real resemblance. George Thompson, the likeable houseman, was "Jockey" because of his size. Head Electrician Johnson, who had operated the first movie projector under Hoover, was happily called "Short Circuit." Even Mrs. Walker, our housekeeper, was known backstairs as "The Tennessee Darling" because of her southern accent.

The White House is practically famous for its nicknames. I remember the time the carpenter's daughter came and asked for Mr. Benton. Not till she added, "He's known here as 'Tojo,' " did they snap to and find him.

And the irony of it all was that, while we had to use our dull, formal names, Mrs. Eisenhower still called her personal maid, Rose Wood, "Rosie," and her husband, "Ike."

By 1956, the First Family was spending a great deal of time at the farm. These trips got me down, because the White House linens had to be hauled back and forth. If I didn't send enough, Mrs. "E" would call for one dozen pillow cases to be sent eighty miles before she would use one of her own. The laundry in the basement was swamped at times, and so was I, because I had to keep a record of what went out and what came back.

I well remember May 24, 1956, because after handling over a hundred sheets, towels, and pillow cases that morning, I began to feel sick— all on my left side. I rested a few minutes, then took the elevator to pick up some clean washcloths from the laundry. When I got to the ground floor, I went straight to the housekeeper's office, because my left arm was becoming numb. It turned out that I was having a small heart attack.

What started out to be a few things turned into a mountain. For three months, I sewed slip covers, curtains, and other household items, and there was no letup. Each week end, when the family went to Gettysburg, Mrs. Eisenhower wanted to take as many things that were finished as possible, and if something weren't finished, she was very displeased about it. I disappointed her several times, but never let it worry me, because I could only do so much in the time that was allotted me.

In June of 1955, invitations were issued to a select group of the White House staff to attend a picnic at Gettysburg to celebrate the thirty-ninth wedding anniversary of "Ike and Mamie" and the completion of the President's house. Four years later, the oversight was corrected, and on June 6, 1959, a buffet supper was held for the entire staff.

Mrs. "E" stood on one of the three stone steps, and shook hands with each guest, making us feel very welcome. She wanted to know if I had bought my yellow flowered dress in California. I told her I had picked it up in a Washington store. Then she said, "It is a real California dress." I felt real proud of my $8.00 cotton dress, especially when Mrs. Robert Anderson, wife of the Secretary of the Treasury, said to me, "I ran over here to tell you how pretty your dress is."

My lifetime of making things over without a pattern had really been rewarded. Even the President got into the spirit of things, and posed happily for everyone who had brought a camera. Later, he graciously said he didn't remember when he had enjoyed himself as much.

Looking at Mrs. "E" as she drank a coke and invited me

to have one too, I couldn't help but think of how really likeable she is. She has an endearing quality that I am sure helped her husband get elected and re-elected. I suddenly thought, "Why, oh why, can't First Ladies be perfect?"

Well, they aren't, and they never were. And they are never as you think they will be from advance publicity. Since everyone parroted the slogan, "I Like Ike," I had thought that the President would have many friends, but he seemed to be clannish and to stick to just a few friends— all millionaires— whom he had known only since he had become an important General, and who were quickly nicknamed "The White House Clan." The leader was George Allen, who also owns a Gettysburg estate.

Backstairs, we speculated that the man behind the "I Like Ike" slogan was really sort of an introvert, who liked to get away from people, and enjoyed painting because it was a solitary occupation. The real extrovert of the family was Mrs. Eisenhower, definitely.

The First Lady seemed never to stop talking, and you would hear her voice and laughter just as soon as she would reach the floor and get off the elevator. She wanted to be an outstanding First Lady, but her health was a great handicap. She had to spend much time in bed, and social gatherings usually turned into a torment with headaches, asthma, weakness, and the inner ear trouble, which made her feel dizzy, and which has thrown her step off balance more than once.

Mrs. "E" spent so much time in bed that, in spite of her feeling about nicknames, she was referred to in hushed tones as "Sleeping Beauty." Even with the servants, she wanted to maintain a gay, holiday air, and she was the first to order a birthday cake made for every member of the help. There were three cakes on my birthday, because I had to share honors with storekeeper Melvern Carter and messenger Shermont Brooks, also born on February first.

Usually Mrs. "E" kept close track of what was going on in the kitchens, by having the food brought to her for tasting, but on the birthday occasions, she would show up in the kitchens. The help said that she only saw the kitchens when she wanted to have her picture taken.

Never has a First Lady received more service, and that led to a housekeeping problem. In the past, there had been three housemen to do the cleaning of the two family floors, but when one houseman left and another retired, Mrs. "E" had three Guamian and Filipino housemen assigned to do nothing but wait on her. They took turns stationing themselves outside her door, to run errands and deliver messages. They also waited on her when she had her bridge friends in, and would go to Gettysburg to take care of her there. That left only one houseman, George Thompson, to do all the heavy cleaning of the second- and third-floor family quarters. And I used to smile when I would read that "Mamie is such a good housekeeper," because I knew that, though the rug might be swept clean of footprints, back in the corners the dust was collecting.

I wasn't surprised when I got the report, from good backstairs authority, that when Eisenhower returned from his last European trip in May, 1960, after the Summit Meeting fiasco, he took one look at the condition of the living quarters, and announced that he wanted the house cleaned up.

Of course, one houseman couldn't do the work of three. The changeover had begun not many months after Mrs. Eisenhower had arrived at the White House. First, she brought in two men from the Navy— Enrique Aflague, a Guamian, and Francisco Lim, a Filipino. Then the third member was added, a Filipino named Jaunito Malapit. All of them had to wait on the First Lady exclusively, and travel to the farm. This arrangement left us short two men upstairs for the whole administration.

Mrs. Eisenhower never wanted anything sent to the

cleaners, and prevented the housekeeper from sending things out to be cleaned. This was entirely her job to look after the upkeep of the mansion. She had to see that rugs, draperies, and all chair and sofa covers were cleaned, without first having to get permission from the First Lady.

But Mrs. Eisenhower wanted the feeling of really running *her* White House, and for the rest of us, permission had to be granted for every little thing. For some reason, if the rugs were brushed clean of footprints, she had a feeling that the house was sparkling clean. Much was made of the business of keeping Mrs. Eisenhower from seeing footprints on a rug before she appeared in any room; everyone became so rug-conscious, that even the police, Secret Service men, and ushers would step around the rugs.

This led to a vastly amusing but disastrous occasion. Mary Jane McCaffree, the social secretary, had become so rug-conscious that while showing some female newspaper reporters the table decor before a State dinner, she said quite sharply, "Please don't step on the carpet!"

Needless to say, the women were shocked. Of course, they didn't know that this was Mrs. Eisenhower's special idiosyncrasy. The witty George Dixon, who writes a column distributed by King Features Syndicate, related the comment of one of the angry newswomen. She had told Dixon, "What the blank did she think we were doing— wearing spikes?"

The man who could really write a book about what goes on, and illustrate it with pictures, is Abbe Rowe of the Interior Department, the man who photographs everything that takes place on Government property in Washington, D.C. I got acquainted with Abbe Rowe, because, whenever the head laundress, Pauline Ferguson, pressed the creases from the tablecloths, I stood ready with my needle and thread to mend any little bad spot in the nine tablecloths that it took for a full-size formal dinner. And Abbe Rowe was there too, to take pictures.

Then I learned that in the Department of the Interior, there is an absolutely priceless photographic record of everything memorable or important that happens in Government. Probably a hundred years from now, the public will be looking at and exclaiming over how we did things in the White House in the twentieth century.

But Abbe Rowe won't be able to reproduce in pictures the amount of interest the various First Ladies have shown in the White House. We had thought that Mrs. Truman had shown a great interest in the running of the house, and was economy-minded, but that was only a prelude to Mrs. Eisenhower, who wanted to put to use her knowledge of budget-living, which she had acquired as a military wife.

She ordered that all leftovers be saved, and the help was afraid to throw away even a dab of something, because she might call for it again at any moment. Another economy measure was cutting down on electricity. When Mrs. Eisenhower first moved into the White House, and saw how dark the interior was, she ordered that all the lights must burn in the rooms, even in daytime, to keep the house from looking dreary. When, by chance, Mr. Crim told her how much the light bill was each month, the lights only burned when it was necessary.

Mrs. Eisenhower would hold daily morning bedside conferences on the running of the household. She would be sitting up in bed writing— here she would spend most of the mornings with her mail. Everyone would come to her— Mrs. Walker, who was really Mrs. Eli Ciarrochi (we simply added a "Mrs." to the Walker when she got married during the Truman administration, because the new name was too hard for us); Mr. West, the head usher; Charles, the butler, and, very occasionally, me.

I remember the day I saw Mrs. Walker carrying to the second floor a plate with four or five little squares of cake on it. I was horrified when I learned that cake mixes were to be used for the teas. Considering the amount we had left over from time to time, I judged that some of the guests didn't like them. The mixes were only used for sheet cake; other cookies and cakes were made by the cooks. I am certain that fewer meals were served during the Eisenhower administration than during any other I have known.

For months at a time, there would be no house guests— only the children in and out— and no parties for young people. All the parties seemed to circle round the older friends— Army buddies— and George Allen, who was like a member of the family.

For a time, Mrs. Eisenhower had a French chef, one of the most famous cooks and pastrymen in the field, François Rysavy, who had cooked for famous people all over the world, from ambassadors to Hollywood stars. But he only lasted at the White House about three years. He let it be known that cooking without onions and garlic was too hard on his nervous system.

The problem was that the President and First Lady did not share the same tastes for food. The President loved onions and garlic. Mrs. Eisenhower couldn't bear even the odor, and Rysavy was torn between their desires. He was ordered by the President to serve a little separate dish of onions on the side, but how could he do that without the odor? Mrs. Eisenhower would say, "I smell onions in *my* house."

Rysavy left, and we heard that he had returned to Hollywood to cook for David Selznick and his wife, Jennifer Jones.

Once I visited Mrs. Eisenhower in her room just after the second Inaugural Ball, and told her how lovely her gown had been. It was perfectly exquisite— citron yellow silk, with an overdress embroidered in beads and tiny pearls, with slippers and evening bag to match. The earrings and necklace also matched. I thought the first inaugural pink gown was pretty, but I have to admit that the yellow was even prettier.

When I told her I thought the dress was very pretty, she said, "I think it is pretty too. The Museum is asking for it already."

The last time she wore the dress, for the King and Queen of Denmark, she told Rosalind Russell, who was a guest, that it was the last time she would wear it, and that the dress was being sent the next day to the Metropolitan Museum in New York. By the time you read this, it should be on display.

But getting back to the bedside visit, Mrs. Eisenhower told me what a strain it had been for her to watch the parade, and how she'd worried about the President too, for fear he would become too fatigued. Then she said to me, "It is nice to have this chat. We seldom see each other."

After I walked out of her room that morning, January 22, 1957, nearly a year passed before I saw her again. I would hear her talking in the hall sometimes when the children were in the house, or she was on her way out, but I was so busy, that I just never took time out to go to her room. When I finally did see her, she said, "Lillian, where have you been?" She was on her way to a movie for her luncheon guests. I told her, "Busy, and when I am not busy, you are."

I used to get very angry with her, and probably she with me. But we developed a warm feeling toward each other, and she gave me many little gifts that showed a personal touch, such as a lavender stole to go with my blue-tinted grey hair. And I reciprocated by trying to find something she wouldn't think of for herself— a candle snuffer for her home at Gettysburg. One year, I gave her a zipper zipper,

to help when the zipper is in the back of the dress. I en-
closed a note saying, "Maybe you won't need this because
you have Rosie."

Back came the reply, "I can use this with or without
Rosie."

I will never forget how kind she was when Mama died.
In fact, everyone at the White House was most understanding. President and Mrs. Eisenhower sent a white Cross
made of carnations. There were flowers and a large dona-
tion from all the employees, some of whom had worked
with my mother through the years.

I had been able to control myself pretty well until I
learned one thing from the practical nurse who had cared
for her those last years. Bertha Davis, who had also worked
for Dr. Montgomery Blair of the Blair House family, told
me how Mama had lived each day for the moment when I
would return from work. She would look at the clock
around 4:00 and 4:30 and say, "It's time for my little Hop-
Skip to come home."

For all our talk and laughter about nicknames at the
White House, I had never known that Mama had had a
nickname for me all the time. And she had hidden it as
effectively as the nicknames of Presidents and First Ladies
are hidden at the White House.

When Mama died, it brought back memories of the last
days of Mrs. Truman's mother, Mrs. Wallace. When Vietta
would go to lunch, I would sit with Mrs. Wallace, and
sometimes read to her, as Vietta did. Mrs. Wallace was an
Episcopalian, and, since I was too, several times she gave
me money to buy candles for my church.

Toward the end, the only thing she would eat was home-
made ice cream, which I would make and feed to her. Mrs.
Truman had been so grateful, that she had sent boxes of
candy home with me for my mother.

When Mama died, in 1953, I needed to get away from

Washington very badly, but it was not until 1954 that I saw my way clear to take a real vacation— a trip to California to see brother Emmett. He had married a beautiful girl from Peru named Fidelia Gallardo, and they were living a story book kind of life in sunny Coronado.

Fidelia, who worked for a catering service, had cooked dinners and luncheons for the John Roosevelt family in Coronado. Once, when FDR came, she cooked the luncheon that his son gave for him, and the President complimented her and said, "How come you don't work for the Government?" She answered, "I look after your children," and the President had been very pleased.

I hated to leave the land of sunshine and water and easy living, but the White House was still much in my mind, and I missed hearing the cheery voice of Mamie Eisenhower as she walked down the halls.

THE MUSIC GOES ROUND
AND ROUND

As I flew back to Washington and my White House home, I reflected on the old jinx— no President has escaped trouble, tragedy, or scandal, or a combination of all three. The Eisenhowers had trouble with sickness and scandalmongers. Before the Eisenhowers had arrived at the White House, the rumors had started circulating behind the scenes, brought in, of course, by guests.

From what I saw of the President around the White House, I would say that he was not at all a "lady's man," but one who enjoyed good male company. He and the First Lady shared an amazing bond that was a joy to behold.

She was the most feminine of the four First Ladies I had worked for, and showed the greatest possessiveness toward her husband. And he paid more attention to her, and made her feel more a bride than the other Presidents did with their First Ladies. I believe that other wives were jealous: Mamie seemed to have everything. Anyway, they just wanted to tear her apart— her reputation and her looks.

People would say, "How do you think Mamie looks with

her bangs and full skirts?" and I would say, "I think she looks like a living doll."

To tell you the truth, when she was at her best, she did too. She wanted to look that way, and she accomplished it. With her poor health and frequent confinement in bed, it was hard to do, but she had a trick that the average house-wife would do well to copy.

The day of a party, she would try on her complete outfit in the morning, make sure that everything suited her, then take it off and go back to bed. When she arose just before the party, she would dress in no time at all, and there was no panic, no missing accessories or buttons. All hooks worked. They had been pretested.

As I walked back into the White House after my vaca-tion, I remembered how I had first met Mrs. Eisenhower. She had stopped by the linen room, and laughingly told me that there would be some babies around the White House. Then, a little later, she'd been back. It had been obvious that she was exploring the White House.

She came to the cedar room, which is across the hall from my linen room. Then she called, "Lillian, what are these things doing in here?"

I answered, "They are White House property, and they belong in there."

Then she said, "Well, this is not *my* cedar room after all."

I said, "No, Madam, this side is yours, and this side is the President's, and this side is for the White House."

Then she wanted to know, "Where will I put my per-fumes? I just can't let them lie on the floor four years."

"You have other store rooms in the attic," I said, and took her on a little tour. Someone had given her the mis-taken idea that the cedar room was hers exclusively. When we got to the room where the tubs and ironing boards were, she said, "What goes on in here?" I told her we used it mostly when the visitors came.

"Well, I'm glad you know what to do. The King and Queen of Greece will be here soon."

She was in a happy mood then, and went downstairs. Later, I would wonder where she would keep her two hundred hats.

I got used to Mrs. Eisenhower's moods eventually. She was a barometer, and you could tell instantly if things were going well or ill for her by the way she responded.

She would have been happy to be with her husband every moment, and she shared his TV western programs, though her own favorites were the daytime soap operas. You might say that she was the first TV fan of the First Ladies. Many a time, the President and First Lady would eat dinner on a tray while watching TV.

Whenever the President was ill— an operation, a heart attack, and a slight stroke— the First Lady would go right to the hospital too, and I'm certain that if she could have suffered his discomfort for him, she would gladly have done so, so much did she "like Ike." She shed tears easily, but most of her tears were for him.

When the President suffered the ileitis attack on June 8, 1956, and had to have an operation, it was a pathetic First Lady who dressed and rushed to the hospital. And, frankly, seeing how sick he was, we were afraid that the First Lady would be coming back alone. Rose Wood packed a bag for Mrs. "E" and took it to the hospital.

We shared all the agonies with her, waiting and watching for the next report. Bulletins were read to the reporters at intervals by nervous, chain-smoking James Hagerty. I think that after the operation, we *all* felt better.

Only then could we laugh about the mix-up of the ambulance that was called from Walter Reed Hospital. It made a mistake by going to the East entrance, where the sightseers come in, and couldn't find the right place to pick up the President. It had to turn around, and come to the North Gate. This drew a small crowd, you may be sure. The President was carried down the grand stairway to the ground floor while I was keeping Mrs. Eisenhower's fitter trapped in my linen room, so she couldn't find out what was happening and spill the beans.

I think it is a miracle of modern medicine that the President was able to overcome such medical handicaps as a heart attack and an operation, and still run for a second term in office, and become, at seventy, the oldest President ever to be in the White House.

Wherever they went— hospitals, Gettysburg, or Denver— the First Lady spent much of the time on the phone to the White House, giving us directions. Especially orders to send this and send that.

I remember that in December, 1959, Mrs. "E" left for Denver to see her mother. The next morning, when I stopped in the housekeeper's office, I saw a feather hat and a pink bed comforter on the leather couch. I said to Mrs. Walker, "Don't tell me you are sending these things to Denver already?" She said, "What do you mean, she hasn't even gotten to Denver yet. She called from Chicago."

When the President had the heart attack in Denver, Mrs. "E" called for a variety of things, but the most surprising one was "turnip greens for the President." Naturally, we didn't ask whether the city of Denver was out of them.

Mrs. Walker looked at me and said, "How many would you send?"

I told her, "No less than half a bushel, to Denver."

We were all very glad when the news came that the President was coming home on November 11, 1955. We watched the TV, and saw him step off the plane. Then all the servants assembled on the ground floor by the Oval

Room door to wait for him. Mr. Crim suggested that we meet him but not tax his strength by shaking hands. When he left the car and came through the Oval Room, there was tremendous applause. He was so surprised that he couldn't speak; he just bowed and bowed all the way to the elevator. These little scenes are very touching between the President and his employees. I think it is wonderful sometimes to let the President know he is still regarded as a human being.

Mrs. Eisenhower was very happy that they were going to the farm for a rest. She would have the President all to herself for a while, and nothing made her happier than that.

Mrs. "E" dared to do many things that broke with tradition, such as riding to the White House in the same car as her husband, after the inaugural ceremony, instead of in the car behind. It is customary for the Vice-President to ride with the President.

People ask me if I knew that Eisenhower and Truman were having a feud. Of course. Everything was known backstairs, even before the Eisenhowers moved in.

I watched from Margaret Truman's bedroom window when President-elect Eisenhower came to visit President Truman, and it was obvious, when he came out, that Eisenhower was angry. When he next came to the White House, to pick up the outgoing President on his way to the Capitol, Eisenhower did not come into the White House. Although Truman was still his Commander-in-Chief, he made the President come out to him. So Ike too broke a few traditions.

And then came a startling sign that Ike did not like Truman, though Truman was supposed to have first voiced the slogan "I like Ike" at the Potsdam Conference in 1945. I was shocked, and so was everyone else backstairs, to see that Eisenhower had ordered the picture of Truman taken down in the lobby of the White House. It had been a custom that the last two Presidents were always represented in the lobby. Ike had both Truman's and Roosevelt's pictures removed.

So Eisenhower and his First Lady both had a little experience in breaking with tradition.

One change I objected to was that Mrs. "E" stopped inviting Heads of State to stay overnight at the White House; from the beginning, she always packed them off to Blair House. Her excuse was that it was more convenient for the guests, but backstairs, we felt that it was really her desire for privacy— a desire she and the President shared.

Much as she loved her grandchildren and her son and daughter-in-law, they stayed on the third floor and not on hers— the second floor. Foreign dignitaries have always stayed on the second floor too, of course. Health may have played a part in it, but I think privacy did too.

Mrs. "E" also cut out the traditional formal parties for top American officials, such as the Vice-President's dinner and the dinner for the Chief Justice of the Supreme Court. The excuse was that it might interfere with the dinners for foreign dignitaries, who were coming to the United States in droves.

Whatever the reason, I will be happy to see the White House return to normal, and I hope the new First Lady will restore the tradition of honoring foreign visitors by keeping them as overnight guests, and that she will bring back the dinners at which the White House honors America's own important officials.

I am not trying to say that we had no entertaining during the Eisenhower administration. There were some very exciting times, and some made even more exciting by a comedy of errors. I can recall the biggest mix-up in baggage anyone could remember. When King Paul and Queen Frederika of Greece arrived, the first royal visitors for the Eisenhowers, part of the baggage went to Blair

House, part to the Embassy, and part to the White House, and nobody could find what they needed.

But, worst of all, the Queen's maid was looking for a small bag, which she had to have at once, so the drivers went to Blair House and brought the truckload of baggage back to the White House and asked the housekeeper to take a look. They had given up. Mrs. Walker asked me to go outside with her to the truck. It had started to rain, but we had no time to cover up. We still didn't find the bag, and rushed inside. The phone was ringing, and I answered for her. It was Mrs. Geaney, housekeeper at Blair House, saying, "O, brother, if you will send the baggage back, so we can get the Prime Minister's clothes, we will dress him and send him over there to dinner."

Then came another ring. The bag that we were looking for had been in the Queen's room all along. They had been practically falling over it as they were calling for help in searching for it.

Then there was President Bayar of Turkey, whose valet distinguished himself at the White House by claiming he did not know how to press his master's suit. We ended up doing it for him, but, oh, what a time we had while we hunted for someone to do it! "Where's George?" became the byword.

There was much worse trouble when Emperor Haile Selassie arrived with his son, Sahle Selassie Haile, who was wearing elevator shoes. It wasn't the elevator shoes that bothered us; it was the shirts he had shopped for upon arrival in the United States, so that he would look very American. The catch was that he had purchased size $14\frac{1}{2}$ shirts and size 14 collars. When "Where's George" came out of the room, after trying to make that royal Prince look presentable, he was absolutely unpresentable himself. He looked as though he had been in a Turkish bath with his clothes on.

And then there was the night Khrushchev and his wife came to dinner, and one of his aides looked at the dark-colored skin of many of the White House employees and actually asked, "Are these your slaves?" Backstairs we had a little fun with that one.

And there was also the night I got the shock of my life when Chief of Protocol, Wiley Buchanen, came right into the powder room with his wife. The Chief of Protocol doing such a thing? I couldn't believe my eyes, and then I noticed that he was holding her lovely green dress against her back. The zipper had given way, and there were only two minutes to go.

I quickly sewed her in, and, as they walked away, I said, "You will have to cut her out of that dress before she can go to bed tonight."

He turned back, smiling, and retorted, "I'm not sure yet. I may just let her stay that way all night, Lillian."

Well, those were two happy people I'd sent on their way.

And then there was the time the wife of a "Little Cabinet" officer lost her petticoat at a White House reception for the sub-Cabinet and independent agencies. There it was— spread out below her on the floor of the Red Room. By a comedy of errors, the petticoat kept changing hands among a bevy of people who didn't know what to do with it, until a butler saved the day by putting a pillow over it and carrying it off.

But there was plenty of excitement backstairs too. I recall the night that the Fred Waring group played for Queen Elizabeth II, and asked for a spray gun. The musicians wanted to spray their instruments with gold. I met the head painter coming out of the housekeeper's office the next morning, looking very forlorn, and I asked her, "What's wrong with Joe?"

She said, "You should see that library wall! It has gold paint sprayed on it, and it may not come off."

P.S. They got it off.

And at that same party, when the dinner was almost over, and the President was making his toast to the Queen, one of the carpenters, who was standing by to help take down the table, thought he heard someone say, "They are out of the dining room." He grabbed the knob of the door— it has to be locked during the serving for security— and shook it loudly, while the President was speaking. We surely thought that everyone would be cashiered the next morning, but to our surprise, we never heard a word.

When Queen Elizabeth II arrived, it was immediately evident that her entourage would be much easier to get along with than the group Mama had had to cope with when the Queen's mother was a visitor back in 1939.

Prince Philip's valet, James MacDonald, with whom I still correspond, had rooms on the third floor, but Mr. White, the footman; Mr. Bennette, the Queen's page; and the maid to the lady-in-waiting, stayed at the hotel, and came in each morning. Their meals were served in the hall on the third floor (the halls at the White House are all furnished like sitting rooms).

This was a congenial group of people to work with. A few minutes after arriving in the house, Miss McDonald, the maid, brought in the Royal blue coat, which the Queen had just taken off, to be pressed, because she would wear it again after lunch. I gave her a hand with this.

There is a difference in what a footman does in this country and what he does in England. Mr. White would put on a red coat, and use the small kitchen on the third floor to prepare the tea tray for the Queen, and serve it in her suite. A footman in this country is usually associated with a horse and carriage or an automobile. Nobody complained or acted haughtily, as the Queen Mother's servants had done.

I was thrilled when Mr. Bennette asked me, "Would you like to have the ribbon from the Queen's bouquet, and one red rose?"

We waited patiently backstairs for Mrs. "E" to make some arrangement for us to meet the Royal couple, as Mrs. Roosevelt had done. One could very easily sense also that the Queen's servants wanted to meet the First Lady, but she never came up to welcome them. By Sunday, which was the last day of the visit, I gave up all hope of any such meeting with the Queen. I happened to be on the ground floor when she and the Prince were returning from one of the many trips that they had to make, and received a bright smile from a distance.

I found out the following morning, after their departure, that the Queen was so anxious to meet the staff, that she had asked her maid to call the housekeeper. Nearly everyone had gone home, so Mrs. Walker; the maître d'hôtel, Charles Ficklin; and Mr. West, the chief usher, were the only three to answer the call. This was one of our greatest disappointments.

I met a lot of famous people at the Eisenhower parties, such as John Foster Dulles, Sir Winston Churchill and Vice-President Nixon. The Vice-President always said the right thing to soothe Mrs. Eisenhower when she was worrying about something. And I still smile when I recall the way he handled one delicate dilemma when she said, "the deep red anthurium from Hawaii and the red carnations don't blend right."

"To the male eye, it looks pretty good," he said, smiling.

I met a lot of famous entertainers too, such as Lawrence Welk. When Welk played for the President, Eisenhower was in a good mood, tapping his foot vigorously to "I've Got Spurs That Jingle, Jangle, Jingle." But then he pressed his luck and asked Welk, "Don't you know 'The Yellow Rose of Texas?' "

Welk replied, "Well, if we don't, we can certainly make it up."

Welk and his band proceeded to do just that. No one could recognize the tune.

I got to see a lot of the idiosyncrasies of actors and actresses and singers as I helped them on the nights of their performances. Some were very frightened because they were about to perform for the President; others took it in stride.

The night Jeanette MacDonald performed, she told me that she had to pass up the delicious dinner, because she had to sing. Some of her favorite dishes, she said, were being served that night— turtle soup, thick filet mignon, corn pudding, artichoke and grapefruit salad, and ice cream with caramel sauce.

I told her, "I will get some of those things tomorrow."

She said, "How I envy you!"

There could be no smoking around Miss MacDonald, though she is not a fussy type. She practiced, then drank a glass of cold water, and sprawled on a couch in the library to rest a minute, thinking nothing about the ivory satin gown she was wearing.

Patrice Munsel had to sip warm tea before singing. She said, "It warms my throat."

Entertainers, I learned, never eat more than a tidbit before singing at the White House. They are too nervous.

Hildegarde was the exception, in more ways than one. First, she wanted to bring her maid and her chauffeur to the White House with her. She got a "No" on this. Mr. Crim told her that he had a maid in the White House who could do anything that she would want done. I got this right from him when he assigned me to wait on her. She made a complete change, saying, "I hope I can get into my dress."

I asked, "You didn't eat dinner?"

And she said, "Oh, yes. I have to fortify myself with food."

I had a tough time fastening her black dress, which fitted skin-tight. She drank four cups of black coffee, and when I thought she would surely burst, she went on and gave a terrific performance.

But the performances I probably enjoyed most at the White House were those of the Eisenhower grandchildren— David, Barbara Ann, Susie, Mary Jean, and their trusty dog Spunkie. We all had a good laugh when the chef, Rysavy, thought the dog was "Skunkie."

What I didn't hear from the kids directly, I heard about from their doting grandmother. I heard all about the chores the children had to do at their Gettysburg house on a corner of the Eisenhower estate. David was making thirty-five cents a week on the lawn; then he complained, and got it up to fifty cents.

"Susie is making her bed so lumpy her mother has gotten contour sheets," Mrs. "E" reported to me one day. Then one year, Barbara Eisenhower wanted to make Easter dresses for Ann and Susie, and I helped her cut them out. She was a no-nonsense mother, and a good, unspoiled person. You could always count on her to say something blunt and humorous. Once when Mrs. Eisenhower set out a bunch of trinkets for the staff, she said, "I have a lot of junk I'd love to bring over here too, to get rid of."

Susan was the most disorganized one, and the one who had to take the most guff from David, who was forever hanging her dolls in effigy, and things like that. David may have acted tough, but deep down he had a tender heart, and when his pet canary, Gabby, died, he buried it with proper ceremony in the Rose Garden.

David's grandfather, though he seemed to take little interest in most of the people in the White House, took a great personal interest in everything pertaining to his grandchildren. He once sent a note to David's teacher. The note required an answer at the bottom, and the President gave it to David for delivery. David came back without the letter.

"What happened to the letter?" asked Granddad.

"I gave it to her," said David.

"Did you ask for the reply?"

"Yes," said David, "but she wouldn't give me the letter back."

"Why?" pursued the President.

"She said she's keeping it." Rummaging around in his pocket, David finally fished out a crumpled piece of paper with the teacher's reply.

School children in general had a special liking for President Eisenhower, possibly because of his friendly grin. He probably got more letters from school children than any other President. But the most delightful evidence of his youthful following was shown to me by Constantine Georgiou, Supervising Teacher at the Demonstration School for Student Teachers in Takoma Park, Maryland.

I didn't copy the President's grammatical and pleasant reply, but I took down in toto the child's letter (it's a verbatim copy of the one he sent) to preserve it for posterity:

Sligo School
Third Grade
October 14, 1959

My dear Mr. President,

I heard today was your birthday. I want to tel you happy birthday. So happy birthday.

I wanted to give you a suit for your birthday present.

You need a suit becos I saw you were wearing only a sport coat on TV. But I cant give you any. My teacher said Sherman Adams got in troble for taking a present. I love you and dont want you to get in no troble.

Love,
Wayne

And speaking of that "troble," I'll never forget when a dinner was scheduled for September 29, 1958, and I was told that I would have to work that night at my usual powder room stand. At the last moment, I was informed that the dinner had been called off, and I was flabbergasted, because dinners are never canceled. So I asked Mrs. Walker, "What happened?"

She said, "Well, it was for Mr. Sherman Adams, and he didn't care to go through with it."

I thought of all this as I tried to make up my mind about when to retire. I had watched the children grow. Soon David would be a "teener." It was hard to believe that in 1960 I was eligible for retirement. I would miss the White House, and I knew it. It had been my whole life.

I thought of how the Eisenhowers had withdrawn more and more into their small circle of friends. I remembered seeing top hostess, Gwen Cafritz, out in the hall, looking very forlorn, because she had no one to talk to. The guests were mostly White House secretaries, and the usual small circle of General Gruenther, and Allen, John and Barbara Eisenhower. I felt like telling her she was lucky she had even been invited. It was time for a change in the White House, and it was time for me to change.

I remember that the White House had seemed even a little more empty when Sherman Adams had left. He had always been so friendly with the help, always greeting us with a smile and a friendly word. We tried to figure out why it was wrong for one man in Government to accept gifts and not another.

And thinking about the Eisenhower grandchildren, I remembered the Roosevelt grandchildren and the Hoover grandchildren. And thinking of loyal Spunkie, who had started life as a little live heating pad for his original owner, John Eisenhower, when he was a soldier, brought back memories of loyal Fala and loyal Rob Roy and Mrs. Roosevelt's Meg, who bit reporter Bess Furman's nose, and a multitude of other White House dogs.

And the feud between "Ike and Harry" brought back memories of Mama discussing the feud between "Taft and Teddy." The new things I heard were beginning to sound like a record I had heard before. It was like that old song "The Music Goes Round and Round," which had made people laugh in Roosevelt's time.

Well, as Mama always said, you can only go one step at a time, and that's really all you have to worry about. One step at a time. But every time I thought I was ready for the giant step, I wasn't *quite* ready.

While I was trying to make up my mind as to whether I would leave the White House, or hold out a few years longer, I often walked around the old parts of Washington that I knew so well. My mind was much in the past, and everything I saw would remind me of something else. I walked by the fashionable Mayflower Hotel and remembered when a walled home for nuns stood there. And I walked past the huge town house that Andrew Mellon had lived in when he was Secretary of the Treasury under Harding and Coolidge and Hoover. We always knew when he was in the White House because of his squeaky old shoes. We used to joke, "Poor man, he can't afford a new pair."

And in Georgetown, I passed the home that had been Lincoln's son's until his death. And I remembered when the Cadillac Company had wanted to give the son a brand new Cadillac for his original two-cylinder one, and Robert

Todd Lincoln had said, "No." He preferred to keep his trusty two-cylinder.

I made my own private little tour of the White House, and I said good-by to the shadows of Presidents past and forever present— to Grover Cleveland's rocking chair, and Abraham Lincoln's circular sofa, and Andy Jackson's sofa and Dolley Madison's gold centerpiece, and Mrs. Eisenhower's 275-piece china collection, and FDR's piano frieze.

I remembered that there was a mysterious sound I used to hear once in a while in the room behind my linen room, which I had finally investigated. As I would approach it, the "swish-swash" would sound stronger and stronger. I would open the door of the work closet, and there would be Moaney, industriously washing Ike's golf balls— swish-swash, swish-swash. I would laugh and walk away. No ghosts there.

I would soon see him busy with another chore— the washing of the famous Eisenhower paint brushes— this time with turpentine. Then he would put them back in a little bucket, ready for action.

I thought of the portrait of young Prince Charles that the President had made, and presented to Queen Elizabeth and Prince Philip— his best painting, to my eye.

I gazed sadly at the floor-to-ceiling Christy portrait of Mrs. Coolidge and Rob Roy in the China Room, and the Healy portrait of Lincoln, sitting above the mantel as if he still presided in the State Dining Room.

Finally I went to see "Perry Como"— known to the outside world as Chief Usher West— and tendered my resignation.

"Lillian," he said, "I hate to see you go— but I envy you." Realizing what a hard job a chief usher has, I knew what he meant.

Then it was time for me to have my little farewell ceremony, just as Mama had once had, and I couldn't believe that was two decades ago.

There was an engraved silver tray for me from the "Remember Me" club— composed of my behind-the-scenes colleagues— who also gave me a gold-plated wall clock.

My farewell gift from the Eisenhowers was a double frame, containing autographed photos of the President and the First Lady. The President's picture was inscribed, "For Lillian R. Parks with appreciation for long and loyal service at the White House and with best wishes. Dwight D. Eisenhower." Mrs. Eisenhower had written on hers, "For Lillian Parks with my sincere best wishes. Mamie Doud Eisenhower."

I thought of how these things would take their place among my treasures, which span fifty years, and had been given to Mama and me— framed photos of other White House occupants, feather fans and figurines, perfumes and bits of finery, the dress in which Mrs. Coolidge had been painted, two of FDR's canes, the ribbon from Queen Elizabeth's bouquet, and a trunkful of other things.

Then I took a look at the Green Room where, through the power invested in President Truman, the American eagle on the tremendous rug had been turned around. President Truman had noticed that the eagle on the U.S. seal was facing the arrows in its claws, instead of the olive branch, so he had decreed that henceforth the eagle would face the symbol of peace.

I looked long and hard at the new green rug with the tremendous eagle that faced the olive branch, and wondered how many women who come to this room after formal dinners, to have coffee before the musicale, notice which way the eagle faces.

I went into the Red Room, where the President takes his male guests to have a liqueur and a smoke, while the ladies are having their coffee, and I thrilled again, as always, to the beauty of the tone-on-tone of red as far as the eye can see— wall-to-wall rug, sofa drapery, and damask silk walls.

At four, I walked down the backstairs and out the south door, through which Presidents had passed every day on their way to their offices, just in time to see Moaney hurrying with the President's golf clubs and cap. Yes, there was the President's head above the hedge. He smiled at me, and I smiled back.

As they walked away, I glanced at the texture of "Ike's" putting green. I hated to leave this place. But I realized that no one could take *this* away from me: the White House was really mine, for always.